he Persian Excursion

D1601391

FRANCE

ITALY

SPAIN

3

Mediterranean Sea

4

5

IRAQ   IRAN

14 12

11

Saudi
Arabia

13

10

6

7

Oman

Yemen

ARABIAN
SEA

9

8

INDIAN OCEAN

ATLANTIC
OCEAN

The Persian Excursion

THE CANADIAN NAVY IN THE GULF WAR

by
Commodore Duncan (Dusty) E. Miller
and
Sharon Hobson

Copyright 1995
The Canadian Peacekeeping Press
Clementsport, Nova Scotia B0S 1E0
and
The Canadian Institute of Strategic Studies
76 St. Clair Avenue West, Toronto, Ontario M4V 1N2

CANADIAN CATALOGING IN PUBLICATION DATA

Miller, Dusty (Duncan E.)
    The Persian Excursion

Co-published by the Canadian Institute of Strategic Studies.
Includes bibliographical references and index.
ISBN 0-919769-78-0

1. Persian Gulf War, 1991—Naval operations, Canadian. 2.
Canada. Canadian Armed Forces. Maritime Command—History—Persian Gulf War, 1991. I. Hobson, Sharon, 1952- . II.
Canadian Institute of Strategic Studies. III. Title

DS79.724.C2M55 1995   956.704'42371   C95-930956-X

The views expressed in this book are those of the authors and are not necessarily those of the Department of National Defence or Maritime Command.

Printed by Arthurs-Jones Lithographing Ltd., Mississauga

Distributed in Canada and the USA by Tanager Press

This book is dedicated to the men and women of the Canadian Forces who sailed aboard the ships in the Arabian Gulf, 1990-91, and to those at home who supported them so well.

Table of Contents

Introduction

The Gulf War was the first time since the Second World War that a Canadian Joint Force Headquarters commanded elements of Canada's sea, land and air forces in a joint and combined combat operation. After the Korean War, the Canadian Forces concentrated training and preparation for war on a scenario that foresaw operations under NATO command in Western Europe and the North Atlantic. The Gulf operation forced us to make rapid changes and introduce new procedures to sustain what eventually became a combat operation half-way around the globe in an area and as part of a Coalition for which we had neither prepared nor planned.

The conduct of the Gulf operation was complicated by Security Council resolutions that incrementally changed the Coalition's tasks from monitoring sanctions against Iraq, to enforcing sanctions, and finally to combat operations aimed at driving Iraqi forces out of Kuwait. Thus national command arrangements had to cater to an increasingly joint force composition, as well as to an increasingly robust and changing set of operational requirements.

That the Canadian Joint Task Force, and the recently formed Joint Staff in Ottawa, were able to manage as effectively as they did, was a tribute to their training, their dedication and their ingenuity. Their experience and their lessons have helped the Canadian Forces make a good start along the developing path of Joint Operations, which constitute for Canada and our allies the bench-mark of post-Cold War military professionalism.

Commodore Miller and Sharon Hobson have compiled an entertaining account of Canada's role in the Gulf War which should be of interest to the military and civilian reader alike. In doing so, they have documented a brief but important episode in Canada's history, and paid tribute to the men and women who comprised Canada's naval commitment to the Gulf War.

General John de Chastelain
Chief of the Defence Staff
November 1994

Foreword

History shows that Canada's military has, except for the latter stages of WWII, been small in numbers and all too often less well equipped than their enemy and their allies. But, history has also shown that what the Canadians have lacked in resources we have always made up for in the quality of our people, our ingenuity, our determination and our belief in basic principles. This book will show Canadians that this aspect of our character is alive and well in Canada's present military. It will relate a first class effort by a first class navy and its embarked helicopters. Their contribution was well beyond their numbers or their equipment capability. It was a contribution better known by our appreciative allies than by the Canadian public. Canadians are modest by nature and do not seek ticker tape parades or trumpet their accomplishments. Our forces in the Gulf returned satisfied that they had done what was expected of them and they were proud of their effort yet all too ready to resume their normal, and much more appreciated, Canadian way of life.

It has taken a recent trip back to Kuwait and Bahrain to make me realize that this story must be told before it is forgotten for it is a part of our nation's history. Commodore Miller, Colonel Lalonde, Mr. Bowden and myself were invited back to receive from the Government of Kuwait the prestigious Liberation of Kuwait Medal. But each of us received something far more significant—we received the genuine emotional warmth of a people and nation who were thanking us for our part in returning their country to them from the terror and horror of a cruel and vindictive despot. Much has changed in Kuwait since the war—most of the destruction in Kuwait City has been repaired or replaced, the dark staining skies of the oil fires no longer bring a sense of perpetual evenings or an impending summer thunderstorm, and only the occasional Iraqi bunker remains in sight as a reminder of the hundreds of similar bunkers that guarded the beach approaches and major intersections of Kuwait City. The sands of time have even shifted sufficiently to hide the mass of twisted metal, clothing and personal effects left along the road to Mutla Ridge where the escaping Iraqi army had been crushed by the allied forces as they tried to go north towards Basra to join the remaining Republican Guards. Life has essentially returned to normal in this tiny nation. But one thing has remained unchanged and that is the sincere Kuwaiti gratitude to Canada and the other multinational forces of liberation. Those sentiments were repeated time and time again during our short return and echoed those I most strongly felt on the day following the Liberation of Kuwait when in front of a crowd of cheering and ululating Kuwaiti, in one of the proudest and most memorable moments of my life, Ambassador Larry Dickenson and I raised the Canadian flag to again open the Canadian Embassy in Kuwait City.

Canadians are an unmilitary people who show a remarkable military capability when involved in a conflict. This book recounts the maritime version of events for the Gulf War. I hope it spurs others, in the land and air forces, to capture their accounts of the conflict through their eyes in order to complete the picture.

Rear-Admiral Ken Summers
March 1995

Authors' Preface

We came together over two years ago to write this book because, despite our different interests and our different backgrounds, we both believed that the navy's story of what it did in the 1990-91 Gulf War was a story that had not yet been adequately told. We wanted Canadians to know what their navy did and how well it had done it. Many of those who have written about the war have tended to overlook or forget Canada's small but important contribution to the allied effort. Canada took on the unglamorous but vital role of keeping the coalition's combat forces supplied. The Canadian navy's professionalism in running that 800-kilometre supply line earned it the respect and gratitude of our allies.

In telling the story, we have chosen to arrange the chapters by type of challenge (preparing the ships, handling command and control, enforcing the embargo, etc.) rather than by chronology. By doing so we hope we have provided a handy reference for those readers who have a particular interest in, say, communications (Chapter Six —"Reach Out and Touch Someone"), while allowing those who have no interest in such a technical subject to skip ahead.

We decided to write in the third person because this is not one person's story, it is the Task Group's. There are times, however, when we thought it better for Dusty to provide a more personal account and at those times the typeset changes to Italics.

This book has benefitted from the support and advice of family, friends, and colleagues. There are many we wish to thank. First and foremost, we would like to thank all those who contributed to this book by giving so generously of their time, knowledge and memories. Among those quoted in the text are: Rear-Admiral Ken Summers, Rear-Admiral Bruce Johnston, Commodore Jim King, Captain(Navy) Roger Chiasson, Commodore Doug McClean, Captain(Navy) Stu Andrews, Colonel Larry McWha, Commander John Pickford, Commander Greg Romanow,

Commander Kevin Laing, Lieutenant-Commander Jim Hayes, Lieutenant-Commander Paul Maddison, Major Pete Nordlund, Chief Petty Officer 1st Class Dave Ashley, and Master-Corporal Patrick McCafferty.

We hope this book does justice to your experiences.

We would also like to thank those who have helped in the production of the manuscript: Lieutenant-Commander Richard Gimblett from the Directorate of History at the Department of National Defence for his detailed comments and suggestions; Dr. Heidi Studer for her careful editing; Clive Hobson, for his help with Chapter One; Diane Larocque for the computer-drawn maps; Daniel St.Cyr, Sue Purcell, Shirley Delahunt, and Susan McNish for their shepherding of the final manuscript through a computer maze; and, Amy Miller for coming up with the title, *The Persian Excursion*—the name used by the sailors in the three ships to describe their mission. We also owe a debt of gratitude to Alex Morrison of the Canadian Institute of Strategic Studies and the Pearson Peacekeeping Centre for having faith in us.

Finally, we wish to thank our families—Naomi Miller; Ron and Peggy Hobson; and Christopher, Nicholas and Amy Miller—as well as our spouses, Ann Miller and Jim Bagnall, for their patience and support.

Duncan (Dusty) Miller
Sharon Hobson
March 1995

List of Illustrations

CHAPTER ONE

"This is what they've paid me for, mum."

"At the request of the Government of Kuwait and the Government of Saudi Arabia, the Government of the United States of America has initiated a multinational military effort to deter Iraqi aggression. The Government of Canada has decided, therefore, to dispatch three ships of the Canadian Forces to the Persian Gulf. Our naval forces, in company with those of other nations, will assist in the deterrence of further aggression."

Prime Minister Brian Mulroney
August 10, 1990

Little more than a week after Saddam Hussein's dead-of-night march into Kuwait and only one day after the first, lightly-armed U.S. troops began landing in Saudi Arabia, there was no bravado or hyperbole in the Prime Minister's voice—just a grim resignation that Canada had to take its place among its allies. This was serious business. Iraq's army, some one million strong, including more than 200,000 in a plundered Kuwait, looked impregnable. Not only was it digging in for the long haul, but it bristled with missiles, 5,000 battle tanks, 10,000 other armoured vehicles, 4,000 artillery pieces, chemical weapons and the other paraphernalia of war. It was considered the fifth biggest armed force in the world.[1]

Set against this, Canada's military contribution looked small. It was anything but. Canada wound up sending 25 per cent of its operational warships to the Gulf along with most of the modern weaponry it had on hand, including specially-equipped helicopters. The ships carried nearly

---

1. The International Institute of Strategic Studies, *Strategic Survey 1990-1991* (Brassey's, London: 1991), pp. 60-61.

1,000 men and women who underwent the most intensive training regimen in Canadian naval history. Their efforts were matched by the military establishment back home that developed the logistics and communications support essential to keeping the Gulf Task Group fighting fit.

This was a baptism by fire. The government had asked for ships and the navy had promised to supply them. But could it deliver a well-equipped task group into a war zone and keep it safe? After nearly four decades of peace, Canada's military leaders weren't sure how well their machine would respond to any war, let alone one conducted in the unfamiliar Arabian Gulf[2] with more than a dozen non-NATO allies. Moreover, the timing was terrible.

With only twelve operational warships[3]—of which only two were less than 20 years old—the navy was waiting for delivery of the first of 12 new City class frigates and four modernized Tribal class destroyers. These ships would be a far cry from the aging warships the navy had been using for the previous 10 years. The new frigates, for instance, were being equipped with top-of-the-line air defence weapons and anti-submarine sensors, as well as computer and communications systems that would provide a command staff with instantly processed information on the threat and the response options in any situation.

The Tribals would be equally impressive combat ships, fully capable of defending a task force from air attack out to a radius of more than 70 kilometres. Equipped as a command ship, and fitted with the latest in anti-air missiles and sonar-dipping helicopters, these destroyers would be at the centre of Canadian operations abroad—whether on NATO manoeuvres or in wartime.

At the navy's operational headquarters in Halifax there was anticipation that, as the navy took delivery of these state-of-the-art warships, it would gradually transform itself from the poor cousin of the NATO alliance into one of the most effective navies in the western world.

Unfortunately, time was not on the navy's side. With nearly a year to go before any delivery, Canada and the rest of the world were plunged into crisis; the navy was expected to respond, despite the fact that neither the Tribals nor the City class frigates were ready. This, however, proved to be a mixed blessing. Because the navy was in the process of acquiring

---

2. While the West usually refers to the region as the "Persian Gulf," its proper name is the "Arabian Gulf."

3. The number includes all destroyers, frigates and auxiliary-oiler-replenishment vessels which were not in the dockyard for maintenance or part of the west coast training squadron.

new ships, its contractors had the modern weapons and sensor systems on hand, ready for fitting in the new frigates and modernized destroyers. In effect, the navy had all the components of three modern warships, but they were in storage across the North American continent, anywhere from California to Halifax, and they would have to be fitted in existing ships. Putting the pieces together to transform three obsolescent naval vessels into combat capable warships was a test of naval ingenuity and dedication.

Fortunately, what the navy lacked in equipment, it more than made up for in people. By circumstance, design or training, the navy had on hand exactly the kinds of skills necessary for converting old ships into new, and for teaching the ships' companies the necessary skills for mounting naval operations against an unpredictable foe, half a world away.

⌘   ⌘   ⌘

Commodore Ken J. Summers knew he couldn't leave Halifax at the beginning of August after Iraq invaded Kuwait. International tensions were increasing and Summers, Chief of Staff Operations at Maritime Command Headquarters in Halifax, and Commander of the Canadian Fleet, knew there would be work to be done if the government decided to join a United Nations (U.N.) action against Iraq. But he was also supposed to go to Norfolk, Virginia for a four-day NATO exercise at the naval headquarters there. He solved the problem by sending Captain[4] Duncan (Dusty) E. Miller, the squadron commander whose ships were to be in the Norfolk exercise.

It turned out to be the right move. Summers was in the thick of things when the government asked the navy what it could contribute to the international action against Iraq. By the time Prime Minister Brian Mulroney announced that Canada would be sending three ships to the Arabian Gulf to help enforce U.N. sanctions, Summers already had put the wheels in motion with the naval staffs in Halifax and National Defence headquarters in Ottawa to get the ships and crews ready for their mission.

Miller, who had been in touch with his superior officer regularly and knew about the Gulf plans, returned from Norfolk in time to arrive at the press conference where Summers was speaking after the Prime Minister's announcement. Miller, who had been whisked from the airport in a car sent by Summers, was in civilian clothes—the airline having lost his luggage—and sat in the back of the room with a dozen reporters, listening

---

4.   All Captains in the book are naval Captains (four stripes), unless otherwise noted.

to his commanding officer. It was only then that Miller learned he was going on the mission as Summers' second-in-command, his Chief of Staff.

The initial problem facing the two men was selecting who else would go on the mission. Miller had, only a month before, assumed command of the First Canadian Destroyer Squadron, which was the one contributing ships to the multinational naval force in the Gulf. As Squadron Commander he was responsible for the co-ordination of all the ships in the squadron, planning and keeping track of their individual taskings. To do that, he had a staff of experts.[5] The problem was that Miller had inherited an almost entirely new staff. Some hadn't even arrived at their new postings in Halifax, and some of them had no experience with working for a squadron commander. One officer, for example, was coming straight from a military college where he had spent three years as Director of Cadets. Although the new staff were all capable officers, Summers was worried that they would have little time to learn their new jobs before heading into a possible war zone. He decided that for a major deployment, it would be preferable to have people who had had either squadron experience or experience in the new weapons systems that were being fitted in the ships.

There was some concern within the navy about hand-picking officers to go to the Arabian Gulf. Some felt that the squadron staff should remain as originally posted so as to give experience to the inexperienced. But there was no choice. Time was at a premium and not all the squadron staff were in Halifax; some were still enroute to their new postings, with their families. There was also a U.S. officer on the staff who was due to be changed in a month's time and couldn't be asked to undertake what could turn out to be a lengthy deployment. Moreover, after the Task Group left Halifax, the squadron would still have to function: there were seven ships in the First Canadian Destroyer Squadron, but only two were going to the Gulf. Therefore, there had to be a residual staff to look after those left behind. Captain Dennis Cronk was to be acting squadron commander in Miller's absence and he was given the original staff. This would give them the chance to work as the regular squadron staff without the added pressure of an international crisis.

---

5. The composition of the squadron staff varies depending on the deployment of the squadron. In the case of the Task Group going to the Gulf, the squadron staff was to include the usual combat, operations, and weapons officers, as well as other specialists such as an intelligence officer, a chemical defence expert, and an army officer.

Summers held a meeting with Miller and Captain Jim King, Deputy Chief of Staff, Readiness. The Commodore told them to go into the navy's personnel computer and get a list of those who would be better suited for the Gulf operation. They did so and came up with about a hundred names of Lieutenant-Commanders who had taken the combat control officers course[6] and who had the necessary experience. Miller and King narrowed the list down to five people, of which they needed three.

Those three—someone to co-ordinate the overall mission (Senior Combat Officer), someone to oversee the day-to-day operations (Squadron Operations Officer), and someone to control the use of the various weapons systems (Weapons Officer)—were to be selected on the basis of talent, experience, availability, and personality. Summers, who can be a fairly intimidating man, wanted people who were innovative, unconventional and unafraid to voice their opinion to the point of arguing it out with him if necessary. He found them.

⌘   ⌘   ⌘

Lieutenant-Commander Greg Romanow had all the prerequisites to be the Task Group's Senior Combat Officer. An extremely intelligent and outspoken man who exudes self-confidence, he could be relied upon to express an idea or opinion without hesitation. His work as an air controller, a navigation officer, and a weapons officer had given him a strong background in tactics for which he had shown a particular aptitude. In addition, he had squadron staff experience, having served on the staff of the Fifth Canadian Destroyer Squadron, before spending a year at the Command and Staff College in Toronto. By the time the call came for Romanow to join the Task Group destined for the Gulf, he was the Acting Commanding Officer of HMCS IROQUOIS,[7] working out of a shore office while the Tribal class destroyer was in MIL Davie's shipyard in Lauzon, Quebec, undergoing a three-year major upgrading.

> *I remember going to Summers about Lieutenant-Commander Greg Romanow, and Summers asked, "What's he like?" And I told him, "He's certainly his own person, he's never going to say 'yes' just because you want him to, and he's probably going to take charge of everything that moves." He said, "Great. Let's get him."*

---

6. A course which prepares an officer for "fighting the ship" (using the ship and all its systems correctly in a conflict).

7. The names of Canadian ships are prefaced by HMCS ("Her Majesty's Canadian Ship"). In this book, we have included the initials only the first time a ship is mentioned.

Getting him was not easy, not because he was needed elsewhere, but because he was on holiday, on the south coast of Nova Scotia, at a cottage without a phone. So the navy called the R.C.M.P. and asked them to go and knock on his door, with the message to report to Miller's office immediately, either by phone or in person. Romanow, who had already started his holidays before the government announced the naval deployment, only knew what he had heard on the radio about what was going on. But when he got the message from the Mounties, he had a pretty good idea of why he was being summoned. He found a phone and called Miller. When he was told he was needed for the Arabian Gulf deployment, he asked only for the afternoon to pull his boat out of the water and winterize his cottage. Then he packed his bags and hotfooted it back to Halifax.

⌘   ⌘   ⌘

Unlike Romanow, Lieutenant-Commander Jim W. Hayes was not unsuspecting. He was just waiting to be called. After all, he had the knowledge and the experience. During his previous year as Squadron Operations Officer in the Fifth Canadian Destroyer Squadron he had been responsible for organizing combat readiness inspections for the ships, and he had been involved in two major naval exercises, one with the British carrier HMS ARK ROYAL.

After the news broke that Canada was sending three ships to the Gulf, Hayes heard that his boss, Captain David Morse, Commander of the Fifth Canadian Destroyer Squadron, was holding a large staff meeting the next day to get things organized for the deployment. Hayes expected that he would be assigned some important task commensurate with his extensive background, and he arrived at the meeting that Saturday morning pumped up with anticipation. He listened and waited as each of the officers in turn was given a role in preparing the Task Group for its mission. Finally, it became clear that the meeting was drawing to an end and Hayes still hadn't received any new instructions. Morse turned to him, and casually asked, "Jim, any questions?" Hayes, not believing he had been left out, managed to ask, "Well, yes sir, do you have any job for me?" Morse's unsmiling face was strangely constrained as he replied, "Well, we're going to be pretty busy around here, Jim, so I want you to command the office." Hayes was floored. He figured he really must have screwed up the last exercise to be left out of the biggest operation the navy had undertaken since the Cuban Missile Crisis.

Feeling badly, Hayes threw himself into his new assignment, which included acquiring special clothing for the ships' officers and crews. He was still feeling pretty dismal, when, a few days later, Captain Morse bumped into Hayes in Maritime Command headquarters, and offhandedly told him, "Oh, by the way, you've been selected for the Gulf squadron staff. Do you want to go?" Hayes didn't need asking twice. In a calm voice and with a straight face he thanked Morse for the honour, and then rushed home to tell his wife and family.

It was only then that the full implication of Morse's question hit him. During a phone conversation with his parents—Hayes' father is a retired Commodore—his mother told him she had been following the story in the news and was worried about his safety. A subdued Hayes quietly replied, "This is what they've paid me for, mum. This is payback time."

⌘ ⌘ ⌘

Lieutenant-Commander Kevin Laing was beginning the job of unpacking 18,000 pounds of furniture and boxes when he heard about the Gulf mission. He and his wife had just moved to Dartmouth, into the first house that they had ever bought, and he was preparing to take over as the commanding officer of the dockyard facilities designed to support the upgraded Tribal class destroyers. After three years on exchange with the U.S. Navy, and a year at Canadian Forces Staff College in Toronto— where he was the top naval student—Laing was looking forward to being eased back into normal naval life. Everything was looking secure and trouble-free—except for the usual problems of settling moving claims and pay procedures. But by the evening of August 12, as Laing watched the increased activity in the east coast port city, and as his friends and colleagues were swept up into the Gulf preparations, he began to wonder how long his peaceful existence would last.

Not long. The next day Captain Morse called and asked Laing if he could help with the weapons training for the re-equipped ships. Laing, who was still on leave before the start of his new job, rooted around in the packing boxes, found his uniform, ironed it, and hurried over to the navy base. There, he met with Commander J.Y. Forcier and Miller, who wasted no time in asking Laing to become the Weapons Officer for the Task Group. Laing considered the request and then pointed out that he was willing but he was worried about leaving when his financial matters were still unsettled. Forcier picked up the phone, called the pay office and told them he wanted Laing's affairs settled immediately. Within the hour, they were, and Laing was the newest member of the Task Group's squadron staff.

Laing was particularly suited for the post of Weapons Officer. A military college graduate, he had later excelled in courses for electronic warfare and combat control—in the latter case he was the top student in the 1984-85 Fleet School's Combat Controllers Course—and had experience as both a weapons officer and a combat officer before spending three years on exchange with the U.S. Navy. There, he was an Operational Test Director on the staff of the Commander Operational Test and Evaluation Force[8] in Norfolk, Virginia. Laing, who was in the surface warfare division, assisted other officers in putting weapons systems, principally anti-air warfare weapons, through their paces before the equipment was declared operationally ready. He had responsibility for the upgraded combat systems of the FFG-7 class of guided missile frigates. It was Laing's posting with the U.S. Navy that was considered critical to the successful operation of the three re-equipped Canadian ships being sent to the Gulf.

> Summers didn't know him, but I assured him that if we were going to have anybody who knew the new weapons systems and the computers, and could put together an operational readiness check for our ships, before they even went over, this was the man.

> A brilliant fellow. He had come first in all sorts of courses and he had just completed a three year program in two years at the U.S. Naval War College[9] and graduated top of his class, while working with the U.S. Navy in Norfolk. We needed him.

⌘   ⌘   ⌘

One member of the squadron staff who did not have to be added or replaced was the squadron air officer, Major Pete F. Nordlund. He had arrived back from Norfolk, Virginia, with Miller, after participating in the NATO naval headquarters exercise, when he was called into Maritime Command Headquarters for a briefing. He got home that night about 8:00 p.m. with instructions to report at 7:00 a.m. the next day to start work on the Gulf deployment. That Saturday, Nordlund watched the

---

8. Operational test and evaluation refers to testing the technical operation of a weapons system. For example, testing to make sure that an air search radar detects an incoming aircraft when it is supposed to according to its specifications. This is done by arranging for an aircraft to come towards the ship at a predetermined speed, altitude, and angle, and checking to see when and where the radar detects it.

9. The Naval War College in Newport, Rhode Island, is an establishment of the U.S. Navy. It is open to officers of allied navies.

people he had shared his office with pack their desks and leave, to make room for three new officers—Romanow, Laing and Hayes—to move in. For a while he wondered how long he would be around and who would replace him.

He had nothing to worry about. Relaxed and good-natured, Nordlund was an experienced scheduling officer who could juggle the Sea Kings' daily training, maintenance and operational schedules. Miller knew him from their time together the previous year, during a major naval exercise. Nordlund was a knowledgeable professional who was known as a hard worker—the perfect officer for the tasking of the five Sea King helicopters embarked in the ships, as well as the analysis of the threats to, and requirements of, the aircraft.

⌘   ⌘   ⌘

In addition to these four officers, Summers wanted to have a Deputy Chief of Staff (Operations), and the Task Group needed a Deputy Chief of Staff (Air) for the Sea King operations. Summers picked Commander J.Y. Forcier, a very smart, computer-literate officer, to oversee the operations side of things. Forcier was available because he was the commanding officer of HMCS ALGONQUIN, which was in refit. As Chief of Staff (Operations), Forcier was responsible for setting up the parameters of a sustainable mission for the ships. For example, he took into account such things as the ships' mechanical endurance as well as the crew's psychological stamina to produce a recommended schedule of 10 days at sea followed by four days in port for the first month of the deployment.

Forcier's planning for the surface side of the operation, needed to be mirrored on the air side. For supervising the operation of the five Sea Kings to be carried in the ships, Summers consulted with Brigadier-General Barry Bowen, Commander of Maritime Air Group. They decided that Lieutenant-Colonel Larry A. McWha, Commanding Officer of 423 Helicopter Anti-Submarine Squadron (HS 423), who was already joining the Task Group as Commander Air—the technical analyst who would assess deficiencies, and make sure both the correct personnel and equipment were available—could also act as the Task Group Commander's Deputy Chief of Staff for Air Operations.[10] McWha was known as a gung ho "pilot's pilot" who would attack his job aggressively and with confidence. He could be counted on to be the first in the cockpit when

10. For a detailed description of Maritime Air Group's preparations for, and experiences in, the Gulf, see Colonel Larry McWha's chapter in the soon-to-be published *Sea Fire to Sea King*, a Canadian Naval Aviation Technical History Project.

either new techniques or equipment had to be tested, always ready to show his pilots exactly what the helicopter could do.

⌘ ⌘ ⌘

In addition to the officers, the squadron staff consisted of 14 other specialists and non-commissioned officers. The majority of these had been in their positions for at least a year and did not have to be changed for the Gulf posting. Signalman Chief Serge Joncas and radioman Chief Dave Ashley, in particular, were considered two of the best in the navy. As Squadron Chief, Yeoman of Signals, Chief Petty Officer 2nd Class Joncas was in charge of all message traffic, sorting out the priorities and making sure the commander got the messages he needed, when he needed them. The quiet and efficient Joncas would also be on the tactical circuit during any manoeuvring of the ships such as would be required for refuelling or stores loading. Chief Petty Officer 2nd Class Ashley, the Squadron Chief Radioman, had been in the navy for 24 years—all of them in communications. His expertise in running the communications centre and maintaining the equipment, as well as his unfailing good humour, were key assets to the Task Group. The staff's coxswain[11] Chief Petty Officer 2nd Class Paul Barry was an old style navy man who could be counted on to provide cool and steady stewardship in tense times. As a weapons expert he also worked with Chief Petty Officer 2nd Class Al Dunn, a radar operator, running the Joint Operational Tactical System.[12]

Petty Officer lst Class Jimmy Hawkins, was the Task Group's air controller. He had a top-level "A" rating which allowed him to direct the operations of a fleet of Sea King helicopters during the day or at night and in all weather conditions. He was also one of the few Combat Air Controllers in the navy, qualified to direct the operations of high-speed jet fighters. Hawkins, however, did not start out with the Task Group, but with the Sea Training Staff. When the squadron staff's air controller fell ill and had to be flown back to Halifax from Gibraltar, the Task Group was lucky enough to have Hawkins step in.

⌘ ⌘ ⌘

The two officers in charge of the Task Group, Summers and Miller, were not specially selected for the duty—instead, they were in the right place at the right time.

---

11. A coxswain is the most senior non-commissioned officer on board a ship. He is responsible for managing the crew, deciding such things as the duty roster and the watch routine.
12. See Chapter 2, p. 23.

In fact, in Miller's case, it couldn't have worked out better if it had been planned. But it wasn't. Canada didn't know in August 1990, when it decided to send three ships to the Arabian Gulf, that it would need more than just an experienced commander. It would need someone who was not only capable of running a large scale supply operation, but was familiar with both the American and the NATO way of operating their navies. Miller, who had been in the navy for 25 years, had acquired those skills and in the months leading up to the Gulf deployment, had honed them.

He was fresh from three years as head of the Canadian Forces Maritime Warfare Centre in Halifax, where he had helped the navy rediscover its tactical focus. He had also served in ships off Canada's east coast for 15 years and had worked with U.S. ships off the west coast for six years, making him capable of working in both a NATO and U.S. naval environment. In fact, in the spring of 1990, as head of the Warfare Centre, Miller was asked to be the Chief of Staff to the Pacific Commander, Rear-Admiral Peter Cairns, to run a Pacific Rim naval exercise. Despite being heavily involved in two other major naval exercises and chairing the NATO anti-submarine warfare group in Brussels, as well as running the Warfare Centre in Halifax, Miller accepted.

There is a difference in how naval operations on the east and west coasts are run and it was a chance for Miller to refresh his memory and acquire new techniques. In the Atlantic, the Canadian navy uses NATO procedures, but in the Pacific Ocean, where there is no major maritime alliance, U.S. Navy's way of doing things tends to prevail. At the time, Miller didn't know that he would soon need to be as familiar with both of these procedures as he was with his right and left hands.

The Joint Headquarters for the spring 1990 exercise was on Ford Island in Pearl Harbor, Hawaii. Fifty-five ships, more than 200 aircraft and 50,000 men and women from Australia, Canada, South Korea, Japan and the U.S. were involved in the exercise, which called for two battle groups to stage a mock battle at sea. One battle group was centered around an aircraft carrier, USS INDEPENDENCE, and the other battle group—commanded by Rear-Admiral Cairns, had the battleship USS MISSOURI, and 21 other warships, as well as a "stationary aircraft carrier" (the island of Oahu). It has several airfields, and a National Guard, as well as units of the U.S. Air Force, and U.S. Marines, all of which was placed under Canadian co-ordination and control.

Miller thus became familiar with the day-to-day operations of a Pacific battle group, and met many of the main naval players. He worked with the commanders of four U.S. aircraft carrier battle groups—three of which would end up in the Gulf.

I had met the various ships' captains and we had established a rapport. It's like anything: if you know the person you're talking to, chances are you're going to get a whole lot more co-operation from them. Ships would sail into the Gulf and say, "Dusty, what the heck are you doing here? What's a west coast sailor doing in the Gulf?" Only I wasn't really a west coast sailor, I had come from the east coast to run that summer's west coast exercise. So it was fun to have these messages come in as soon as the ships arrived, and we instantly had a rapport.

In June, after he returned to Halifax, as one of his last acts as head of the Warfare Centre, Miller ran an intensive two-week Maritime Command exercise out of Bermuda. A Buccaneer aircraft squadron from the U.K.—an electronic warfare squadron which simulates air attacks on ships—and the British aircraft carrier HMS ARK ROYAL participated in that exercise. It gave Miller a chance to get to know the British commanders and ships, and the capabilites of their Buccaneer squadron—all of which would come in handy two months later when Miller was sent to the Gulf.

In addition, the exercise provided experience in the workings of another key aspect of the coming Arabian Gulf deployment: one of Canada's Tribal class destroyers, HMCS ATHABASKAN, functioned as the command and control ship—a role she was to reprise in the Gulf three months later.

Because the Tribals were being upgraded, the crew of ATHABASKAN were told that they had—at least on paper—the same equipment as an anti-air warfare destroyer. This forced the ship's operations team to learn the capabilities of the "new" weapons systems, and to pay more attention to the air side of things than they had done before. Normally, they would have focused on anti-submarine warfare (ASW) matters, almost to the exclusion of other threats. Dealing with the air threat in an exercise gave the operations room staff a taste of what was to come—an attack by aircraft and missiles would be one of the main concerns in the Arabian Gulf.

Miller returned home to Halifax at the end of the Bermuda exercise and in July, began his new job as Commander of the First Canadian

Destroyer Squadron. Almost immediately, Miller was sent down by Summers to Norfolk to act on his behalf as the anti-submarine warfare commander for a NATO exercise. It involved staffs from two aircraft carriers, the nine-ship Standing Naval Force Atlantic (STANAVFORLANT), and two other battle groups from the U.S. Atlantic force, practicing the latest ASW techniques on the U.S. Navy's tactical computers.

So in the few months before leaving for the Arabian Gulf, Miller had the unique experience of commanding and controlling two very different naval operations—one on the east coast and one on the west coast. He had met and established good relations with many of the navies that would be participating in the action against Iraq. And finally, he had worked on the premise that a Tribal class destroyer would be used as a command ship, equipped with anti-air warfare weapons.

⌘　⌘　⌘

It was more than good fortune that found Summers in command of the Canadian Task Group—it was a mistake. A 27-year-old mistake. When he showed up at the Canadian Forces recruiting centre in 1963, he didn't really go to join the military, but rather just to get information about joining. Kenneth and Margaret Summers, however, wanted their eldest son to join up and get his education at the Royal Military College. Kenneth Summers accompanied his son that day and when the recruiting officer asked Ken which branch of the service he wanted to join, he hesitated, thought for a moment, and was about to reply "Air Force" for no particular reason, when his father said, "Navy, of course."

Summers received his college education and grew to love military life. A clever man with a hands-on approach to command, he specialized in command, control and communications. During his postings at National Defence Headquarters in the office of Director Maritime Requirements (Sea), he helped set the philosophy and the design of the operations room of the new Canadian Patrol Frigates. During a later posting as Director Maritime Force Development, Summers had worked on the 1987 White Paper, helping to chart the way ahead for the Canadian navy. During his sea time, he had served in three of the navy's modern DDH-280 Tribal class destroyers, including as Commanding Officer of HMCS ALGONQUIN. Later, during his year as commander of the Second Canadian Destroyer Squadron in Esquimalt, Summers was involved in some significant exercises with the American navy in the Pacific.

By 1989 he had been promoted to Commodore and moved back to the east coast as Chief of Staff, Operations, and Commander Canadian Fleet. In the latter capacity, he was the Flag Officer who went to sea on major international exercises, taking on responsibilities such as anti-submarine warfare commander for the NATO force. In August 1990, Summers, as Commander Canadian Fleet, was given his greatest challenge: to put together a task group for deployment to the Arabian Gulf.

⌘   ⌘   ⌘

At their first meeting in Miller's office, the new squadron staff immediately set about the preparations for getting three ships with highly trained crews to the Gulf. Everything needed to be done. The navy was going to an area of the world where it had never operated with equipment it had never used. Forcier and Miller had to go through the tactical plans that had been developed by Canadian allies during other skirmishes in the region. Romanow acquired the navigation charts and began planning the ships' passage. He also had to work closely with the Sea Training staff to plan the crew training en route to the Gulf.[13] Laing began work on detailed weapons control orders for the new weapons systems which were being fitted in the ships. Hayes had to schedule a trials program to test all the weapons, sensor, and computer systems before the ships left Halifax, as well as plan for the ships' departure. McWha was to supervise the stripping and re-equipping of five Sea King helicopters for their new role, and Nordlund scheduled the air crew trials on the refitted aircraft. It was a massive undertaking, made that much more arduous by the knowledge that it had to be completed within a mere two weeks!

While the initial planning was underway by the squadron staff, there was still the question of who else should go on the Gulf mission. There was a finite number of berths available, so that the number of experts and specialists sailing as part of the Task Group was limited. ATHABASKAN has a normal complement of 275 officers and men, while the smaller HMCS TERRA NOVA usually has 214. HMCS PROTECTEUR usually carries 250 officers and crew but was built with about 300 bunks. Over the years the extra bunks had been removed; for the Gulf expedition, they were put back in—cadged from another supply ship, HMCS PRESERVER, which was in refit at Halifax-Dartmouth Industries Ltd.

---

13. An invaluable training aid, the Sea Training Staff oversees the operations of a ship to make sure the ship's company attains the required readiness standards. In the case of the Task Group, there were five or six trainers in each ship: a Weapons Chief, an Engineering Chief, etc. They spread themselves around the ship, taking notes on the exercise being run, and then they would debrief the ship's officers and crew, telling them where they were deficient.

For all three ships, the navy put bunks in nooks and crannies that had never had bunks—some of which were a very tight fit and only suitable for lean crew members who didn't toss and turn much in their sleep—and extra bunks were put in all the officers' cabins, except the Captains' and their Executive Officers'.

The space constraints forced the squadron staff to examine carefully every position and decide if that crew member was essential to the operation. For example, they looked at whether or not they needed a Padre and decided that with the prospect of fighting and the associated battle stress, a Padre was essential. But they could not have a Padre in each ship; they could only take two.

In addition to the regular crew members, there were eight bunks in each destroyer for the army's air defence personnel. PROTECTEUR had two air defence batteries, one on top of the hanger and one on the fo'c's'le,[14] and thus had to find room for 16 air defence personnel.

Each destroyer carried a doctor and two medical assistants instead of the usual practice of each ship having just one medical assistant with one doctor for the entire Task Group. In addition, there was an extra medical team in PROTECTEUR put together by surgeon Captain Larry Myette. The 15 extra medical staff comprised a complete surgical team (surgeon, anesthesist, and four nurses, as well as x-ray and operating room technicians). In putting the team together Myette was anticipating combat injuries such as blast, burn and ballistic wounds. The Defence Department sent a medical expert to Halifax to educate the medical team on the treatment of wounds caused by chemical warfare.

The Task Group also had to find space for an increased air department. PROTECTEUR was to carry her full complement of three Sea Kings instead of the usual two, which meant an extra crew of four. The only way to accommodate an extra crew was for Lieutenant-Colonel Larry McWha to be one of the aircrew—for a "pilot's pilot" this was the ideal solution. At Maritime Air Group's urging, the navy also made room in PROTECTEUR for an additional Safety Systems Technician, a Non-Destructive Test Technician, an Aviation Metalsmith and an Aviation Machinist to bolster the supply ship's aircraft maintenance detachment. Major Doug Foster, Shearwater's Aircraft Maintenance Officer, who accompanied the Task Group to its forward operating base in Bahrain, was needed to oversee the completion of the aircraft's original

14. The part of the upper deck that is located forward of the mast nearest the bow.

modifications and any subsequent ones. Two more Aircraft Maintenance Officers—air force Captains Don Feltmate and John Madower—also joined PROTECTEUR's air department. There was, unfortunately, no room in the ships for any company technical representatives to help solve new problems with the equipment fitted in the Sea Kings; the air group would be sailing with the knowledge it had and no more.

A Sea Training Staff and various civilian technicians for the ships' equipment travelled with the Task Group as far as Gibraltar. The ships had a total of 34 cots which could be used for a temporary period—they cannot be taken into a battle zone because they are not bolted down—and thus were suitable only for the week that the Sea Training Staff was on board.

If pushed, the Task Group could use a system of "hot bunking"—a not very popular way of accommodating extra personnel—whereby one bed is used by two crew members, one using it during the day, and one during the night. However, that option was thankfully just a failsafe, and never had to be used.

In addition to these essential personnel, the navy wanted to have some bunks available for members of the press. It managed to reserve four bunks in PROTECTEUR—the only ship which could accommodate women—for members of the press. The various visiting delegations of politicians and admirals also had to be accommodated, so there was a sea cabin in ATHABASKAN kept available.

Normally the commander of the fleet (Summers) and the squadron commander (Miller) are not in the same ship at the same time. To accommodate both of them in ATHABASKAN, Miller slept on a hide-a-bed in Commander John Pickford's[15] sitting room. Once Summers moved ashore as Commander of the whole Canadian operation, Miller moved into the Squadron Commander's cabin.

When the Task Group finally sailed, ATHABASKAN had on board 313 personnel, TERRA NOVA 249, and PROTECTEUR 372. PROTECTEUR, which was carrying the increased air and medical departments as well as two of the army's air defence units, had 70 people on board who had never been to sea before in their entire lives.

---

15. The Captain of a ship is a title, regardless of rank. The Captain of ATHABASKAN was Commander John Pickford; the Captain of TERRA NOVA was Commander Stu Andrews; and the Captain of PROTECTEUR was Captain Doug McClean.

CHAPTER TWO

Making Do With What You Have

It's the Canadian way: take a whole hodgepodge of equipment and put it together and make it work. We've taken a Dutch fire control system and married it with an Italian gun in the Tribal class destroyers, and it works, and everybody looks at this and asks, "how on earth did you do that?"

Canadians do it, Canadians make it work. The U.S. works on brute strength and the latest technology, and if it's simple, even better. Some of the Europeans work on very intricate and complex systems. The British produce good solid equipment—if it's built to withstand a direct hit, it's British. And Canadians have looked at all of this and said, 'Yeah, there's a time to be able to use each of those philosophies—let's put them together.' And it's the putting them together that's the challenge. That's where we excel.

In the days before the government announced it was sending three ships to the Gulf, Commodore Ken Summers held meetings with his key staff to discuss the options for Canadian naval involvement in the Gulf. Although there had been no government decision to participate in the enforcement of an economic embargo, there were very strong suggestions that this could happen. In that event, the navy had to be prepared. Summers, therefore, had to know what would be feasible in a short time frame—what threat could be expected, what ships could go, and what equipment could be fitted in the ships to counter the threat.

If the navy was indeed to send a self-sustaining task group, it would have to include a command ship—that meant a DDH-280 destroyer had to be a part of the excursion. The 280s are the only ships in the Canadian navy which have the space and equipment to support a squadron commander and his staff. But not all four of the navy's DDH-280s were available: two were in the shipyard at MIL Davie in Lauzon, Quebec, undergoing a major modernization program, and a third was on the west coast. That left ATHABASKAN.

If the task group was going to stay in the Gulf any length of time—as was expected would be the case—a supply ship would have to go as well. Two of the navy's three replenishment ships were unavailable: one was on the west coast and one had just entered Halifax-Dartmouth Industries Ltd.'s shipyard for a scheduled refit. That left PROTECTEUR.

While a 280 and a supply ship might have been sufficient, Summers and his people preferred to add one more ship to make up a task group. There were two to choose from: TERRA NOVA and FRASER. TERRA NOVA, a 31-year-old Improved Restigouche destroyer, was the preferred option because she was the only ship equipped with the new defensive Canadian Electronic Warfare System.

Even before the ships were chosen, National Defence Headquarters was working on what equipment would be required. Canadian destroyers carried mainly anti-submarine warfare systems, and supply ships had no weapons systems at all. The ships selected for the mission were going to need a substantial amount of work to be ready for what would confront them in the Gulf. The Iraqis had no submarines but they did have sophisticated fighter/bomber aircraft and Exocet missiles—the ones that rose to fame for the damage they inflicted on British ships during the 1982 Falklands war. The Arabian Gulf had also been heavily mined during the Iran-Iraq War of 1980-88 and Iraq was believed to be adding more mines as it became apparent that the international community would respond to the invasion of Kuwait.

Because of the nature of the threat, the navy decided to remove the anti-submarine warfare equipment from the ships (including the mortars, anti-submarine rockets, and some of the sonar transducers) and use the freed-up space for anti-air weapons and other specialized equipment. The ships would also have to be fitted with some kind of mine countermeasures equipment. Additionally, because the Task Group would be intercepting shipping and enforcing an economic and military embargo, the ships would need various sizes of guns which could provide a graduated response to vessels who ignored the U.N.'s request that they stop, provide information, and allow themselves to be boarded.

Working closely with National Defence Headquarters in Ottawa, Summers and his staff had the responsibility of figuring out what, given the time constraints, could reasonably be fitted in the ships. As a first step, Summers chaired a meeting of his staff, the captains of the three ships, and the navy's engineers, to discuss equipping the ships. The next step, however, presented a major problem: how to proceed? With such a wide range of equipment being put into three ships at once, the navy's usual painstaking planning process could not be used. There was only one way to proceed: a huge meeting was convened at the Maritime Headquarters. This meeting included the ships' commanders and their operational officers, the chiefs of staff of the navy for Materiel, Personnel, and Training as well as the Commanding Officer of the Ship Repair Unit, and workers from the dockyard, including electricians, shipwrights, riggers, and armaments specialists, who came with their relevant engineering authorities. Sitting around the huge meeting room, with diagrams and blueprints spread over the conference table, this staff began the process of identifying what had to be done to install each piece of new equipment. Starting with a relatively simple system, the 40mm Bofors gun, the commanding officer of each ship said where he wanted it installed. The representative from the rigging shop would determine if there was a problem with the placement, and then the engineer evaluated the power requirements. And on it went, until the installation of every piece of new equipment had been sorted out. They had the plans, and were in the process of installation within a day. From then on, it was a matter of keeping track of the progress on a daily basis, making changes as needed.

Captain Jim King, Deputy Chief of Staff, Readiness—a major co-ordinator at these meetings—ascribes the success of this novel approach to ship planning to the quality of the people involved. "Based on their experience and their knowledge of our systems and what could be done, people were not reluctant to make very key decisions about what was possible and how they could compromise. So we went from equipment to equipment, from ship to ship, and decided where it would all go and what changes would have to be made."

Summers' staff maintained a catalogue of equipment systems and the schedule for fitting each of them in the ships, as well as the other concurrent activities such as bringing on board stores, changing and training personnel, and adding medical facilities. The catalogue was critical to helping the staff answer four key questions: could they get the equipment in time?, could they fit it in time?, could they train their people in operating it?, and could they support it?

The task of fitting the equipment in the time allotted fell to the Ship Repair Unit (Atlantic) working with the Naval Engineering Unit. The commander of the repair facility, Captain Roger Chiasson, had no more than two days warning of what was to come. During the initial planning, no one fully understood the enormity of the undertaking. He says that in retrospect, "if we had been given time to prepare and if we had known what the schedule was, I think we would have scared ourselves out of our wits and said this is totally impossible." Ironically, the navy was lucky that time was short.

Chiasson had taken command of the unit only three weeks before, on July 16, having come from the Canadian Patrol Frigate program where he was Deputy Project Manager at Saint John Shipbuilding Limited in New Brunswick. (The personal contacts he had from that job occasionally came in handy when he needed to track down equipment sources for the refitting of the three ships going to the Gulf.) His whole career, however, had prepared him for the task at hand. An engineer by classification and training, he has managed ship refits and new construction most of his naval life of 30 years. He had been dealing with the Ship Repair Units on both coasts and he knew their capabilities. He is modest in describing his role in the ship repair process: "I made up my mind very soon after I arrived that the last thing I had to do was tell this place how to fix ships. And that is still the way I run this place. I do not get involved in the detailed direction of fixing ships." Chiasson believes in surrounding himself with competent people and delegating the work to them. It's a management style that paid off for this monumental task.

Lieutenant-Commander Graham Chamberlain was the Production Operations Officer at the Ship Repair Unit. The job was a high-pressure one because he functioned as the customer focus point, keeping his finger on the pulse of the day-to-day operations. He was on leave the Friday the government announced it was sending ships to the Gulf, but on Saturday, August 11 he appeared at Chiasson's office door, saying he was ready to get to work. Chiasson put Chamberlain and Acting Production Commander John Bouchard, the senior civilian on staff, in charge of the work.

One of the reasons that the Ship Repair Unit was able to get the ships ready to sail inside of two weeks, was the co-operation the navy received from the workers and their unions. The rules governing the division of work amongst the various trades were tossed aside, as everyone pitched in to get the job done. The result was about 90,000 person-hours of work in two weeks. Workers, organized into three shifts, worked around the clock. In the first four days, more than 500 workers had logged over

5,000 hours of overtime. By the end of the two weeks, the workers had put in 40,000 person-hours of overtime. Although there have been suggestions that the workers' main motivation in doing the work was the overtime money they received, Chiasson doesn't believe it. He says the average earnings in overtime for the two weeks was only about $2,500—hardly enough to justify the hard work and unflagging dedication he witnessed. Rather, Chiasson is convinced that it was a matter of national pride—"People were walking around with Canadian flags in their hardhats, and they were basically ready to work until they dropped."

Civilian dockyard workers, known as dockyard mateys, are the mainstay of the Ship Repair Unit. These are the men and women who do the technical and the mechanical work of the shipyard: crawling under and over the various bits of machinery, soldering wires, greasing here, bolting there. Normally they have the luxury of time and meticulous scheduling to carry out their work, but in August 1990, speed was of the essence.

Chiasson remembers one day in particular, when he had been on the bridge of PROTECTEUR, talking to Captain Doug McClean and his Executive Officer. Chiasson was returning to his office and as he was about to cross the gangplank, he saw a fairly small, frail worker with a huge "Santa" sack thrown over his shoulder. The bag, stuffed full with insulation, was big and bulky, and the small man was running down the jetty with it. He reached the gangplank, ran up it and disappeared through a door into the ship, ignoring Chiasson and the other officers, who had to step aside quickly to avoid being run over.

On another occasion, the Deputy Minister of National Defence, Robert Fowler, and numerous other senior officials were visiting the Ship Repair Unit. They were in the cable shop, one of the critical shops in the refit process, and were lined up watching the activity. All of a sudden everyone felt a wire moving amongst their legs—two workers were running out and measuring cable right where the high ranking officials were standing. It was another example of the dockyard mateys having a job to do and they were going to do it, regardless of who got in their way.

The Defence Department helped the refit program by streamlining the procurement process. Things were done on the strength of a phone call and then followed up with the appropriate paperwork. Lieutenants found themselves exercising enormous power as they phoned for such things as pieces of communications equipment, and demanding that it appear within minutes. There was little argument. The officers got what they wanted, where and when they wanted it. Usually all equipment requests filter through the base supply organization, but there was no time for that. Flatbed trucks were travelling all over the continent, picking up the necessary supplies. Aircraft were dispatched to pick up key components. Materiel began arriving before the Ship Repair Unit put in the requisition—forward-thinking young officers in headquarters would take the initiative and organize with a supplier for the delivery of equipment that they knew would be needed. But while a seven-tonne mount for a Close-in Weapon System was a fairly obvious requirement, identifying all the cables and connectors that went with it was more of a challenge and the responsibility of the Ship Repair Unit. Chiasson recalls that his Materiel Support Officer, Lieutenant-Commander Bob Alce, had a bunk installed in his office and, except for one night, spent the entire two weeks at the repair unit. Chiasson says, "Things were coming so fast and so heavy that Bob's staff would just go out on the jetty every morning and find out what had arrived."

The ships' staff also worked around the clock, helping to install the new equipment, advising the engineers and the dockyard workers, and ensuring the safety and security of everyone on board.

Industry, too, did its part in getting the ships ready. Locally, the Ship Repair Unit contracted with various private companies such as Halifax-Dartmouth Industries Ltd., for a total of about 10,000 person-hours of work. Nationally, major contractors such as Paramax Systems Canada of Montreal and Saint John Shipbuilding Limited of New Brunswick, co-operated with the Department by pirating weapons and sensors systems from the Canadian Patrol Frigate and Tribal class destroyers, and responding to urgent requests for spare parts, testing, and field service engineers.

The Assistant Deputy Minister (Materiel) organization had to keep track of all the systems, cabling, connectors, spares and miscellaneous items used from other ship programs—and it had to be ready to deal with the practical and legal backwash if companies were unable to meet their contracted deadlines for those projects. Surprisingly, however, when the final tallies were in, the diversion of major weapons systems from the Tribal upgrade and new frigate programs did not have a significant impact on the completion of those ships. But the systems were of profound importance to the three ships sent to the Gulf.

Command, Control and Communications Equipment

ATHABASKAN, a Tribal class destroyer, was built to function as a command ship. It had the space and the command and control systems to accommodate a squadron commander and his staff. But the backup plan for command and control was not so straightforward: Summers wanted PROTECTEUR to function as the alternate command ship during those times when ATHABASKAN was in port. This was a new concept for the Canadian navy. Although the U.S. Navy uses its replenishment vessels as command ships, Canada has always steered clear of the idea because it has never viewed supply ships as tactical vessels.

Nevertheless, the navy transformed PROTECTEUR from a logistics ship to a command and control ship—quite a leap for a vessel that had only a rudimentary operations room. Into this sparsely-equipped centre, the navy fit two command and control systems—the Automated Data Link Plotting Systems. Produced by Litton Systems Canada Ltd. of Toronto, this computer system was designed to replace the manual plotting tables that the navy used to have. It displays the information from the ship's sensor and weapons systems which detect, classify, and track aircraft, ships and submarines. This information can be sent to other ships' computers via a data-communications system called a Link 11, which also had to be installed in PROTECTEUR. Finally the navy fitted the new operations centre with the controls for the new weapons systems, and extra air conditioning to keep the electronic components cool in the heat of the Middle East.

ATHABASKAN, as command ship, was already equipped with a command and control system, the CCS-280. TERRA NOVA had an Automated Data Link Plotting System and Link 11 set on board.

All three ships were equipped with a Joint Operational Tactical System (JOTS) which provides a picture of the ship traffic in a region. The display is not automatically updated by radar inputs as the situation changes but requires manual updating based on information received by, and rebroadcast from, a central source—in the case of the Arabian Gulf deployment, an American ship. In Canada, the JOTS is usually found only in the command ship of a task group, but for the Gulf deployment, the system was put in all three ships and the software upgraded.

All the ships were fitted with an International Maritime Satellite (INMARSAT), a commercial satellite communications system. INMARSAT provides ships with worldwide data and voice communications via satellite and commercial telephone systems. By hooking an American cryptographic system, the Secure Telephone Unit (STU III), into INMARSAT, the satellite can be used to send and receive coded voice and facsimile communications. In ATHABASKAN, the antenna was fitted on the area above the bridge. However, one of the fire control radar antennae—large spherical antennae which are characteristic of the Tribal class destroyers—obstructed reception over a 15-30 degree arc. Consequently, the ship's heading at the time of transmission on the INMARSAT, would have to be taken into account, and occasionally changed so that the receiver and transmitter would be pointing towards the satellite being used. But as Miller says, "This was no great operational problem as we're used to that because we have on-board helicopters. We're used to having to change the ship's heading to fly into the wind to land and launch the helicopter."

The ships were also fitted with the Demand Assigned Multiple Access Satellite Communications (called DAMA/SATCOM for short), a military satellite communications system. Instead of the more traditional single channel per carrier type of system, DAMA/SATCOM has a pool of satellite bandwidth available that is automatically allotted to users according to their priority. Once a user has transmitted a message, the bandwidth is automatically reallocated.[1]

Air Defence Equipment

The long-range capabilities of modern weapons make it essential for a ship to be able to detect and identify an enemy at great distances—it's much easier to destroy an aircraft or ship before they launch their weapons, than it is to shoot down a small, low-flying, supersonic missile. Easier, but not easy. One of the major threats facing the ships going to the Gulf was the possibility of an Iraqi fighter aircraft firing missiles at the Task Group from up to 70 km away. To counter that threat, the ships needed modern sensors to detect the aircraft, and sophisticated weapons to shoot down either the jet or the missile.

All electronic equipment has a unique electronic signature[2] which can be detected and identified by specialized electronic support measures equipment. In PROTECTEUR, that equipment, which was quickly

---

1. Mark Hewish, "Satellite communications: more bandwidth and terminals needed", in *Defense Electronics & Computing* (Supplement to *International Defense Review* 9/1991), p. 109.
2. James F. Dunnigan, *How to Make War* (William Morrow and Company, New York: 1988), p. 362.

acquired and fitted, was the British Kestrel System. Kestrel is a broadband electronic support measures system which gives the ship the bearing of intercepted radar emissions from ships, missiles and aircraft. Kestrel also has its own automatic computer operated threat library, which, when fitted in PROTECTEUR, was configured to the Arabian Gulf so that it could identify the source of the radar emissions in that region. For detecting aircraft and surface ships, the supply ship had only a commercial navigational radar, good for a radius of about 50 kilometres—sufficient for normal peacetime activities but not for operations in the Arabian Gulf. To improve the ship's detection capabilities, the navy fitted PROTECTEUR with the SPS-502 radar, which has both navigation and surface search capabilities.

Instead of Kestrel, the navy equipped ATHABASKAN with the ALR-76 electronic support measures receiver. Previously fitted in the navy's Tracker coastal patrol aircraft which were taken out of service in 1989, the ALR-76 is a listening device which tells the ship when it is being targetted by a missile's or aircraft's radar. Like Kestrel, the ALR-76 receiver came with a threat library.

ATHABASKAN was already equipped with an electronic support measures receiver, the WLR1, which was left onboard. Although it is an older, slower piece of electronic warfare equipment, it has an advantage over more modern systems: it provides the operator with the detailed analytical information needed to identify the source of the emission, such as a Mirage or F-18 fighter aircraft. Systems such as Kestrel, although computerized and very fast, do not give a full analysis. They merely search their libraries and give the operator a choice of what could be the source of the emission.

The most sophisticated electronic warfare system was already in TERRA NOVA—the Canadian Naval Electronic Warfare System (CANEWS) manufactured by MEL Defence Systems Ltd. of Stittsville, Ontario.[3] It combines the best of the old and the new: it is a fast, computerized system like Kestrel yet it is analytical like the WLR1. CANEWS provides instantaneous detection, identification and warning of air threats.

Once a threat was detected, the ships would need weapons systems to protect themselves. Only one of the three ships was already equipped with an air defence system: ATHABASKAN carried Sea Sparrow missiles

---

3. MEL has since been taken over by Lockheed Canada Inc. of Ottawa.

and two quad launchers—retractable arms fitted with four missiles that swing over the side of the ship for firing. These radar guided missiles are capable of shooting down enemy aircraft out to about 14 kilometres. The navy left this system onboard, but just before the war started, the missiles were upgraded.[4]

One ship fitted with a local defence system, however, was hardly sufficient. All three ships would have to be re-equipped to handle the threat posed by Iraq's aircraft and missiles.

The most sophisticated piece of equipment placed in all three ships was the Block 1 Phalanx Close-In Weapon System (CIWS, pronounced Seawizz), a last ditch defence system for use against low-flying aircraft and anti-ship missiles such as the French-built Exocet. The Phalanx is a six-barrel, 20mm Gatling gun, which fires high density shells at a rate of 3,000 rounds per minute, effectively throwing up a wall of steel. The automatic, self-contained system has its own tracking radar and a range of about a mile. It can track several targets at the same time.

As soon as word came down that the ships were likely to be fitted with a Phalanx Close-In Weapon System, Commander Stu Andrews of TERRA NOVA was determined to get one for his ship.

> I knew that there was one over in Dartmouth for use by the naval armaments people. I didn't know if there were any anywhere else, but I did know there was one there. So I grabbed my Combat Systems Engineer and told him, "I don't care what you've got to do, but I want that one," figuring a bird in the hand was better than two in the bush. So whatever influence that he had on the process, we got the one from Dartmouth. I was very pleased—now I knew we had one.

Unfortunately, his pleasure didn't last for long. That system had been used for maintenance training and it is likely that the wear and tear of student use and the constant taking apart and putting back together was responsible for the problems that plagued it during the Gulf deployment until its eventual replacement in late December 1990.[5] Andrews says the other two ships received brand new equipment, "straight out of the cartons," and "I've been kicking myself ever since."

---

4. See Chapter Seven, pp. 136-138.
5. See Chapter Seven, pp. 130-132.

To fit the CIWS in ATHABASKAN and TERRA NOVA, the anti-submarine mortar system had to be removed from the stern—which was not a loss because the submarine threat in the Gulf was nil. PROTECTEUR had two CIWS fitted, one on top of the aircraft hanger on the stern and one on top of the bridge. Because ships' hangers are made of aluminum they do not have the strength to support a piece of equipment weighing a total of about 10 tonnes. So the shipyard engineers fashioned one-metre-wide steel beams to run across the top of PROTECTEUR's hanger and pilotage which were attached to the vertical joists and thus could transfer the weight of the CIWS from the hanger to the ship.

In just 24 hours, the power and cooling water were connected for the seven-tonne CIWS mounts in ATHABASKAN and PROTECTEUR, and their mechanical operations tested. The procedure, called being "set to work", usually takes two weeks and the Canadian efficiency absolutely astounded the field service representative from General Dynamics. Miller remembers the attitude that produced the quick results.

> I'll never forget going down to the dockyard and watching the workers actually place this thing on the quarterdeck of ATHABASKAN. I stopped and talked to the dockyard matey who was hooking it up after the base had been welded onto the deck. I said, "How's it going?"
>
> "It's going just fine," he said. "There's 267 little contacts that I have to solder here. Each of them has a little different colour wire on it and I have to put the little different colour wire on the little solder that belongs to that wire and I'm not allowed to get them mixed up. And I'd be doing a whole bunch better if I wasn't talking to you, Sir."

This particular piece of equipment had never before been fitted in a Canadian ship. It was available because it was going in the 12 new patrol frigates. The navy took four from that program and installed them in the ships going to the Gulf. Because the navy was preparing crews for the new frigates, the Task Group was able to get two crew members who had completed the CIWS training course. But there was a definite learning curve associated with operating the equipment.

The Phalanx Close-In Weapon System is a computerized system which can be programmed to fire at a specific target. It could be told, for example, to fire only at aircraft going faster than 140 knots which is the top speed of the Sea King helicopter and thus was a way of ensuring that the Task Group's own choppers weren't accidentally shot out of the sky.

> *But the first time the system was shut down for maintenance, we made a startling discovery. After working on the system, the operators had switched it back on. At about the same time, one of our Sea King helicopters had just left the ship for a training exercise. As the helicopter moved away from the ship and gained speed, the Phalanx gun suddenly started whirring around. It was completely unexpected and made everyone jump. What the heck was going on? The operators quickly checked the parameters of the system and figured out that when they shut it down for maintenance and then turned it back on, it reloaded the baseline memory, not the reconfigured program. The baseline program called for the system to fire at anything going faster than 90 knots. Fortunately, the system was not on automatic so although the gun whirred around tracking the helicopter, it didn't fire.[6] From then on, whenever the system was switched on after being shut down for maintenance, the operators re-entered the parameters.*

For further air defence, the ships carried a total of 32 members of the 119th Air Defence Battery out of Chatham, New Brunswick. These army personnel were equipped with a shoulder-launched, optically-guided, short-range missile system. These missiles were initially "Blowpipes," which the army had in stock, but they were later replaced by newer "Javelins" acquired from Shorts Brothers in Ireland.

The ships were also fitted with chaff systems. Chaff is a passive air defence system consisting of rockets which explode in the air, releasing strips of metal which confuse aircraft and missile guidance systems. The chaff rockets are launched at the very last minute. Depending on their type, the explosion releases either glowing magnesium strips which are so hot they seduce infra-red (heat-seeking) guided missiles away from the ship, or a cloud of metal foil strips which confuse the enemy's radar.

In addition to its regular onboard chaff system, ATHABASKAN was fitted with the newer Shield system. Shield rockets are fired automatically by a computerized system once a threat is detected. The system assesses

---

6. The CIWS has three settings: automatic, which means it will track and fire at anything within the entered parameters; manual, whereby it will track a target but will only shoot when someone flicks the appropriate switch; and standby, where the system doesn't track or shoot but will alert the operator that there may be targets out there.

the threat and searches its computerized databank for the appropriate response—what type of rocket to fire (either magnesium or metal foil strips), and in what pattern around the ship. Each rocket round is made up of seven small canisters that explode one at a time with a few seconds between each one. Each burst burns for about 30 seconds.

PROTECTEUR was given the Shield system, in addition to the Super-Rapid-Blooming Offboard Chaff (SRBOC), a standard metal chaff launcher. A SRBOC launcher was fitted onboard each side of the bridge, with each able to launch several canisters of metal foil strips.

TERRA NOVA already had the SRBOC on board, but it was given an additional decoy system, the DLF-2, or as it is more commonly referred to, the Rubber Duck. This is dropped off the ship in a canister which then inflates to a large tetrahedral figure. Because of its large radar cross section, the missile is fooled into homing onto the DLF-2 and away from the ship.

Perhaps the most controversial piece of equipment that was fitted in the three ships was the 40mm gun—one on each of the port and starboard sides of the ships—that came from the military's stock.[7] The 40mm or Bofors guns were built in 1943 and had been used in Canada's last aircraft carrier, HMCS BONAVENTURE. After she was decommissioned in 1970, the Bofors guns were sent to Germany where they used to defend the Canadian bases against air attacks. When the army bought a new low-level air defence system in the 1980s, the Bofors were returned to Canada and placed in storage where they remained until the Arabian Gulf crisis. The fact that there were no electronics in this very old mechanical system was perceived as an advantage: the Bofors is unaffected by deceptive measures such as chaff. When a ship fires chaff into the air, all its own radars can be affected, including its fire control radars. But the Bofors, because it's manually operated, is still usable.

It has a range of 5,000 meters and a firing rate of 120 rounds per minute—and the military had plenty of ammunition on hand. The gun, which fires a tracer round that burns as it flies to show the gunner where his stream of fire is going, uses ammunition armed with a proximity fuse: the shell is detonated once radio waves inside it detect the presence

---

7. There is an apocryphal story passed around by the media that one of these guns came from a museum. That is not correct. While there was one in the Maritime Command museum, neither it nor the parts for it were considered for use in the Task Group ships because it was a much older version of the gun. The authors would like to thank Lieutenant-Commander Richard Gimblett of the Directorate of History for the research on this issue.

of a nearby ship or aircraft. Using proximity fuse ammunition means the gunner doesn't have to score a direct hit to do a lot of damage to small ships and aircraft. Although the 40mm gun was designed for anti-air warfare, its primary use in the Gulf was to make a good splash in front of a vessel that refused to stop or turn around.

Anti-Ship Weapons

TERRA NOVA was the only ship fitted with the McDonnell Douglas' Block 1C Harpoon surface-to-surface missile system.[8] This powerful, high-tech weapon has a range in excess of 70 miles (112 km) and can do tremendous damage to most ships. It moves at subsonic speed and uses an active homing radar for guidance. Because the navy is putting the Harpoon in its new patrol frigates, it had the weapon system in stock. Fitting the eight launchers of the Harpoon system aboard TERRA NOVA was a painstaking task. First the anti-submarine rocket torpedo launcher (ASROC) had to be removed, and then the Harpoon system had to be installed absolutely plumb level to the deck, and machined in place. Cabling then had to be laid to the operations room about 50 metres away not only for operational control of the weapon, but for targetting: the system's over-the-horizon capability requires the use of shipboard detection, location, and identification systems.

Once the equipment was fitted, the operators had to be certified to use it. Because the navy had crews in courses preparing for the new frigates, there were crewmembers available who had completed their courses on the Harpoon system. But they still needed to pass certification exams conducted by the U.S. Navy, a process which normally takes three weeks. Maritime Command didn't have three weeks—it had three days. Consequently, the American officials arrived in Halifax to bear witness to TERRA NOVA doing the impossible: within three days the ship and eight operators and technicians were certified, or at least certifiable.

The two destroyers were already equipped with a main gun—two 3"(76mm)/70 (Mk6) guns aboard TERRA NOVA and a 5"(127 mm)/54 OTO Melara Compact gun in ATHABASKAN.[9] PROTECTEUR had originally been equipped with a 3"(76mm)/50 (twin mount) at her bow

---

8. ATHABASKAN was not fitted with the Harpoon system because there was no room—the ship has a short quarterdeck.

9. When describing ship guns, the first figure is the inside diameter of the gun barrel, and the second figure is the length of the barrel in calibres. For example, 3"(76mm)/70 means the gun barrel has a diameter of 3 inches (or 76mm in the metric system) and a length of 210 inches (3" x 70 calibres).

but the navy had removed it a few years earlier because it was continually being damaged by heavy waves. The dockyard reinstalled it in less than 12 hours. That was possible because of the dedication of the workers, typified by one young surface weapons technician that Summers remembers. The sailor, who normally worked in the Fleet School, was on holidays somewhere in Nova Scotia when the activity in the dockyard began. When he heard about the refits, he said to himself, "They need me." Leaving his family at the cottage, he returned to Halifax and supervised the installation of the 3"(76mm)/50 gun aboard PROTECTEUR. Summers says, "At that stage of the game, people weren't really keeping track of who was who. Some people thought he was part of the ship's company, other people thought he was working in the dockyard, but it didn't make any difference; he was there, and that was his baby." After the work was finished, the sailor reached the obvious conclusion, "They need me over there." Summers says,

> That's when the question about who he was came to light. This guy, who had done all this on his own initiative, was now going to be left behind. But he wanted to go. When I was made aware of it, I said, "Make it so." Any guy that would take that type of interest in what was going on, and wanted to be part of it, he should go.

For firing across the bow or protecting a boarding party, the ships would be able to use the .50 calibre machine guns[10] which were fitted onboard the port and starboard sides of the ships. These fire at a rate of 450 rounds per minute, and like the Bofors are manually aimed. There were six .50 cal guns in ATHABASKAN and PROTECTEUR, and four in TERRA NOVA. In ATHABASKAN, one was right above Miller's living quarters, on the port side. It was hard-mounted to the deck, and when it was fired—as it was on a daily basis for training and to make sure it remained functional—Miller felt like he was living inside a tin drum. When he couldn't take it anymore, Miller would visit the operations area on the starboard side—usually just at the time when the crew would start firing the gun bolted to that deck.

Mine Countermeasures Equipment

The navy purchased three mine avoidance sonars from C-Tech in Cornwall, Ontario, and fitted them to the ships. This omni-directional fish-finding sonar uses a short pulse length sonar wave to detect very

---

10. A .50 cal machine gun uses ammunition that is 1/2 an inch in diameter (.5 inch).

small objects. Based on its fish-finding capabilities, the navy expected it to be able to detect mines out to 4,000 metres and as close as 200 metres. The system was tried in Halifax to make sure it worked, but because the water in Halifax harbour is considerably different from that in the Gulf, the Task Group would have to wait until it got to warmer climes before being confident.

The mine avoidance sonars were placed in the anti-submarine sonar domes underneath ATHABASKAN and TERRA NOVA. Putting the sonars in PROTECTEUR required jury-rigging. The ship has a swing-down dome for a sonar and it was empty, but the navy chose not to fit the mine avoidance sonar there for two reasons. First, the increased draught of the fully loaded supply ship was already a navigational concern in the shallow waters of the Gulf, without the addition of a sonar dome on the bottom of the hull. And, second, it would have put the sonar too far below the warm surface layer of the Gulf to be of any use detecting floating mines. Consequently, the navy decided to fit the sonar at the bow. The hastily designed structure to which the sonar was attached protruded off the front of the ship like a small horizontal oil derrick, 17 feet below the water line. There were problems attaching it because PROTECTEUR has an ice-reinforced bow. The workers, who were working underwater, kept breaking their drill bits as they tried to drill the necessary holes in the hull. By the time the Task Group left Halifax, the divers had only managed to drill a third of the holes. The job would have to be finished in Gibraltar.

ATHABASKAN and TERRA NOVA were fitted with Racal's Hyperfix system, an accurate electronic navigational system which uses fixed shore stations to determine the ship's location. The system is accurate to within 3 metres at ranges of 40-50 kilometres from shore.[11] There were shore-based installations in the Arabian Gulf, and by fitting the two destroyers with receivers, it allowed them to fix precisely the location of a detected mine. The ships did not use it extensively in the Gulf, but the system was very much appreciated when the ships had to travel through a mine field by following a previously navigated clear channel. The Hyperfix allowed them to be sure they were in the channel. The Hyperfix systems were already in stock, because they were to be fitted in recently acquired minesweeping auxiliary vessels.

---

11. Thomas G. Lynch, "Canada's Interim Minesweeping Vessels," in *NAVY International*, January 1991, pp. 21-23.

Special Fits

In addition to new weapons and sensors, ATHABASKAN was fitted with new engines. The ship has two cruise engines and two main engines: three of those four were changed in order to give the ship the longest time before maintenance became necessary. (The fourth engine was relatively new and had more than enough maintenance-free hours of life left.)

All three ships also carried Rigid Inflatable Boats (RIBS). These high-speed, extremely seaworthy, manoeuvrable boats were also from the new frigate program. They could be launched very quickly by a newly fitted hydraulic crane on the quarterdeck and were to be used by boarding parties sent to inspect merchant vessels. Those boarding parties would be carrying light sub-machine guns, equipment not normally carried on board ship until the Gulf crisis.

Finally, there was a concern about weight. The DDH-280 destroyers, of which ATHABASKAN is one, have to be carefully balanced. The naval engineers have always made sure that when fitting new equipment, something is removed or shifted in order to maintain the stability of the ship. In the case of the Gulf deployment, there were a great deal of new, and heavy, systems going onboard. To counteract this, weight savings had to be made elsewhere. Commander John Pickford decided to help out by ordering the ship's staff to remove all extra furnishings—which amounted to 90 tonnes of equipment. This included extra paper, rope, chains, lockers, false deckhead panelling, pictures, every second chair in the wardroom, messes, and cabins, and every second mirror in the washplaces. Pickford says removing the so-called "creature comforts" aboard his ship helped out with the weight problem, but it accomplished another objective as well: "it was important to set the tone for the ship's company. This was not going to be another NATO exercise. We didn't know what was going to happen."

In preparation for the hot climate, the decks were painted white to reflect the sun—an idea gleaned from the British experience in the Gulf, which paid off by reducing the temperatures inside the ships by about 5-10 degrees Celsius. The air conditioning systems in all three ships were completely stripped down, cleaned, and recharged, ready for the increased demand put upon them by both personnel and the sensitive electronic equipment. The ships were also equipped with extra desalination machines which proved extremely efficient: throughout the deployment the crews had sufficient water for drinking, cooking, and showers, despite consumption being double that used in cooler climes.

Sea Kings

The five CH-124A Sea King helicopters which were to accompany the ships to the Gulf also had to be modified. They, like the ships, were fitted out for their primary mission of anti-submarine warfare, and thus had to be re-equipped for a surface surveillance role in the Gulf. Immediately after being informed that the ships and their helicopters would be going to the Gulf, a team of staff officers from Maritime Air Group Headquarters produced a list of equipment that they believed could be fitted in the aircraft in the time available. The equipment included:

- a forward-looking infra-red (FLIR) sensor for night surveillance;
- a global positioning system for accurate long-range navigation;
- stabilized day/night binoculars and night vision goggles;
- chaff and flare launchers for self defence;
- radar warning receivers to warn against detection by hostile fire control radars;
- laser warning receivers to warn against detection by hostile target designators;
- an infra-red missile jammer for defence against heat-seeking missiles; and,
- a door mounted machine gun.[12]

The aircrew were provided with nuclear, biological and chemical defence suits, and cooling vests, as well as armoured seats and personal body armour.

To make room for the new equipment the sonar system and sonobuoy receivers were removed from the helicopters, but they were sent to the Task Group in shipping containers in case a submarine threat materialized from one of Iraq's allies, such as Libya. In addition to re-equipping the five helicopters going to the Gulf, Maritime Air Group approved the modification of a sixth helicopter to remain in Shearwater as a spare. It could be used for research, development, evaluation, and training in support of the air group in the Gulf.

The air force's connections with the United States and Great Britain through officer exchange programs came in very handy during the Sea

---

12. For more technical information on the modifications to the Sea Kings, see, Martin Shadwick, "Sea King Update," in *Aviation & Aerospace*, January 1991, pp. 12-14.

King re-equipping. McWha says "for example, we got the chaff launchers because of relationships that we had with people who had been on exchange in the United States. We knew people down there who could make the right connections to get us that gear. In fact, we were able to get it even though there was a great demand in the U.S. Navy." Maritime Air Group used the same networks to obtain information and training help for some of the equipment. According to McWha, "we managed to get people from the U.S. Marine Corps to give us training on air combat manoeuvring and evasion tactics for helicopters to get away from Iraqi fighters."

As the engineers, support personnel and test crews began work on the Sea King modification program, it quickly became apparent that the plan to produce one prototype aircraft with all the modifications finished was an impossibility. There was no Sea King which had in it the type of equipment being put in the Gulf helicopters—the air force was working from scratch. The re-equipment involved a lot of wiring and electrical work as well as large amounts of metal cutting, bending and riveting. For example, all of the antenna mounts had to be designed and manufactured. Because all of this took so much time—a commodity in extremely short supply—the engineers decided to install the various modifications concurrently in different aircraft so that they could all be tested—and redesigned if necessary—during the same two weeks. Only once the equipment had been properly fitted and approved in one aircraft could it be installed in the others.

By the time the Task Group was ready to sail, all the different pieces of equipment had been tested and approved, but none of the five helicopters had a complete, working fit of the new mission suite. The remainder of the work would have to be done en route.

Personnel

To protect the more than 900 officers and crew sailing to the Gulf, the navy stocked up on sunscreen, sunglasses, and Canadian-designed Tilley hats—the latter an inspiration of Lieutenant-Commander Jim Hayes. Hayes owned a Tilley hat and knew what a great piece of headgear it was: cool, protective, and virtually indestructible. He thought it would be an ideal piece of kit for the ships' companies. To that end, he sewed his squadron crest on the front of it, and wore it in front of Commodore Summers. Hayes got the desired reaction. Summers liked the hat so much he approved its acquisition for all members of the Task Group. Thereafter, Hayes' colleagues referred to him as "Jim Tilley."

Plans and Training

Vice-Admiral Robert George, Commander of Maritime Command, charged Summers with the responsibility for preparing both ships and crews for their mission. It was a mind-boggling task which required wide-ranging experience and a dependable staff. Summers had both.

The afternoon progress meeting with representatives from headquarters, the navy's operational staff, Maritime Air Group personnel, training staff, supply, and engineers from the Ship Repair Unit was held in the conference room at Maritime Command Headquarters. These specialists reviewed the ships' and crews' progress over the previous 24 hours and adjusted, as necessary, the plans for the next 24. With Summers overseeing the planning and progress of the entire operation, from refit through training to deployment, the rest of the squadron staff concentrated on specific aspects of the preparation.

Miller and Commander J.Y. Forcier were responsible for developing the tactical plans for the naval task group. In this, they found the allies immensely helpful. An officer from the Canadian Defence Liaison Staff, London, Lieutenant-Commander Graham Day, flew to Halifax with the operations plans and some of the publications that the Royal Navy used in their Armilla Patrols—regular patrols of the Southern Gulf, which the British began in 1980 to protect merchant shipping during the Iran-Iraq War. There were also two U.S. officers in fleet school who had operated in the Gulf, and who were able to provide invaluable tactical advice.

Forcier and Miller went through all these documents in detail. Each sitting with a stack of publications about a foot high, they would read as fast as they could, taking concise, one line notes, on any information that could prove important to the Canadian ships and their mission. For example, in one engineering section was the warning that upper deck fresh air intakes must have a filter over them to protect against the extremely fine sand that blows around the Middle East. What the Americans found worked best was a piece of foam, placed on the inside and the outside of the intakes, that allowed air to penetrate, but not sand. Miller and Forcier took note of that and gave the information to the squadron's chief engineer, who then went to the supply people. They hopped in a car, drove to Canadian Tire, bought rolls of foam, and that very day, chopped it up and began placing it over the air intakes.

Through the Fleet School's Combat Division, the navy began preparing the ship's operations staff for the large number of radar contacts they would be faced with in the Arabian Gulf. The training staff tried to swamp the operators by injecting as many contacts as they could onto the radar screens. Fortunately, the Fleet School and the Maritime Warfare Centre had British and American exchange officers who had actually been in the Gulf on various operations. They put together a training package of what the Canadian crews might be faced with in the Gulf.

Each of the three ships had two combat teams, so that operations could continue around the clock. For two intensive days, August 20-21, each of the six teams, along with the squadron staff, tested equipment and worked through every scenario the Maritime Warfare Centre and the Fleet School thought the Task Group might encounter in the Gulf. At that time, however, the navy believed its area of operations would be the Gulf of Oman, and therefore, the training was aimed at coping with the traffic and threat in that area. Fortunately, given the later change to the Task Group's operational area, the training staff included everything from possible surprise attacks to an all out war scenario. The squadron staff also went over PROTECTEUR's dual roles of replenishment ship and 'destroyer.' Using a supply vessel for patrolling and interdicting shipping was a new concept and the operational details required clear definition.

Myriad details and questions emerged for every facet of the deployment. The navy did its best, if not to answer every question before the ships sailed, at least to come up with the options to be tested en route. For example, with regard to the interdiction of merchant ships and the insertion of a boarding party to check the cargoes, who should be in the boarding party? What weapons do they carry? Should they wear a flak jacket and if they do and they fall out of the boat, would they sink? Do they wear a life jacket and a flak jacket? (The navy finally decided that the boarding party members should wear a flak jacket and a small, inflatable life jacket.)

Once the theory and the shore-based training was complete—or as complete as there was time for—the crews and ships had to be sent to sea for equipment trials. The Naval Engineering Unit (Atlantic) put together a list of trials that the three ships had to undergo before leaving Halifax. That was the easy part. Much harder was figuring out how to get all three ships through the extensive trial program in just two days. That scheduling job fell to Lieutenant-Commander Jim "Tilley" Hayes working with the Engineering Unit.

All three ships had to exercise at the same time, but on staggered schedules. For example, PROTECTEUR would be on the degaussing range, testing the effectiveness of her degaussing coils—electronic coils that go around a ship to reduce her magnetic signature—while ATHABASKAN would be testing her chemical warfare defences and electronic warfare system. Then PROTECTEUR would test her chemical warfare defences, while ATHABASKAN tested her echo sounder (a piece of equipment which measures the depth of the water beneath the hull) and gyroscope (the ship's electronically operated compass), and then moved to the degaussing range. Meanwhile, TERRA NOVA would be testing her electronic warfare systems. To complicate the scheduling further, when the ships began testing their search radars and their guns' automated tracking systems, the navy had to arrange for aircraft to fly in at specific times and altitudes. Fortunately, the interservice co-operation was tremendous: the air force provided the necessary CT-133 Silver Stars and CP-140 Aurora aircraft at a moment's notice, whenever asked.

Over the course of the trials, all the ships' weapons systems, except the hand-held Javelin close-in air defence system, were fired. They were not, however, fired at targets; the purpose of the exercise was to make sure the weapons would function, and that the control systems in the operations room actually worked. The firings also served to build confidence in the crew members using the weapons. Accuracy trials, however, would have to wait until the ships were en route to the Gulf.

Because of the number of trials which had to take place in 48 hours, with each ship's exercises dovetailing with another's, a problem with one ship would be felt throughout the at-sea trial schedule. Fortunately, most of the problems were small. For example, TERRA NOVA had trouble with her gyroscope. This is not an unusual occurrence, and in short order the ship's electronics technicians ripped out the faulty one and replaced it with a new one, so that she could get on with her next trial.

The crews became extremely efficient at fixing any equipment problems that cropped up during the trials. For example, putting new equipment in a ship changes the magnetic signature of the vessel and it may also interfere with the degaussing coils. Some cables, especially those of the Phalanx Close-in Weapon System, would create interference if they were too close to the degaussing cables. In ATHABASKAN that problem was solved by moving some equipment two feet to the left. As each ship found and corrected a problem, it would call the other two ships and alert them to a possible problem and solution.

For the first gruelling 36 hours, the crews underwent one trial after another, without a break. The next 12 hours of trials were at a slightly slower pace. At the end of the two days, the individuals had begun to work together as a team, and their minds were focused on the seriousness of the situation.

To give them time to visit with their families and say their goodbyes, the ships' crews had a one-day break before sailing for the Gulf. Even PROTECTEUR, despite some problems during the trials,[13] and the time-consuming task of taking on the fuel supply for the task group, was able to complete everything in time for her crew to get the well-deserved day's leave.

⌘   ⌘   ⌘

At the very start of the two week undertaking to ready the ships for their Arabian Gulf mission, Miller and his wife, Ann, hosted a barbeque for the squadron staff and their wives. Miller knew the families were extremely worried about the deployment because they had been bombarded with information on T.V. and in the newspapers about the Iraqi invasion of Kuwait, about Hussein's threats to the west, and about the possibility of battle. It had left everyone tense. Miller wanted to reassure them by privately going over the details of the preparations and the elements of the mission with them.

It was a good move. By informing and reassuring the families, they were ready for the media attention, an inevitable part of the mission. The very next morning after the barbeque, Wendy Dunn, wife of Chief Petty Officer Al Dunn, ran into a slew of reporters as she left the married quarters at Shannon Park. Asked if she knew about her husband's tasking, she was able to answer honestly and calmly that she knew all the details and was confident in the navy's ability to carry off the mission without any unnecessary risk to its people. Her composure and assurance in a time of personal upheaval was a public relations coup for the navy. It underlined that the authorities were not rushing into this commitment blindly but were carefully planning and preparing for the mission.

---

13. The Close-In-Weapon System was still being welded onto the deck when PROTECTEUR needed to get to the degaussing range. Because the scheduling was so tight, Captain Doug McClean decided to take the ship through its degaussing trials while the dockyard workers were still working on the CIWS, much to the surprise of the head of the dockyard.

The barbeque served another purpose for Ann Miller, Dusty's wife. She had an important task to hand to someone that night, and she picked her candidate carefully—Chief Petty Officer Dave Ashley. She did not know him well, but she knew he had an irreverent sense of humour, and that was what was needed. Knowing her husband's tendency to become impatient in tense situations, she said to the Chief, "Just keep Duncan laughing. Don't let him get too serious." It was that request that helped set the tone of the briefings held every evening at 1900 after Miller took command of the Task Group in October.

CHAPTER THREE

With a Little Help from Our Friends

On a sunny August 24, 1990, thousands of people gathered in Halifax harbour to wave goodbye to the Canadian ships and wish them well in their mission. Lining the public wharves, standing on rocks, and jammed onto pleasure craft, families, friends, Haligonians, and others felt the intense pride and sadness of sending ships off to a war zone. At 2:00 p.m., while bands played and people cheered, HMCS PROTECTEUR moved towards the open sea, followed by TERRA NOVA and ATHABASKAN. The five Sea King helicopters assigned to the ships followed them in formation, landing on board just outside of the harbour. "Operation Friction" was underway.

Unbeknownst, however, to the people waving and cheering on the shore, TERRA NOVA was in trouble. Within ten minutes of sailing, one of the ship's two primary generators had failed. Commander Stu Andrews, looked out to the thousands of people waving, the officials saluting, and the bands playing, and said, "I don't care. We're sailing. I'm not telling anybody we're not going." So the ship steamed forward on one generator until it was out of sight of Halifax harbour. Then Andrews quickly arranged for a replacement part to be flown to Gibraltar while his engineering staff beavered away at an interim fix.

TERRA NOVA's mechanical problem was not the only worry for the Task Group's officers and crews as Canada's eastern shore faded in the distance. As they went about their duties, they couldn't help but wonder whether or not they were sailing to war, where in the Gulf of Oman they would be operating, how the environment would affect them and their equipment, what kind of support to expect, what they would be doing and how they would be doing it, and, finally, when they would return. Although their questions would be answered as the journey progressed, at that moment, they were truly sailing into the unknown.

Overshadowing all of the operational questions, however, was another, more mundane, personal one: would the squadron staff work well together? Most of the staff already knew each other—the Canadian navy is a small organization—but that's not to say they all got along. With so many strong personalities in a confined space, there were turf wars that had to be fought. Even before leaving Halifax, McWha, Summers' Deputy Chief of Staff (Air) had managed to cross swords with the Commodore by not showing up for an official ceremony. But McWha, who was juggling three different jobs, had felt his responsibilities lay with his air department and the choppers, and was busy helping with the aircraft.

The two weeks spent getting ready for the deployment had been so busy, there had been no time for the men of the squadron staff to get to know each other and become friends. They had each been fully absorbed in their own duties and responsibilities. Now, with what had been the toughest two weeks of their lives behind them, they could look up from their desks and their papers to see who they would be expected to live, eat and sleep with for the next many months.

The command set-up had the trappings of a touchy situation, starting with an unusually heavy assemblage of brass: a Commodore (Summers) in charge of the mission, a Naval Captain as his Chief of Staff (Miller), a Commander and a Lieutenant-Colonel as Deputy Chiefs of Staff (Forcier and McWha), as well as three Lieutenant-Commanders (Hayes, Romanow and Laing) and a Major (Nordlund). The military abides by strict rules of seniority but all of these fiercely independent and strong-willed men were used to calling the shots to some degree. They also knew they were there specifically because they were not the types to say "yes sir" to every suggestion. They were there to give voice to ideas, doubts, and arguments. Consequently the first week at sea proved noisy and raucous as each officer tried to win support for his way of doing things. But by the time the ships reached Gibraltar, a peace had been obtained, and as the men adjusted to their roles, the staff coalesced as a team.

What drove the officers to overcome their personal differences during that first week at sea, was their determination to make the mission a success. That mission began with training—and, not surprisingly, it proved to be the first source of disagreement that had to be argued through and resolved without rancour.

Summers had been told by his commanding officer, Vice-Admiral Robert George, that he had been given the best equipment and the best people, but it would all mean nothing if Summers didn't train them properly. That, Summers says, accounts for "my total preoccupation between Halifax and Gibraltar with the training." He wanted to start training at a fairly advanced level, especially on the air defence side of things. The squadron staff disagreed. They believed that, after the hectic activity of the previous two weeks, the training on board ship had to move more slowly. Summers reluctantly agreed to an approach that started at a more basic level and increased substantially with each passing day.

In devising the training schedule, the staff knew they had to be demanding, but not to the point of exhausting everyone. The question was, where to draw the line? The crews had to be tested to their limits, but they still had to be ready and alert when they arrived in the area of operations. The training program set up to meet that criteria included keeping close tabs on the workings of all the ships' crews, and adjusting the schedule and the tasks when tiredness began wearing people down.

Part of that process involved changing the approach of the Sea Training Staff. Extremely rigorous and efficient groups of officers, chiefs, and petty officers, these teams are greeted by ships' crews with apprehension. Although the Sea Training Staff are there to help the crew members become more proficient in their jobs, they are unreservedly demanding and critical in how they go about that. What Miller did not want was for the criticism to become so intense that it became demoralizing for the men and women who had been "working their butts off for the last 10 days and were tired." So he convened a meeting in ATHABASKAN in which he discussed with the Training Staff, headed by Commander Mike Pulchny, the philosophical underpinnings of the training. Miller made it clear what this was to be: in his words, "Don't pound the living daylights out of these people the first few days, because we're going to go nowhere." He explained the need for the crews to come together as a team before they reached the Gulf. To that end, he wanted the Sea Trainers to hold off on the criticism, and instead be helpful. He told them, "If the ships' companies are coming up with good ideas, you must listen to them." He said to "be patient, be nice," and assist the crews by documenting the new procedures.

This was completely contrary to the Sea Training Staff's usual draconian approach. Because the Trainers are seen as "the authority," they generally discount what crew members say and tell them to do their jobs the way the books describe—no ifs, ands, or buts. This time, however, things were different. The Sea Trainers had little experience with the new weapons systems, while the crews had been training on them. There was initially some questioning of whether or not this new approach would work, but Pulchny threw his support behind the Captain's request, and the training team adapted.

It worked. After the meeting, the mood on board the ships changed. The tension dissipated and the crews went about their work in a serious yet relaxed manner. That attitude was a necessary component to the success of the training. Usually on naval exercises the biggest criticism lobbed at ships' companies is that they do not take the business seriously enough because they know it's not real and they act accordingly. But not this time. The crews knew they were going into a war zone, and they undertook the exercises en route with single-minded resolve.

Initially, the ships' captains wanted the squadron staff to put together a daily schedule for weapons exercises. But surprisingly, Miller refused and told the captains it was their responsibility to put together their own program for weapons training. This was a novel idea to the navy: everyone usually looks up and asks for direction. Miller would only give them a guideline on how many drills should be done in a week, but he wouldn't lay out a detailed program for training each watch on each weapon system.

Commander Stu Andrews, commanding officer of TERRA NOVA, says "the speed with which we went across didn't allow for a huge amount of time for interchange of ideas amongst the three ships. So it was a terrific experience for freewheeling, getting people together and coming up with ideas from all ranks. I made it very clear to my crew that nobody had a monopoly on good ideas." The crew responded with ideas on everything from operational procedures to organizing the watches and setting priorities—taking into account the extra duties imposed on the ship by the installation of the new weapons systems and the requirement to keep a lookout for mines. Because there were not enough crew members to do everything all at once, duties were organized as to what was most important at the time. For example, when not otherwise needed, the cooks and stewards were used for mine watch. Andrews says, "they were probably the best that we could have had because it was an unusual duty for them. So they were dead keen and very attentive."

PROTECTEUR had perhaps the hardest training job ahead of her. As a supply ship, she was not used to having any weapons systems on board. Not only did the crew have to learn how to use the weapons, but the ship as a whole had to adapt to battle tactics. The mindset in a destroyer is quite different from that of a tanker. For example, PROTECTEUR (and Canada's other two auxiliary-oiler-replenishment vessels, PROVIDER and PRESERVER) had no "action stations" plan, where the alarm goes off and crew members take up their positions with the weapons, more people go to the engine room and the operations room, and different officers go to the bridge. The supply ship's action state is "replenishment stations" which is used when another ship is coming alongside for fuel or supplies. Other than that, the supply ships have only "emergency stations" which are sounded when a ship is in distress and the crew members are required to act to save themselves or others. So a whole "action stations" organization had to be designed for PROTECTEUR, and it had to be done for nearly 400 people, instead of the normal complement of 20 officers and 240 crew members.

In addition to the need to implement an "action stations" plan, the supply ship had another unique problem. None of the five Sea Kings in the Task Group had a full fit of its new equipment. That meant the modifications would have to be completed en route. Because of that, PROTECTEUR's air department was particularly hard pressed during the Atlantic transit to finish the modifications on the aircraft while at the same time participating in the general crew training for combat and damage control. In addition, the supply ship's operations room was still not finished, with the satellite and other hookups still to be completed while the ship was underway and training.

The Task Group as a whole also had to adjust to the different type of operations it would be undertaking in the Gulf. The navy had not been involved in intercepting and boarding merchant ships since the Second World War; the navy's prime mission for the past 40 years had been anti-submarine warfare. Fortunately, the navy had already begun the process of expanding its capabilities in the realm of air defence.

Traditionally, when Canadian ships participated in multinational NATO exercises, they were split up and made part of larger groups, with the Canadian vessels reporting to a foreign commander. But for the last several years, Canada has wanted to have a more meaningful role in the NATO exercises. About five or six years ago, Canada put its metaphorical foot down. With the growing importance of passive towed array[1] expertise—a leap forward in surface vessel technology—the Canadian navy demanded

---

1. Passive towed arrays are sonars which are towed on lines far behind the ships and listen for the sounds of other ships and submarines.

a larger role in order to practice these anti-submarine warfare skills. NATO was initially not enthusiastic, but after Canada said it would participate with only one ship, not a full task group, the alliance gave Canada the role of anti-submarine warfare commander for the exercise. For several years, that's the role that the Canadian navy has played.

Anti-submarine warfare is much different from anti-air warfare. Defending against an air attack demands an immediate reaction, while hunting subs is conducted like a chess game in three dimensions. It requires thought, organization, and a thorough knowledge of the ship's capabilities. Miller believes that it was that type of methodical, meticulous training that allowed the ships to move quickly and competently into air defence.

> *We knew, over the last several years, that we had to start moving from the slow-moving anti-submarine warfare side to the fast reaction anti-air warfare side, and that's where we trained ourselves in our annual Maritime Command exercises. We made ourselves the anti-air warfare co-ordinator even though there were more capable allied ships in that area. So here they are saying, "Wait a minute, we've got this capability." But we'd say, "yeah, we know, but this is our exercise and we want to learn your capability, so how about you send a few officers over to our ship, and help us out." And they did. So even though we didn't have the actual weapons systems, the fact that we said we did on paper, meant that we had to think anti-air warfare in a serious way. And that paid off in spades in the Gulf for ATHABASKAN.*

The transit across the Atlantic was used as an intense air defence training period, as crews became familiar with the Phalanx Close-In Weapon System, Sea Sparrow missiles, Bofors guns, and chaff systems. The chaff system in particular led to some hair-raising moments.

Captain Doug McClean, PROTECTEUR's commanding officer, says no one on board was familiar with the Shield system fitted each side of the ship. They knew that each infra-red rocket round consisted of seven small canisters that would explode one at a time with a few seconds' interval and that each burst of chaff would burn for about 30 seconds. But PROTECTEUR's crew had no idea how long it would take to reload the system and fire again. So en route to the Gulf, McClean decided to try it. The plan was for the ship, closed up at "action stations," to fire a few rounds; then the loaders for the system, who were inside the bridge protected from the blast of the Shield, would run out, get some more rockets out of the lockers, reload the launchers, get back inside the bridge, and fire the system again. It was quite a blustery day, and the wind was off the port beam. PROTECTEUR's crew had read the books and looked at the diagrams but they still had one question: do you use the port or starboard launchers when there is a port wind? So McClean asked the Sea Trainers and the Weapons Chief said, "Sir, you always fire the windward launcher." With that, PROTECTEUR fired the launcher.

The first thing that surprised them was that the canisters did not fly off the ship a couple of hundred yards as expected, but only went about 50 yards. As the first one exploded, McClean said, "Boy, that's pretty damn close." He had no sooner voiced that thought when he realized to his horror that the burning chaff was drifting toward his ship. Still burning, it landed on the fo'c's'le. By then the second explosion had occurred, and there were still five to go. The Commander of Sea Training turned to McClean and quietly asked, "Is there any way we can stop it?" There wasn't: when one goes, the next six follow.

As the fire rained down on the deck—the deck of a ship filled with fuel and ammunition—one of the army air defence troops tried stomping it out. No luck—it lit the bottom of his boot on fire. McClean, watched helplessly as "he's busy now trying to put his shoe out—and the deck's still burning." Miraculously the ship (and the crewman with the burning boot) emerged unscathed from the seven bursts of chaff, but McClean learned two lessons from the experience: "Not to fire the windward launcher in a strong beam wind ... and Sea Trainers don't know everything." This latter point came as a surpise to McClean who used to command a Sea Training unit.

As a last-ditch defence against an air attack, each ship had on board an army air defence unit from 119 Air Defence Battery based in CFB Chatham. ATHABASKAN and TERRA NOVA each had eight army air defence personnel and PROTECTEUR had 16. In addition, there was an army officer, Lieutenant Paul Romeo, on the squadron staff. The air defence units, operating shoulder-launched Javelin air defence systems, faced a couple of training problems, including getting used to using a hand-held system on a moving deck. Because PROTECTEUR was not heaving as much as the two destroyers, the army personnel started their training by all moving over to the supply ship. The move also enhanced safety by having all the operators working together under the close eye of their range safety officer, Major Dan T. Cook, who sailed with the Task Group to Gibraltar. Then there was the problem of a target.

We had an Aurora CP-140 aircraft follow us over and it dropped flares and the army fired the first set of missiles at these flares. But they found that the optical guidance system was very light-sensitive and therefore these bright flares were not a good choice for target practice. Someone suggested we should do the same as the British which is use a Sea King helicopter, hovering on the horizon, just outside the range of the missile, and have the air defence units fire at that. Well the pilots didn't think that was such a hot idea! And even we had some sympathy for them. So we didn't do that. Instead, we found that a Very pistol fired from the ship provided a good enough target. The Very pistol looks like a sawed-off shotgun and fires a flare which is not as bright as those dropped from aircraft. The army managed to train itself using it as a target.

Usually these soldiers get to fire one missile about every one-to-two years, but en route to the Gulf, they fired about 60 missiles—many of which were the Blowpipes that had been sitting in the army's inventory for some time and would soon have had to be disposed of if they were not used—giving everyone a chance to fire a couple of missiles each. The men became extremely proficient, and the navy was confident of the air defence units' abilities to detect and engage the smallest of targets.[2]

While the army was getting its sea legs, the navy was getting re-acquainted with a land force weapon system—the army's Bofors 40mm air defence gun. Being manually aimed and operated, it was not a difficult weapon to figure out, but it did require some experience to use it effectively. The crew members put in many hours of practice, firing at targets placed on the ocean surface at varying distances and angles from the ships.

The ships used paraflares to train their crews on the use of the .50 cal machine guns. These small, handheld rockets were fired into the air and when they reached the top of their trajectory produced a bright light and a parachute. Drifting back down to the ocean, the paraflares made excellent targets for the machine gunners.

Helping to train the ships' crews while at the same time training themselves, were the air departments. Because not all the new equipment had been fitted in the Sea Kings before the Task Group left Halifax, none of the air crews had had a chance to fly the fully modified helicopter.

---

2. The army air defence units, because they were using optically guided missile systems, were on duty for daylight hours only. Dusk and dawn were deemed to be the hours of greatest threat.

As Major Pete Nordlund describes it, "when we sailed on the 24th of August, we were sailing with a helicopter that was completely foreign to us in many ways." During the transit across the Atlantic the aircrews not only had to get used to operating the new equipment, but they had to develop tactics for using it. They also had to practice operating the aircraft while wearing chemical warfare protection outfits.

Nordlund says the aircrews figured out for themselves exactly what training they needed. "They got up there, got a feel for the equipment and how to use it, and then slowly they came up with a training package to improve their capabilities." Nordlund paced the crews so that they would not exhaust themselves, but made sure they all flew at least once a day.

Practicing and training wasn't limited to the Task Group's new equipment. The ships' companies had to become accustomed to working while wearing cumbersome chemical defence gear and the medical staff also had to be exercised. In particular, they had to be prepared for a large number of casualties. So as part of the en route training, the Sea Kings transported "casualties[3] to PROTECTEUR, 20 at a time to test both the ship's readiness to transport injured personnel from the flight deck to the surgery, and the medical team's ability to handle that kind of emergency.

Helping through all the exercises, was HMCS FRASER, a 33-year-old St. Laurent class destroyer which accompanied the Task Group as far as Gibraltar. She proved absolutely invaluable as an objective observer and judge of the Task Group's capabilities, and as an all-purpose "enemy." The ship laid "mines" in front of the Task Group, acted as a merchant vessel for boarding operations, built targets for the crews to fire their weapons at, and undertook surprise attacks to test the Task Group's responses and readiness.

Although the crew of FRASER did not serve in the Gulf, they were an invaluable part of the multinational effort against Iraq.

Commander Jay Plante, the ship's captain, had found the magic that a worked up, enthusiastic and professional surface ship's crew could weave. It was amazing. They kept calling over to PROTECTEUR for more wood to make targets. When we asked them how many they'd made, they said "about 50"! What we accomplished en route to the Gulf couldn't have been done without FRASER.

---

3. Not real ones; they were crew members made up to look like they had suffered various injuries such as burns, broken limbs, abdominal wounds, etc.

Gibraltar

Upon reaching Gibraltar on September 2, the ships underwent some routine maintenance. At the same time, divers finished fitting the mine avoidance sonar at the bow of PROTECTEUR, and TERRA NOVA had the barrel of her 3" gun changed in order to be sure that it had the longest possible operational life ahead. The three ships were also fitted with radar absorption material—the first time for Canadian vessels. The navy had checked the radar signatures of the three ships and had ordered the material beforehand so it was ready when the ships arrived. Maritime Command told the ships' captains that although it was unable to provide an exhaustive analysis of where best to place the radar absorbent material, it could tell them where the 90 degree angles were and where the signature could and should be reduced. But Maritime Headquarters added that once fitted, the ships would have to be put through a series of relatively lengthy trials, taking time that the Task Group didn't have.

Conflicting with the suggestion that the Task Group take the time to do trials off Gibraltar was a French offer for the ships to spend 12 hours off Toulon working with their aircraft which would simulate an attack by Exocet missiles. The squadron staff and ships' officers talked it over and decided to skip the Gibraltar radar absorption trials. They reasoned that having the material would be better than not having it—it would reduce the ships' signatures even if it hadn't been fitted in exactly the right place. MARCOM was not happy with the decision. But to Miller and Summers, there was no other option.

> We had a choice of doing MARCOM's trial, knowing that we fitted the radar absorption material, or taking advantage of the French offer to exercise us with their Mirage aircraft, which is flown by the missile head of an Exocet. To my mind there was no choice. I was going to take the French offer after leaving Gibraltar. We had to spend time getting to Toulon where we would work with the French, so I told MARCOM to tell us how we could do our own, shorter, trial of radar signatures.

So in the meantime, following instructions from MARCOM, the Task Group flew a Sea King helicopter around each ship to collect the radar signatures. That information was then used to determine steaming guidelines for the ships when they were in the Gulf. For example, at dusk and dawn—considered the most likely time for an attack—the ships adjusted their operations in order to steam in a way which presented the smallest radar signature to an attacking Iraqi aircraft, based on what the staff believed was the most likely approach for such an air attack. This could involve a ship sailing in the northern part of its patrol sector until 2:00 or 3:00 in the morning and then steaming on a southerly route from 3:00 to 6:00 a.m.

> *I think these kinds of things are clever, they have to be done, and they're asking 'what if?'. What if we get attacked at this particular time, how do we react. And everybody was thinking that way. And very quickly the ships' crews realized we're not being stupid out here, we're being very clever. That makes all the difference in the world to the individual sailors and their morale when they realize everyone really does know what they're doing.*

Before leaving Gibraltar the ships and their crews were put through an intense three-day exercise designed by Lieutenant-Commander Greg Romanow (the Sea Training Staff went ashore, having completed their job of getting the crews to the point of a readiness check). Working with Canadian and allied air and naval officers, he scheduled and co-ordinated the whole plan, which included everything from interdiction and boarding of a ship, to a small vessel dropping a mine in front of the Canadian ships—requiring a fast stop or manoeuvre—up to a full out attack, simulated by Canadian CF-18, CC-147 Challenger, and CP-140 Aurora long range maritime patrol aircraft as well as British Tornado, Canberra[4] and Buccaneer[5] aircraft and Boghammer fast patrol boats.

According to Romanow, "probably the hardest thing to co-ordinate is an operations room, because every piece of weaponry that has been added—from the machine gun to the Phalanx CIWS—has to be under the control of the combat officer. We had to co-ordinate all the communications, the orders, what they could and could not do, and what the rules of engagement were." The ships' companies had worked on that throughout the Atlantic crossing and now Romanow was going to see how well prepared they really were. He was also going to test one other person.

Summers asked Romanow for a briefing on the plan, before the exercise started. Romanow replied that he didn't think it was a good idea—making Miller wince and Summers glower. Displeased, Summers asked curtly, "Why not?" Romanow didn't miss a beat. "Well, essentially it's your decisions that are going to keep us all alive, and we kinda want

---

4. The Canberra aircraft used for the Gibraltar exercise was an electronic warfare control platform.
5. The Buccaneer is a low-level, high-speed attack aircraft.

to see how you'll do, Sir." Summers, though shocked, acceded to the setup. Romanow, alone of the squadron staff, was in control of the exercise.

Seated by himself at a console in the operations room, equipped with radios for communicating with the various aircraft and ships, Romanow orchestrated one of the most intensive tests ever of Canadian naval capability. The main event was the air attack.

> *The simulation was a Challenger aircraft coming out, with two CF-18s under its wings, to make it look like one aircraft on the radar. We were trying to make it look like a Mirage aircraft armed with Exocet missiles. At some stage of the exercise, the CF-18s would "fire," leaving the wings of the Challenger and aiming straight for the ship. There's nothing more demoralizing in our exercises than having those two CF-18s zooming by, and then hearing the weapons officer say, "For exercise, ENGAGE."*
>
> *We had to get them before they got us. The first time it happened in Gibraltar, you could hear the Phalanx system whirr around, lock onto both CF-18s, simulate fire, ... and then the aircraft went by. Morale went way up. But I said to Summers, "That's once. But they've got a couple more scheduled in here. Let's just hope this is consistent, and it doesn't matter what watch is on." Because we had to make sure both watches could do the same thing.*
>
> *The next two attacks went exactly the same way. Perfect. I called my staff on the other two ships and said "ATHABASKAN got hers. There is no problem here." And the staff on both TERRA NOVA and PROTECTEUR came right back, and said, "Yep, no problem here."*
>
> *Summers and I looked at each other and said, "Hot dog! They've got it. They've figured it out. They're ready for anything to be thrown at them."*
>
> *This was one of the few times when Summers went to the bridge of ATHABASKAN and made a "Well Done" pipe. Morale soared.*

The Royal Navy provided some of its vessels for the Canadian ships, deployed in three sectors off Gibraltar, to practise their interdiction techniques, including a shot across the bow and a boarding. The British also provided their Fleet Readiness and Air Defence Unit (FRADU) from Yeovilton. These electronic warfare aircraft are used to simulate enemy aircraft in an attack on ships. But because the British exercise package was not quite what the Canadians needed—it was geared to peacetime operations in the southern Gulf—Summers and Miller put together their own training exercise. The FRADU was initially piqued at the Canadian decision to design a different program, but on reflection, agreed to participate in it.

Although these exercises and others like them convinced the squadron staff, the ships' captains, and the ships' crews that they were ready to handle the threat in the Gulf, it wasn't so easy to convince their superiors back in Canada. And they remained unconvinced until Vice-Admiral Charles Thomas, Vice Chief of the Defence Staff, visited the Task Group in January. Thomas, especially, was skeptical of the Task Group's operational readiness because in his previous post as Maritime Commander he had sent a couple of ships out on surprise exercises, and they had performed badly.

Knowing that, Miller made sure that when Thomas came aboard the ships in January he heard from the sailors, because he would probably not believe the commanders who would be trying to present their capabilities in the best light. Thomas went through the normal intelligence briefs, toured the ships, and spoke to as many crew members as possible. He was convinced: the ships' crews were well trained and ready to fight.

East to Suez

At the end of the Gibraltar exercises, Summers and Commander J.Y. Forcier, Deputy Chief of Staff (Operations), left the Task Group to fly to a meeting of the national commanders of the countries sending ships to the Middle East to enforce the U.N. sanctions against Iraq. Miller, who was Acting Commander of the Canadian Task Group in Summers' absence, began moving the ships to the degaussing range at Augusta by tracing a route from east of Majorca, South of Sardinia, through the Strait of Messina. He chose that route as a precautionary move, because Libya's intentions at that point in the crisis were unknown and unpredictable. Libya was also the only country in the region which could pose a submarine threat. The Libyan navy had six Foxtrot submarines, which although obsolescent and probably not all operational, added to the unpredictability problem and made the Task Group cautious.

On the way to Augusta, off the coast of Toulon, the French provided, as promised, an Atlantique aircraft fitted with an Exocet missile head to test the ships' air defences. Flying the aircraft as if it was an Exocet missile, the pilot flew toward the ships, using the missile head's radar to guide the plane in for the attack. To defend against the attack the ships used tactical manoeuvres and chaff. Firing the chaff successfully took some practice—the three ships fired more in that one exercise than the Canadian navy fires in a year—but the results from the 12-hour exercise were edifying. The small TERRA NOVA, fitted with radar absorption material, and firing its chaff while manoeuvring appropriately, was almost invisible to the Exocet. The larger ATHABASKAN, equipped with a helicopter hanger and two helicopters, was almost as successful but could not hope to seduce the missile completely. While the destroyer was able to develop the necessary tactics to increase the odds of warding off an attack, it couldn't guarantee a 100 per cent success rate—it would depend on other factors such as the heading and speed of the ship, the direction the attack was coming from, and what else was going on at the same time.

Only PROTECTEUR did not fare well. It did not really matter what the supply ship did, she was a big target. Even using radar absorption material to reduce her signature by 50 per cent, PROTECTEUR still presented a 50 per cent larger target than ATHABASKAN. Also, being a tanker, the ship was unable to manoeuvre as quickly while firing her chaff. There was no way around it: she would have to rely on her two Phalanx Close-In Weapon Systems as the main defence against a missile attack.

The ships had already been degaussed in Halifax, but because the magnetic influences in the earth are different for different latitudes and different climates, the Task Group decided to take advantage of the Italian range at Augusta to do it again nearer the Gulf. Canadian technicians flew over from Canada to work on the monitoring equipment and help the ships reduce their magnetic signatures.

The ships also took advantage of their time in Sicily to test their mine avoidance sonars for the first time. There were a whole range of trials that had to be completed on this piece of equipment. By dropping a transponder in the water in various locations, each ship was able to test detection capabilities at different ranges, for all 360 degrees, under different conditions. (Detection ranges will vary depending on such things as the sea state, salinity, water temperature, and the speed of the ship.) The tests demonstrated that the ships were able to detect the transponder at a great enough distance for them to react with a manoeuvre that would avoid impact.

Well, it was long enough for the destroyers to react. PROTECTEUR was a different matter. Even before leaving Halifax, Captain Doug McClean had expressed skepticism that the mine avoidance sonar attached to the bow of his tanker would be effective. The detection range would not be sufficient for the supply ship to stop, because once it gets going, it is like a freight train which cannot be stopped or turned quickly. Even with a detection distance of 500 metres, the ship would not be able to react fast enough to avoid hitting a mine.

Summers and Forcier, flying via a Canadian military Challenger jet, met up with the Task Group in Augusta. Miller met them at the airport, and noted that Summers was quiet on the ride back to the ships. When Miller asked him what had happened at the meeting, Summers said he did not want to talk about it until they were back in the operations centre of ATHABASKAN. The reason became very clear upon arrival.

Summers asked Lieutenant-Commander Greg Romanow, the Senior Combat Officer, Lieutenant-Commander Kevin Laing, the Weapons Officer, and naval Lieutenant Dan Langlais, an intelligence officer seconded from National Defence headquarters, to join him, Forcier and Miller in the operations room. There he explained that Canada was being asked to deploy its ships, not in the Gulf of Oman, but on the front lines in the central Gulf. Their reaction, spoken almost in unison, was short and to the point—"Are you crazy?" Romanow was especially incensed that Summers was considering changing the deployment. The Lieutenant-Commander had spent 20 hours putting together a plan for the Task Group's deployment to the Gulf of Oman. He had put all the necessary messages out on the airwaves, he had scheduled the ships' rotations, and he had collected, written, and organized the necessary documentation to support the deployment. He was understandably aghast: all that work down the drain.

But Summers insisted. The deployment had to be considered seriously.

When the Task Group had left Halifax, the preliminary plan had been for it to undertake embargo enforcement operations in the Gulf of Oman, just outside the Arabian Gulf. This, however, was not carved in stone, and the government knew the plan could be amended as other nations joined the operation. When Summers attended the multinational meeting in Bahrain on September 9 and 10, the allies discussed using a sector approach to divide up the enforcement operation—there would be individual national patrol areas for each navy deploying to the region. Each navy was asked where, in the Arabian Gulf, Gulf of Oman, and

Red Sea area it intended to deploy its forces. Australia, Britain and the United States already had ships in the Gulf of Oman; the southern Gulf off the United Arab Emirates, was the preferred operating area of the British, Dutch, Italians and French. Meanwhile, Summers, buoyed by the air defence proficiency of his three ships during the training exercises en route, had, upon arrival in Bahrain, spoken with an American Admiral and told him that Canada wanted to do something significant, not just be a bit player.

Although the main enforcement work was to be done in the central Gulf, at the conference it was apparent that most of the coalition partners were opting for more southerly deployments. But Summers looked at the plans, and decided that the higher profile central Gulf area might be better for the three Canadian ships. After all, the crews had demonstrated an extremely effective air defence capability, and the ships were equipped with a satellite communications system that was compatible with the Americans. The other allies either used a different satellite system or were relying on High Frequency.[6] This caused Summers to be concerned "that if I was in with the rest of them in the southern Gulf, maybe word of a missile attack would not get to me." In terms of warning, it was obviously better for the Canadian ships to be close to the more northerly American ships.

To Summers, the conclusion was obvious: "the place for us, the one that was most professionally challenging, the one that had the highest visibility for Canada, and the one that as a naval commander I would be most comfortable operating in, was the central Gulf, as opposed to the southern Gulf or Gulf of Oman." But reaching that conclusion was not the same as making the decision. That could only be done by the government. Summers needed an objective assessment of the situation to present to National Defence headquarters in Ottawa. That's what he asked his staff for back in ATHABASKAN.

Summers wanted a staff paper which would assess the capabilities of the ships and their weapons systems; the self-defence capabilities of the ships; how well trained the crews were and what they could conceivably be expected to handle; what weapons the Iraqis could use against the Canadian ships—in particular what would be the range of the Exocet missile which Iraq uses on its Mirage fighter aircraft; and the possible areas of deployment for the Canadians—the Red Sea, the Gulf of Oman, the southern Gulf, and the central Gulf.

---

6. See Chapter 6 for information on the ships' communications systems and the problems with High Frequency radio waves.

Summers gave the five men their secret assignment at midnight on September 11-12. They had only eight hours to brief Summers on their conclusions and a total of 24 hours to prepare the final 30-page staff paper. That kind of staff effort would normally take six months back in Canada. To meet the 8:00 a.m. deadline, each officer took an area and then, using a comparative approach, they discussed each one. Their conclusion was that the Task Group was compatible with the U.S. forces operating in the central Gulf, the Canadian ships did have adequate self-defence systems, and if an American Aegis cruiser, with its immense anti-air warfare capability, was placed between the Canadians and Iraq, then the deployment was definitely possible. In fact, not only was a central Gulf deployment feasible, but the officers had given Summers enough information for him to conclude it was the best contribution that Canada's navy could make, and it would provide the highest profile for the small naval force.

One thing the officers did ask for, however, was air support. Although the U.S. had promised to provide air cover, their fighters would only be operating in a couple of areas of relevance to the Canadian Task Group. The officers felt they would be happier with more coverage. Their request, contained in the report submitted to Summers, was relayed to both Vice-Admiral Robert George, Commander of Maritime Command and to General John de Chastelain, the Chief of the Defence Staff. General de Chastelain relayed the report's recommendations to the Prime Minister and his "war cabinet" and quickly got the approval he needed for the Canadian ships to patrol the central Gulf. At the time, the government was already reviewing the option to send a squadron of CF-18s to the region. The Task Group's concern over air cover provided further rationale for the deployment of fighter aircraft.[7]

Defence Minister Bill McKnight later explained the decision to the Standing Committee on External Affairs and International Trade by summing up Summers' initial analysis: "The reason the operational area was selected, where we are operating today in the central part of the Persian Gulf, was that it provided the best opportunity for the Canadian task force to do good work." Pointing out the proximity of other naval forces in the area, McKnight added, "It allowed [the Canadian ships] to function in an environment that gave the men and women the best protection we could achieve."[8]

---

7. Ross Howard and Kevin Cox, "PM orders jet squadron to Persian Gulf," in *Globe and Mail*, Sept. 15, 1990, p. A1.
8. Standing Committee on External Affairs and International Trade, *Minutes*, Issue No. 67 (October 25, 1990), p. 18.

The patrol sector the squadron staff selected for Canada was in the central Gulf just outside the range of an Exocet missile, as launched from an unrefuelled Mirage aircraft. Most importantly, Miller and his officers did not want to operate the supply ship PROTECTEUR any further north without close protection. So PROTECTEUR, which was designated the alternate command ship, was assigned a relatively safer sector in the central Gulf which would allow her to participate in the interdiction mission, and if necessary, conduct boardings, while also being available for replenishing allied ships.

The ships left Augusta and proceeded to Port Said at the mouth of the Suez Canal (see Map 1). Somewhere near the Ionian Sea, Captain McClean thought he detected a problem in PROTECTEUR. He was asleep in his bunk when he was awakened by a "THUD" against the ship's side. Every ship has its own noises and motions, and because McClean was new to PROTECTEUR, he wasn't sure what he'd felt. He knew there was nothing out there but it really felt like the ship had hit something. He called up to the bridge and asked about the noise. He could only imagine the officers rolling their eyes as they assured their new captain that everything was fine, and that the ship had just been hit by a big wave. But McClean, despite the skepticism of his officers, knew what a big wave felt like, and he was pretty sure this was something more. He became suspicious that the mine avoidance sonar may have been damaged. So at the first opportunity, which was Port Said, McClean sought approval from the port authorities to send divers down to check out the sonar. The approval was denied, most likely because of the heavy traffic and high level of tension in the port.[9] It wasn't until the Task Group reached Great Bitter Lake, half way down the canal, that McClean was able to confirm his suspicions: the mine avoidance sonar was gone.

Before the ships could pass through the Suez Canal, tradition demanded that the government issue an Order-in-Council putting the crews on active service. Although military personnel are always considered to be on active service, if the government wishes to send them into high risk situations—as the area from the Suez Canal onwards was considered to be—there is a tradition that the government consult Parliament through the mechanism of an Order-in-Council. For political reasons, that was delayed.[10]

---

9. A ship sending divers below has to fly an international flag signifying its actions. Because of the general anxiety over a possible terrorist attack on the Suez Canal or its users, a ship flying such a flag would make other vessels in the area very nervous, wondering just what exactly the divers were doing.

10. Lt(N) Richard Gimblett, "Multinational naval operations: the Canadian Navy in the Persian Gulf, 1990-91," in *Canadian Defence Quarterly*, August 1992, pp. 25-31.

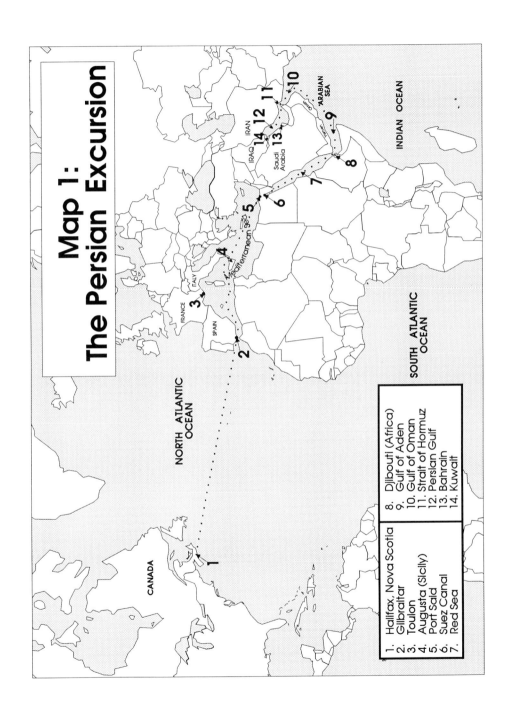

Map 1:
The Persian Excursion

1. Halifax, Nova Scotia
2. Gibraltar
3. Toulon
4. Augusta (Sicily)
5. Port Said
6. Suez Canal
7. Red Sea
8. Djibouti (Africa)
9. Gulf of Aden
10. Gulf of Oman
11. Strait of Hormuz
12. Persian Gulf
13. Bahrain
14. Kuwait

Under the National Defence Act, such an Order-in-Council must be tabled in the House of Commons within 10 days of approval by the Governor-in-Council. But the House was in summer recess until September 24 and the government did not want to recall it early. Therefore, the Order-in-Council was not issued until September 15. To make sure that the ships did not enter the war zone before then, the visit to the NATO facilities in Augusta, Sicily, had been extended to 48 hours.

The Suez Canal and the Red Sea

Travel through the Suez Canal has to be arranged beforehand: one convoy goes southbound to Great Bitter Lake and then one goes north. The Canadian ships were put in a holding anchorage at Port Said, along with Britain's HMS GLOUCESTER which had paid the required extra tariff to be the lead ship going through the canal.[11] There were about 20 ships in the convoy of which the Canadians were a part: the warships were first in line, followed by a collection of merchant ships including three huge Cape vessels which the U.S. had filled with Reserve soldiers and military equipment. Ironically, an Iraqi tanker was also in the convoy.

The evening before leaving Port Said, the crews had their first taste of Middle Eastern culture. They were entertained on board their ships by the "Gulli Gulli Man"—a magician dressed in the traditional white robe of the Arabs from which he produced, by turns, each of the 12 live chicks he had hidden inside! The ships' companies also had an opportunity to buy Middle Eastern goods from local traders who set up their displays in the ships' hangers. But these merchants were not allowed to just mingle with the foreigners; everything had to be arranged by a middle man. He would negotiate on a crew member's behalf with certain traders to whom he had given a "mini-monopoly" for certain ships.

The ship convoy left Port Said just after midnight on September 16 and began the 14-hour journey through the very narrow Suez Canal. The Egyptians were on the alert for possible terrorist attacks on the allied warships. Along the fortified sides of the canal were vehicles filled with Egyptian troops armed with machine guns, ready to protect against an attack. The manned outposts which appeared at regular intervals along the length of the canal were a source of interest to Hayes. "You had to

---

11. To be the lead ship costs more because it will not be held up if any of the ships in the convoy breaks down. Conversely, the last ship in the convoy, which has to hope none of the others experience problems, pays the least amount of money. The Suez Canal has been known to be blocked for up to two days while engineers figure out how to move a disabled ship.

wonder about these poor guys who were there, what they did wrong to be stationed in the desert. They would wave to us as the ships went by, and I often wondered, are these guys calling for 'help' or just being friendly?"

But the threat that these outposts were defending against was taken seriously and the Canadian ships were put on a war footing for the journey, keeping their 40mm and .50 calibre guns manned. The danger of attack and consequences of war were made emphatically real as the ships passed by the remains of burnt out tanks and trucks on the east side of the canal—remnants of another conflict, 23 years before. With every passing kilometre, the Canadians became more aware that they were leaving the familiar behind and entering a new and dangerous part of the world.

The trip through the Suez marked not only a psychological change—from the relative peace of the Western world to the conflicts of the Middle East—but also a climatic one. The temperature soared to over 40 C, and the air became steamy. At this latitude, Hayes' foresight in equipping the ships' companies with Tilley hats was especially appreciated. The Canadian-made headgear protected the top of the wearer's head from the direct heat of the sun and the hat's brim provided a small area of cool shade for the face.

When the convoy reached Great Bitter Lake, it anchored in order to let a north-bound convoy pass. The Task Group used the time to test its (remaining) mine avoidance sonars. ATHABASKAN launched its Rigid Inflatable Boat with a home-made "mine"—a garbage bag filled with tin foil—and moored it fairly close to the surface using a danbuoy (a portable floating buoy). The small boat moved the target "mine" to different locations around the ship, testing the mine avoidance sonars' 360-degree capability, and determining its useful range. At the end of the test, the Task Group felt confident that the system would detect a mine at about 500 metres, a long-enough range for a destroyer to react.

The brief stay in Great Bitter Lake also revealed a potential problem with the ships' radars. A bird flew down the starboard side of ATHABASKAN and the radar picked it up. "Unknown contact, 085, 1,000 yards, closing" rang through the ops room as the combat team desperately tried to figure out what was going on. When the staff finally figured out that the "unknown contact" was a bird, the immediate flood of relief was followed by a new worry: were the radars going to pick up birds flying in the Gulf? That would certainly raise the tension level if the ships thought they were under attack every time a bird flew by. But it turned out that the incident was the result of an exceedingly unusual condition: the surface of Great Bitter Lake was so smooth that the radar beam sweeping it was picking up everything.

The convoy continued its southbound journey to Port Suez. There, as the Canadian ships neared the point where they would offload their pilots, the crews were met with a welcome surprise: all the members of the Canadian embassy as well as many from the Canadian community in Cairo had motored down and were waiting there, cheering and proudly displaying three huge Canadian flags while waving smaller versions and holding signs wishing the sailors well. As the ship's companies heard "Oh Canada" playing from the shore, they choked up. The "tough" navy men lined the decks in silence, holding back tears by coughing and clearing their throats. Hayes says "we were stepping into the great unknown, and to have a bunch of Canadians there rooting us on was very moving." Commander John Pickford agrees that the embassy's actions "boosted morale and made you feel proud to be a Canadian," but he adds that there was a bittersweetness to the moment because "it was also our last link with Canada."

Entering the Gulf of Suez, things became decidedly busier in the operations room. The number of contacts on the radar screen increased to about 30 an hour from a more usual five or six—the Canadians were being introduced to what was to become their normal operating pace for the next five months. As the Task Group passed through the patrol areas of the U.S. carriers in the Red Sea, they could monitor the ship-to-ship communications. Hearing the Americans challenging merchant ships using the standard businesslike hailing language caused the Canadians to rethink their plan of operations.

> We decided to make our challenges more personable. We were practicing in a very military fashion and then on our radios we were able to hear how this worked in the Gulf. And we thought, 'these are merchant ships. Maybe we should be a little nicer.' So we changed the challenging statements from "This is Canadian warship. What is your registration?" to "Good morning Captain, how are you this morning? This is Canadian warship and we're here conducting operations in accordance with United Nations Resolutions 661 and 665. We'd like to ask you a few questions."

The first practice session with the new script underlined the need for the challenge to be conducted by a crew member who felt confident and was able to think quickly on his feet. A nervous sailor, in a slow, stilted, voice, read, "Good....morning.....captain, how.... are.... you.... this ..... morning?" Not only did he sound like a machine, but it was evening, not morning—he had neglected to substitute the appropriate salutation! As Miller says, *"That's* why we practice!"

In the Red Sea just north of Djibouti, the Task Group had its first heart-stopper. A Sea King, flying off ATHABASKAN, lost an engine when a fuel pump failed.[12] The helicopter, later nicknamed the "Persian Pig," was on its way over to HMS GLOUCESTER to pick up Commodore Summers and some of the Task Group's officers who had been invited to view a demonstration of the helicopter method of lowering a boarding party onto a vessel—a method subsequently adopted and used by the Canadian Task Group in the Gulf. The Sea King's engine flamed out just as the aircraft was approaching GLOUCESTER. The pilot, air force Captain Chris Charlton, and his crew tried to relight the engine, but no luck, and the aircraft continued to head for the water despite full power in the remaining engine. A few feet above the water's surface, Charlton managed to level the helicopter and as his crew members dumped more fuel, he gained a couple hundred feet of altitude. Unfortunately, by dumping the fuel, there was no longer any way the helicopter could make it ashore; the crew had no option but to try and land aboard ATHABASKAN.

Although the aircraft has two engines, it cannot hover on just one: it must have forward motion for the wind to help keep it aloft. A Sea King operating on one engine in the hot, humid air of the Middle East needs at least 45 knots of speed to land aboard a destroyer.[13] The crews of ATHABASKAN and PROTECTEUR immediately came to action stations, and ATHABASKAN's captain, Commander John Pickford, had his engineer crank up the ship's engines to their maximum, bringing wind speed across the ship's deck to 33 knots. At that point, Charlton brought the Sea King in parallel to the ship, and deciding the Fates were with him, swiftly moved over the flight deck, and landed ... heavily, with a foot to spare between the helicopter's tail wheel and the deck edge—an incredible feat of piloting.

---

12. "Canadian helicopter lands safely despite engine failure" by Paul Mooney, in *The Ottawa Citizen:* Sept. 19/90, p. F15.

13. When the air is hot and humid, it is less dense. When the air is less dense, the turning blades do not produce as much lift.

Even before the Task Group reached the Arabian Gulf, the immediacy of danger caused the ships to take some extraordinary protective measures. At its southern end, the Red Sea narrows to about 35 km, and is bordered by Yemen on its eastern shore and by Ethiopia and Djibouti on the west. That narrow body of water, the Bab El Mandab Straits, was a high risk area for the Task Group because of a possible threat from Yemen which had yet to declare its intentions over Iraq's invasion of Kuwait. The Yemeni armed forces were equipped with Silkworm missiles—a Chinese-made missile with a 100 km range. After consulting with the British ship HMS GLOUCESTER which had continued on with the Canadian ships after transiting the Suez Canal, the Task Group decided to move through the Straits under cover of darkness. As a precautionary measure, each ship's crew was brought to increased readiness, with all weapons and sensors switched on and ready to fire.

After transiting the Straits without incident, the Canadian Task Group parted company with GLOUCESTER. The British ship continued on to the Arabian Gulf while the Canadians sailed into Djibouti for a brief rest and resupply, as well as a briefing from the French navy.

Djibouti, which was the Task Group's last stop en route, was not a very pleasant layover for the Canadian ships. They stopped there to obtain fuel and fresh food supplies. Djibouti, a poor nation, went to a lot of trouble to get fruit and vegetables for the Canadians. Unfortunately, as the piles of produce sat on the jetty, the supply officers could see that they were insect infested. If the produce was taken on board it would contaminate the food already in stock. It was a sensitive situation which required a gentle touch. These poor people, after all, had done their best to supply the Canadian ships. In an attempt to show appreciation and to avoid any suggestion of insult, the Canadians, who had already paid for the supplies, donated them to the local population.

There was a similar problem with the fuel: it contained more contaminants than the Canadian ships could take, particularly ATHABASKAN which has gas turbines. PROTECTEUR, therefore, decided not to top up her holding tanks, but to wait until docking in Bahrain.

In addition to the replenishment problems, the ships' crews were exposed, some for the first time, to close-up views of poverty, starvation, and political violence. During the Task Group's brief stay in Djibouti, Summers took his squadron staff out to dinner at a local French restaurant and then for a beer at a bar that was the local watering hole for French legionnaires. A few days later the ships heard that a militant faction had thrown a grenade into that same bar and killed four people. The whole Djibouti experience left the ships' crews grateful that they were Canadians. Hayes echoed the thoughts of many of those on board when he wrote home that he wished his children could spend a day in Djibouti so they could appreciate what they have in the West.

The two days and one night in Djibouti were not wasted. TERRA NOVA was able to take on board a company service representative for its Phalanx Close-In Weapon System which was exhibiting problems, and ATHABASKAN used the lay-over to transfer by crane to PROTECTEUR the ailing "Persian Pig" Sea King helicopter. Also, the French have a large naval base in Djibouti and they were extremely gracious to the Canadians during their short stay there. The Admiral of the Indian Ocean Command briefed, in French, Summers, Miller, and the three ships' captains on the situation in Iraq and the Gulf.

> The generosity of the French was indicative of the special relationship between France and Canada. It reminded us that Canada benefits from increased global ties because it is a bilingual, bicultural country. The French were generous with both their hospitality and their information, giving us some special insights on Iraq's military capabilities.

The Arabian Gulf

It took the Task Group four days to reach the Strait of Hormuz after leaving Djibouti. Before sailing through, Commodore Summers ordered all personnel sporting beards to shave them off so that the chemical warfare gas masks would fit snugly—a stark reminder that the ships were entering a potential war zone. To make the most out of this otherwise traumatic event, the ships raffled off the right to shave the individual beards, with proceeds going to the United Way. ATHABASKAN's coxswain paid $70 for Commander Pickford's beard to be shaved off, and Commodore Summers paid $70 for removal of the captain's mustache. But Pickford, who had had his beard for 13 years, decided to keep some facial hair and saved his mustache.

The historic passage through the Strait into the Arabian Gulf was commemorated in a message from the Task Group to Admiral Robert George, Commander of Maritime Command, and National Defence Headquarters. The title, at Pickford's suggestion, was "Far Distant Ships"—a reference to Canada's World War Two naval history as chronicled in a book of the same name. The message signalled the success of the misson so far, and included the line "Per Ardua Ad Mare"—a naval twist to the former Royal Canadian Air Force motto "Per Ardua Ad Astra" which means "Through Adversity to the Stars."

While the occasion was historic, the actual transit of the Strait was kept very quiet and low-profile. The Iranians had Silkworm missiles set up along their coast and the Strait was known as "Silkworm Alley." The Canadian ships sailed through at night, with their weapons and sensors in the "standing to" state, the same as during the transit through the Bab El Mandab Straits. It didn't, however, go as smoothly.

Half-way through the passage, the electronic warfare equipment in TERRA NOVA detected a Silkworm missile to the south of the Task Group. TERRA NOVA immediately reported it to the operations room in ATHABASKAN, and everyone went through an agonizing few moments as they wondered if they were coming under attack. Hayes, who was Squadron Watch Officer, puzzled over the contact, and then told everyone to relax. He knew that the Silkworms were to the north of the Canadian ships, so a missile to the south did not make sense. It had to be a false alarm. It was.

The Task Group's arrival in Manamah, Bahrain on September 27 was Miller's first encounter with Middle Eastern bureaucracy. PROTECTEUR was not allowed along the same jetty at which the other two Canadian ships and allied vessels were docked. Instead, she had to sit at anchor 10 kilometres offshore. This was to be a persistent problem, with the tanker being prevented from docking every time she tried to come into port. The reasons varied. Sometimes it was because of the amount of fuel being carried and the possibility of an accident. But there was an American amphibious carrier in dock which had almost as much fuel on board as PROTECTEUR. Another time, the reason was that ships of PROTECTEUR's size were too difficult to manoeuvre in harbour. But the carrier was bigger than the Canadian tanker. Captain McClean was also told by the Bahraini authorities that the quality of their pilots was somewhat suspect and they did not want to put the Canadian ship in danger. But when McClean offered to use his own team to bring the ship in, the Bahrainis replied that it was compulsory to use their pilots.

The first time it happened, both Summers and Miller tried to persuade the Harbour Master that the ship was part of the Task Group and that docking near town was necessary for her crew to have some rest and relaxation time, as well as for some maintenance work to be done in the ship. The Harbour Master was unbudgeable.

This was my first indication that in the Middle East, the status quo is all important. When the status quo is that your ship is at anchor 10 kilometres away, that is the way it will remain. You may pull out all sorts of stops to get alongside and if you get there, you can stay forever as far as they're concerned. Because that is then the status quo. That gave me an insight into Iraq and Kuwait. The fact that the Iraqis had invaded Kuwait and were there, saying this is now Iraq, was therefore, to them, the status quo.

By day two of what was to be an eight-day visit, frustration was mounting. Summers and Miller had tried everything, every argument to get the Harbour Master to let PROTECTEUR into port. Then, almost by accident, they hit upon the solution.

I had gone personally to the Harbour Master to present him with a crest of the First Canadian Destroyer Squadron as a gesture of goodwill—a traditional act whenever Canadian navy ships visit a new port. After I presented him with this I continued to make our case for bringing PROTECTEUR alongside. I said, "don't you realize, it's our command ship that's out there, 10 kilometres away?" Well, that did it. He could relate to that because the U.S. command ships were alongside the jetty, so he picked up the phone, and called the tug master. Then he said, "Well, the tugs are on their way out to bring PROTECTEUR alongside." I thanked him very much and very quickly, because I had to get out of there fast. I knew the captain of PROTECTEUR wasn't aboard his ship.

Miller got hold of PROTECTEUR's Officer of the Watch to let him know what was happening. Usually that officer could have taken the ship alongside using tugs, but in that area of the world, where the Canadian ship had never been before, it was much preferable to have the captain aboard. Captain McClean, who had stopped off in ATHABASKAN on his way ashore for a game of tennis, got word that his ship was to be moved. He immediately called PROTECTEUR to tell his Executive Officer and the engineer to raise steam. Steam-driven ships require a long time to produce the necessary power to get underway. At the time of McClean's call, the ship, which had been sitting at anchor for two days, had cold engines, and was facing a four hour wait before it would have enough energy to move. Usually a captain only orders his ship to raise steam when he is on the bridge, ready to go, not 10 kilometres away. But this was an unusual situation and the rules didn't apply. McClean took one of the Task Group's fast rigid inflatable boats over to PROTECTEUR and as soon as he arrived, phoned the Harbour Master ... and lied. The engineer was rushing the steam process, but the ship still needed another 30 minutes before it would be ready. McClean did not tell the Bahraini that; instead he said his ship was weighing anchor now, and would be getting underway in the next few minutes. He knew that if PROTECTEUR did not move quickly, the Harbour Master would very likely change his mind and make her stay at anchor offshore. So the tanker, escorted by a Bahraini tug, began to creep towards the harbour on one boiler, with the second one firing up a few minutes into the journey.

PROTECTEUR was able to take its berth dockside that time, but because the problem occurred every time the ship tried to go into Bahrain, McClean preferred to go to Dubai and Jebel Ali in the United Arab Emirates.

CHAPTER FOUR

SCUDS, Sand, and Sea Snakes

Picture the central Arabian Gulf. The war between Iraq and the allies has started, and the Iraqis have already fired a couple of SCUD missiles at Israel. But now there's a SCUD missile on a southern trajectory heading towards Bahrain where Canada's Joint Headquarters is based.

As soon as we knew that the missile was heading to Bahrain, I called Commodore Summers who was in the headquarters there. I asked him if he was all right, was there anything we could do, did he need to be evacuated in the event that the SCUD hit near there and released a chemical? I wanted to be prepared with a contingency plan if we needed to get him and his staff out of there fast.

Summers, who was in his chemical warfare suit, replied in a muffled voice, "No, it's okay, we're all right—but stay on the line." On the ship's data link I could see the SCUD approaching Bahrain, and over the phone line in the background I could hear someone counting down in a slow, steady, unemotional, voice —"Two minutes to impact... One minute to impact ..."

That SCUD actually hit about 30 miles north of Bahrain and we all breathed a huge sigh of relief.

Over the next few weeks, SCUDs went towards Bahrain several times, either passing overhead on their way to Qatar or hitting short of Bahrain. On each occasion Summers used a standard procedure of establishing radio-telephone contact with the Air Task Group, the Field Hospital, our Naval Task Group, and the detachment in Riyadh.

The people in the Canadian headquarters were under a fair amount of stress during these times, and when I called Summers to see if he and his staff were all right, our conversation followed the same course as the first time.

*By about the seventh or eighth time, I had become rather complacent
and I didn't bother calling him. And I got an immediate flash message
on the ship's teletype, "Miller call Summers immediately." I thought,
"Oh God, the one time I haven't called him and he's in trouble and
needs help."*

*I grabbed the phone and dialled his number, wondering how bad things
were there. When he answered I blurted out "Is everything all right?
Are you okay?" and an irate voice, thankfully muffled by the gas mask,
came down the line at me, "Everything's fine! .... But Why Didn't
You Call Me, You _____ ?!"*

Complacency was the enemy and a constant threat. Unlike World
War II or the Korean War, there was no shooting going on for the first
three-and-a-half months of the Task Group's deployment. It became easy
to forget the imminent danger. Yet the long days of standing watch with
nothing happening except for the occasional hailing of a merchant ship,
were arguably the most dangerous time for the Task Group: if Saddam
Hussein wanted to launch a pre-emptive strike, that was the time to do it.

Consequently, the air threat preoccupied those standing watch in the
operations rooms of the three ships. Iraq's air force had 30 high-speed
Mirage F1 fighter aircraft[1] which were equipped to carry Exocet anti-
ship missiles. Most of the fighters were located in the northern part of
the country, but they could be forward-based in the south. Prior to the
coalition's entry into the war in January 1991,[2] the Iraqis regularly
practiced attacks on ships by flying five or six of their Mirages
simultaneously towards the allied force. The Mirage pilots, flying in
international airspace, knew there was an invisible line which demarcated
a safe zone. Flying beyond that line would leave the Mirages open to
defensive allied fire; the Iraqi pilots always turned back before they got
to that point.

Despite those practice runs, the allied commanders believed the chances
of Iraq actually staging a successful attack with the Exocet missile were
not very good. That analysis, however, did little to reassure the ships'
companies of ATHABASKAN, TERRA NOVA and PROTECTEUR,

1. International Institute for Strategic Studies (IISS), *The Military Balance, 1990-1991* (Brassey's, London: IISS, 1990), p. 106.
2. The war can be deemed to have begun with Iraq's invasion of Kuwait on August 2, 1990. North Americans generally consider, however, that the war began when the allies began bombing Iraq in the early morning hours of January 17, 1991 (Baghdad time). This book subscribes to the view that the war began August 2.

sitting on the front lines of the multinational forces. The incoming Iraqi Mirages always managed to raise the "pucker factor" among the crews.

The Iraqis also had four Chinese-built Badger medium-range bomber aircraft each capable of carrying two Silkworm missiles. But the aircraft's slow speed and medium altitude make it vulnerable to fleet air defences. Even if an aircraft did manage to release a missile, its relatively slow speed of Mach 0.9 would make it an easy target for a ship's point defence system. Consequently, the Task Group did not feel the Badger-Silkworm system presented a major threat.

However, there was concern about the possibility of a surprise Iraqi air attack being staged by having the aircraft travel down through the coastal mountains in Iran, so as to avoid detection by the naval forces. These aircraft could then emerge closer to the allied ships and be able to launch their missiles at very close range, reducing the allies' reaction time to just seconds. Not only would the Iraqis be able to use their Mirage and Badger missile-equipped aircraft for such an attack, but there were indications that Iraq had modified two small Lear jets to carry the Exocet missile, and thus they also could be used in such a way.

Iraq had seven Super Frelon helicopters which were capable of both carrying Exocet missiles and laying mines. Using helicopters to attack ships, however, is a dicey tactic. On the one hand, the Super Frelons could be modified to operate from oil platforms and drilling rig supply vessels, reducing their distance from targets, and enabling them to stage their attacks from almost anywhere. On the other hand, helicopters are slow-moving aircraft vulnerable to air defence systems and when fully loaded have a limited range.

The Su-24 Fencer is a Soviet-built fighter bomber, capable of carrying a combination of air-to-surface weapons. It was stationed in Central Iraq and had the range to be a threat to the Task Group, but there were indications that the 16 aircraft—which had only been acquired in late 1989—and crews were not quite up to combat standard.[3]

The shore-based SCUD missiles could have been fired at the ships. Most of the missiles had a range of about 300 km although the Iraqis had developed two versions with extended ranges: the 600 km range Al-Husayn and the 900 km range Al-Abbas.[4] While theoretically they could be fired at maritime targets, in practice the missiles would not be precise

---

3. IISS, *Strategic Survey, 1990-1991* (Brassey's, London: IISS, 1991), p. 62.
4. *Ibid.*, p. 61.

enough to hit a ship. But that wasn't much comfort when a couple of times the reported Link trajectory of SCUD missiles passed within a mile or two of ATHABASKAN, and the crew wondered if by some incredible piece of bad luck, the thing would drop out of the sky onto their ship.

Not only did the Task Group have to worry about a missile threat from Iraq, but there was also some concern about both Yemen and Iran. Yemen, which was equipped with Soviet-built SS-21,[5] Frog-7[6] and SCUD[7] missiles, had not declared outright for Iraq, but neither had it condemned Baghdad's action. For that reason, the allied ships were on alert when passing through the Bab El Mandab Straits at the south end of the Red Sea. Iran had not announced its support of either side in the Iraq-Kuwait crisis; its actions could not, therefore, be predicted. Because Iran had a battery of Chinese-built Silkworm missiles along its coast at the mouth of the Gulf, the allied ships remained vigilant while transiting the Strait of Hormuz.

The Iraqi naval threat consisted mainly of eight Osa class fast patrol boats which carried Soviet-built Styx surface-to-surface missile systems.[8] Iraq also had access to Kuwait's more modern guided-missile patrol boats which were seized after the invasion.[9] While these Iraqi and Kuwaiti vessels did pose a threat in the northern Gulf, none was equipped with short-range missile air defence systems, leaving them vulnerable to anti-ship missiles as well as rockets and bombs.[10]

For the navy, throughout its deployment in the Arabian Gulf, the major concern was mines. There are two basic types of ocean mine: contact or influence. Contact mines are usually tethered and explode upon contact with a vessel. Influence mines are activated by the pressure wave of a passing vessel or its magnetic or acoustic signature. Magnetic and acoustic influence mines can be tethered or laid on the ocean floor; pressure influence mines are always bottom laid. It has been estimated that the Iraqis laid 1200 mines in ten separate areas around the Kuwait coastline.[11]

---

5. *Military Balance, 1990-91*, p. 121. A surface-to-surface missile with a range of 120 km.
6. *Ibid.*, p. 122. A surface-to-surface unguided missile with a range of 70 km.
7. *Ibid.*
8. *Ibid.*, p. 106.
9. *Ibid.*, p. 109.
10. See, David Foxwell, "Operational lessons: contending with Iraq's patrol boats," in *International Defense Review*, No. 5/1991, p. 466.
11. Captain Richard Sharpe, RN, *Jane's Fighting Ships, 1991-92*, editorial, p. 47.

Moored mines were a threat to shipping only in the extreme northern Gulf but drifting mines were a threat throughout the northern and central area, as they followed the currents and formed a crescent pattern that ran down the western side of the Gulf and then across from Qatar towards the eastern shore. The Canadian ships had undergone two degaussings to protect them from mines, and ATHABASKAN and TERRA NOVA were also equipped with mine avoidance sonars. In addition, there were mine lookouts in each of the three ships continuously during daylight hours. But perhaps the single most important piece of mine countermeasures equipment was the Sea King helicopter. These aircraft, fitted with forward-looking infra red systems and carrying an alert and well-trained crew, were able to locate mines in the Gulf both during daylight hours and at night. Flying out ahead of the task group, low over the water, they kept the ships aware of any danger.

Once a mine was located, the ships could hand disposal over to the Explosive Ordnance Destruction (EOD) teams. These men were trained to dispose of any detected mine by swimming out to it and putting a plastic explosive on it to blow it up. Alternatively, if the navy needed a sample of the mine to learn more about it, the teams were trained to disarm and retrieve it.

Because of the Task Group's equipment and training, Miller believes "we were the best prepared of any of the warships in the Gulf to counter the mine threat."

Then there were the chemical weapons. These were assessed to be of the least threat to the navy because they could only be used over a relatively small area. In the unlikely event that they were used, ships could close their external ventilation systems, and sail out of the contaminated location. Also, chemical weapons would have to be carried to the ships either by aircraft, which would likely not get through the allied air defences, or by a SCUD missile which would have to hit a ship in order to burst open—an unlikely scenario given the SCUD's inaccuracy. But the fact that Iraq did have chemical weapons and because Hussein had shown he was willing to use them[12] the ships' crews had to become proficient in donning, working in, and getting out of special nuclear-biological-chemical warfare (NBC) suits.

Up until the Gulf deployment, the navy had not put much emphasis on training to fight in a chemically contaminated environment. Crews

12. The Iraqis used chemical weapons against Iran in 1984.

had practiced dealing with nuclear fallout by closing down their ship, but actually to don cumbersome protective gear for any length of time, was virgin territory.

The Task Group practiced en route before it arrived in the Gulf region, in a two-hour training session. Naval Lieutenant Geoff Frusher, the resident nuclear-biological-chemical defences expert, visited each of the three ships and gave every individual two-hours worth of NBC training with the protective equipment. The suit consisted of a neck to feet, one-piece jumpsuit, large boots to wear over the normal footwear, gloves, and a mask.[13] The end result was an unidentifiable crew member who resembled a large insect. The ships' companies had to learn how to do their jobs while wearing the suit, and also how to remove it when entering a protected area of the ship without contaminating either themselves or the closed-off area.

Canadian warships have an internal air system called the Citadel system, which comes into play when the ship is closed down to protect against a nuclear, biological or chemical attack. The sealed ship's internal air pressure is higher than the atmospheric pressure outside, so any leaks will be from inside to outside. PROTECTEUR was built with the Citadel system in a part of the ship, but Captain McClean discovered, to his dismay, that over the years the system had been allowed to atrophy as money for all-embracing ship refits had become scarce. He says,

> ... she had not had a functioning Citadel system for many years—in other words we couldn't get positive pressure inside the ship. So I put together a team, and on the way over, we worked day and night to reinstitute the Citadel. By the time we got there, we had the right sort of positive pressures inside those areas of the ship that were meant to be used to protect people from nuclear-biological-chemical contamination. There's nothing like incentive to get the job done!

Citadel entry ports, equipped with air filters, resemble the divers' hatch found in submarines—small spaces in which the NBC special equipment must be removed before the sailor can enter the ship. Removing the outfit in a small space is difficult enough, but the added

---

13. The mask was constructed so that it could accommodate a straw, allowing the sailor to drink. There was no provision, however, for any subsequent urination. Fortunately, those on board a ship could expect to have to wear these outfits for only a short period of time, until the ship sailed clear of the contaminated area.

catch is it must be done without bare hands touching the outside of the suit. Crew members go into the entry portals in twos, in order that each person can help the other. Suits are left in the decontamination chamber.

Learning to use and function in those unwieldy suits was expected to be difficult, but the initial training session with Summers' staff revealed an unexpected problem.

> *We did our first exercise just off Gibraltar. I remember it because we spent about six hours in this suit. That's probably the longest that you would ever spend, because at sea, you can at least steer away from a chemical cloud. We were so hot in these things, and people started to get grouchy after about the second hour.*
>
> *We went through all of our drills, inside the ship and outside the ship, fighting the ship wearing these strange-looking costumes. When we went to action stations, everybody went into the operations room and Commodore Summers was there. He had a chair as the Task Group Commander. I was going to be to his right as the Squadron Commander.[14]*
>
> *At this first action station, I sat right next to the Commodore in what was usually the Squadron Watch Officer's seat. I was sitting there, with the communicators right next to me, talking to other ships, and I get a WHACK across the back! Then a voice screams at me, "WHAT ARE YOU DOING IN MY CHAIR?!!!" It's Lieutenant-Commander Jim Hayes, who is the fellow who normally sits there, and he thinks it's the signalman, or whoever, sitting in his chair. I turned around and right away I could see his eyes open wide with an expression of, "Oh my God, I just hit the Squadron Commander! What have I done?!"*
>
> *We learned something from that. With these NBC outfits, we needed to identify ourselves. So we put rank insignia on the front and the back so that people would know who they're talking to—or who they're about to hit.*

The Sea King air crews have different protection gear than that issued to the ships' crews. In addition to the mask and the protective overalls, the air crews had to wear a charcoal hood and suit and four layers of gloves. To cool the wearer who was wrapped in this "cocoon," the air

---

14. *"In fact we worked out that during these times, I would more than likely be the command presence on the bridge, which meant that I had to put on a flak jacket and a crash helmet, on top of all the NBC stuff. It fit, but it was desperately uncomfortable and hot."*

force supplied cooling vests. This was essentially a T-shirt with surgical tubing running through it connected to a container of ice water and a portable power source that pumped the cool water through the shirt. In order to prolong the wearing time, the air detachments had bought Canadian Tire coolers which they packed with ice and carried on board the helicopters to keep the suit supplied with cool water.

The air force plan for operating in a chemical warfare environment is for its people to reuse their suits: in other words, it would not be disposed of after the wearer is exposed to chemical or biological agents. Therefore, the suit has to be removed without any of the inside surfaces being contaminated, hung up so as not to touch and contaminate any other suit, and then put back on when needed. Because there is no room in a Sea King for the air crew to put their chemical protection gear on when they thought they might be running into a contaminated area, the air crews always wore most of the equipment when operating the aircraft after January 16. The air crews quickly adapted to wearing the chemical protection outfits because they were used to wearing cumbersome immersion suits during their normal operations in the Atlantic. However, there were some frustrations. The helmet, for example, which was larger than normal in order to cover the gas mask, had a more restricted field of vision requiring the wearer to turn his head to see things instead of being able to just look to the side, or down, with his eyes. Also, the extra layers of gloves effectively removed the wearer's tactility, so that he had to look at what switches he may or may not have his hand on.

Underlying all of Iraq's readily apparent military might was perhaps the most worrying threat of all—a terrorist attack. Many in the Task Group believed that Hussein would not wait to face the combined might of an international coalition, but would use terrorist attacks to pick away at the growing military presence before it entered the war. For the navy, that meant all fishing boats (dhows) and small civilian aircraft approaching the ships would have to be viewed with extreme suspicion—they could be loaded up with explosives or be carrying fighters armed with hand-held missiles. To add to the navy's worries, the Arabian Gulf was filled with fishing dhows, not just from Iraq but from Iran, whose moves in the Gulf crisis could not be predicted.

Terrorism was a special concern in or near harbours. That threat was brought home to Lieutenant-Commander Kevin Laing immediately on the Task Group's arrival in Manamah, Bahrain.

Shortly after we passed the Bahrain bell, I, as the Staff Watch Officer received a report of a terrorist attack and the piracy of a merchant vessel outside Damman, a port less than 100 kilometres away. I went up to the bridge of ATHABASKAN and observed the striking down of .50 calibre machine gun mounts and ammunition for our entry into harbour. I also noticed several small dhows and speed boats within a mile or so of us. I suggested to the captain of ATHABASKAN, Commander John Pickford, that maybe we should leave a couple of mounts up and be ready, just in case. As it turned out we were quite safe but we just didn't know it at the time and we couldn't take anything for granted.

Ultimately, terrorism did play a part in the Gulf war, but not as the navy had envisioned it through armed dhows or small aircraft. Instead, the terrorism took place in the Kuwait oil fields. The fires set there by the Iraqis produced huge clouds of acrid, black smoke that blocked out the sun for miles in every direction. While within range of this ecological catastrophe, Sea Kings were unable to fly and the number of people who were allowed onto the ships' upper decks was kept at a bare minimum. Those that were needed there had to wear surgical masks. When it rained, the ships were covered with a sticky, oily soot that was almost impossible to clean off. The engineer (the on-board scientist) kept a close eye on the amount of carbon monoxide in the air, which turned out to be within the range of what is acceptable.

The oil gushing from Kuwaiti pipelines into the Gulf also was a source of concern to the ships. Oil in the water flowing through the intakes would foul up the cooling system, clogging the pumps and tubes and possibly stopping them completely. As it happened, the oil released into the Gulf was thin enough that it did not hurt the machinery, and in any case, most ships were able to circumvent the slicks so as to avoid any problem. Also the water intakes on the heavily laden ships were far enough below the sea surface that the oil did not get sucked inside.

In addition to the manmade threats that would confront the ships in the Gulf, there were the natural hazards—beginning with the climate. The bad news was that most days the temperature was above 40 degrees Celsius with near 100 per cent humidity. The good news was that the weather was incredibly stable.

The poor weatherman got a really hard time, because the weather never changed. The big news was "there might be a cloud!" Everyone would rush to the upper deck to see it, because they hadn't seen one for several months. It did get more exciting towards January, because in the winter the wind whips up every three or four days. But there's a cycle, and once we figured out the cycle, we didn't need the weatherman. So he was kind of like a Maytag repair man.

Sometimes, to make things interesting while the weatherman was presenting his report, the staff would sit and try to see shapes in the lines drawn on the weather charts. One day, everyone claimed to see a "duck"—everyone except me. While the weatherman was talking, I kept asking, "where's the duck, where's the duck?" The next day, Chief Dave Ashley used a computer graphics program to draw a duck the size of an 8-1/2 by 11 page. He came into the briefing room, dropped the drawing in front of me, and said, "Can you see the duck now Sir?"

The daily outside temperatures of over 40 degrees translated to over 50 degrees inside such places as the closed-up aircraft hangar and engine rooms. Master Corporal Patrick McCafferty, an air technician in PROTECTEUR, described the discomfort in the aircraft hangar in his diary:[15]

The helos gleam from constant washings and rubdowns with light lubricants and with the hangar door and hatches open it's almost bearable to work on them. But we dread when the sun goes down. At approximately 1600 hours all hatches and doors are closed to prevent any white light from escaping the ship and 'darken ship' is piped. The hangar is lit with mercury and tungsten lights which add to the heat in the hangar. Temperatures routinely top 150 degrees and with the humidity at 90 per cent it seems worse. All our tools are like wet bars of soap squirting from our hands. We regrease the helos every 25 hours on our supp[lementary] checks. It's amazing—almost as soon as we put the grease in, it oozes out almost in a liquid form. We all use fibre weave paper towels to wrap around our heads, waists and wrists to soak up the sweat. I can't believe how much of it we actually use but the show must go on.

---

15. The diary excerpts are used with permission of Master Corporal Patrick McCafferty.

Relief was infrequent and fleeting. Even the morning ritual of shaving and showering didn't help much. As McCafferty described it, "When you shave there is enough sweat that you don't need shaving cream. After showering you feel almost fresh but by the time you reach the hangar you are soaked in sweat again."

Aware of the problems caused by the excessive heat and too much sun, the medical staff put extra effort into making sure those on deck covered up with either clothes or sunblock. One of PROTECTEUR's medical officers, Lieutenant Kenneth Cooper, commented to a reporter, "The biggest threat to the sailors is not Iraqi Exocet missiles. It's the sun, the heat and dehydration."[16]

With time, however, the ships' companies did acclimatize to the heat and some even began to like it.

> You don't realize how well your body has acclimatized until you get visitors from out of town—flown by helicopter out to the ship, just arrived, and for the first three days they are perspiring, going around washed out, dragged out. Yet here we are, all putting sweaters on because it goes down to 72°F and looking at them as if to say, 'what's the matter with you?' You realize that your body has acclimatized to the environment that you're working in. It's quite remarkable.

But while the people acclimatized, the equipment did not, and the ships' operations had to be modified to handle the increased heat. The ships tried to reduce radiated heat from light bulbs and pipes by using red lights instead of white lights, and turning off the hot water as much as possible. The ships also restricted access to the upper deck to stop the cool air inside from escaping. While in the Gulf, people had only one door—an air lock door—by which they could get outside; usually there are four or five ways to gain access to the upper deck. Maintaining cooler temperatures inside the ship was so important that ATHABASAKAN detailed a Petty Officer solely to look after the air conditioning system.

The cool air that was being so preciously guarded, was not easily come by. The ships had to keep their air conditioners operating full blast to stop the electronic systems from overheating. Even then, the below deck areas were not what could be considered "cool"; they were just not as hot as outside. The problem was that the air conditioners used sea

---

16. Andrew Phillips, "Risky Mission," in *Maclean's:* October 1, 1990, p. 27.

water in their operation, and the water in the Gulf was as warm as a tub of melted butter.

Steam-driven ships, such as TERRA NOVA and PROTECTEUR, also have intakes which feed in water for the boilers, and all the ships use sea water to cool the engines. In the Gulf, these circulation systems would occasionally be blocked when sea snakes were sucked into the intakes.

More poisonous than a rattlesnake, these three to ten feet long reptiles would gather on the surface of the water during calm seas and sun themselves, so that the sea around the ships would seem to be fairly alive. Hayes, who was spending his waking time in the operations room, always made it a point to get up on deck at least once during the day to get some sun. While there he would look down at the water and count sea snakes. One time he counted, in the space of 30 minutes, 50 snakes.

The ships' surgeries were equipped with anti-venom but it was really just for morale purposes: the snakes were referred to as "two-steppers" because if they did bite someone, the victim would only live long enough to take two more steps. The one disadvantage the snakes had was their small mouths—they could only bite in places they could grab such as between the fingers or toes (their favourite spots) or any extra flab on a person's body. The snakes also could not bite through a diver's wetsuit, which made it possible for the crews to clear their ships' intakes without any casualties—although the experience was not without its excitement.

The water in the Gulf is like a lake, so wind coming in from across the wide expanse of desert in the northwest makes for choppy water in the southeast. Occasionally the wind produced a swell of about 20 feet— not much in the open ocean, but in the shallow water of the Gulf it was enough for ships to go aground if they were at anchor.

And there were even the occasional sandstorms to watch out for at sea. It's possible for one to whip up and blow right across the Gulf, although luckily none did during the Task Group's deployment. Still, blowing sand was a problem whenever the ships and aircraft were near land. The sand is not granular like North American sand, but rather is the consistency of flour. This 'brown flour' coats the ship and gets into everything. It was especially hard on the helicopters which had to be kept, even when fully armed, in their hangers.

No one serving with the Task Group had had to operate under such conditions before. As the men and women toiled away in the oppressive heat, patrolling the Gulf and hailing merchant ships, the realization that they would likely find themselves in the midst of a vicious shooting war was never far from their thoughts. And the officers in charge of the Task Group were no less aware of the heavy responsibility they had for making sure that everyone came back alive, and that Canadians would be proud of the way the ships and crews had discharged their duties.

CHAPTER FIVE

"We're a Canadian Group here!"

The first couple of times we came across a vessel which we thought we should board under the U.N. mandate, we reported this to the co-ordinator, which was a U.S. ship, and asked whether or not we should board. The reply came back no. I then asked, "did you confirm that it has been boarded previously?" There was a 10 or 15 minute delay and then the reply came back, "no it hasn't been boarded." I said, "Well, we're a Canadian group here, and under our terms, we have to board this vessel, because it says it's going to Iraq. And we boarded it.

Military command and control arrangements are complex at the best of times, but they can become downright complicated when various countries team up to fight a common enemy. As evidence of this, one need look no further than Defence Minister Bill McKnight's description of the command and control arrangements which he gave to the House of Commons in January 1991, just after Canada was given responsibility for the multinational Combat Logistics Force:

> Canada has tactical command of assets, materiel and personnel of other nations. That being said, the over-all command of the assets of all the collaborating nations involved in the hostilities ... fall under the over-all command of General Norm Schwarzkopf. That being said, we must recognize that when Canada accepts tactical control and command of assets and personnel of other nations, naturally Canada has assigned the tactical control of its assets to the over-all command.[1]

---

1. House of Commons, *Debates*, January 17, 1991, p. 17198.

McKnight's description was accurate but confusing. The overlapping and interconnecting of the various legal authorities do not lend themselves to succinct explanations. Unfortunately, answers like McKnight's are viewed by the media and the general public as just so much political gobbledygook aimed at covering up what they consider to be the real explanation: that Canada had relinquished control of its forces to the U.S. to be used in whatever manner the Americans thought best. But that was not the case. Here's how command and control worked during the Arabian Gulf crisis.[2]

Neither Canada, nor any other country, ever gives up national command of its military forces. Although a multinational commander may be given the authority to use Canadian ships in specific operations, the government retains the final say of whether or not those ships can be used in that way. Therefore, the Canadian Task Group, from the time it left Halifax, until the time it returned, was under national command.

The next step down from national command is operational command—the authority to plan and execute military operations with the available ships, aircraft, and other assets. In the Canadian navy, operational command usually rests with the Commander of Maritime Command, but it can be transferred to another national or allied commander. For the deployment to the Arabian Gulf, operational command rested initially with the Maritime Commander and then with the Joint Commander, Commodore Ken Summers.

The Joint Commander and the Joint Staff

When the naval Task Group left Halifax, it was operating, as per normal, under the operational command of Maritime Command Headquarters. Commodore Ken Summers had been in charge of the Task Group on its way to the Gulf, and Captain Dusty Miller had been his Chief of Staff or second-in-command. The journey had been one of challenge and accomplishment, and by the time the ships docked in Bahrain, the officers knew they had three ships that were ready for combat. They were buoyed by the crews' achievements and they were looking forward to demonstrating the renowned Canadian "can-do" attitude.

But after the Task Group docked in Bahrain, the squadron staff noticed a mood change in Commodore Summers. Although they did not know

---

2. In this chapter, the authors have attempted to simplify what are extremely complex concepts which have been developed and refined over long periods of time by Canada and the NATO allies.

it at the time, Summers had been told by General John de Chastelain, Chief of the Defence Staff, that he was to be moved ashore to become the commander of a Joint Headquarters. Like any dedicated navy man, Summers would have preferred to stay at sea. But the need for a Joint Commander was pressing because Canada's participation in the Gulf had become more complex. The deployment of a squadron of CF-18s as well as army units (the army was supplying base security forces for the CF-18 squadron in Qatar and air defence forces for the ships, as well as engineers and supply technicians), in addition to the three ships, required a one channel Canadian command in the Gulf. Back home in Ottawa, National Defence Headquarters was realigned into a Joint Staff (JSTAFF) configuration[3] and it had taken over operational command of the Naval Task Group from Maritime Command. The navy was still responsible, however, for support of its ships, aircraft and personnel in the Gulf. To this end it set up a Logistics Detachment in Bahrain.[4] In practical terms, this meant the ships in the Gulf would get their mission directives from the Joint Staff and their supplies through Maritime Command.

The Joint Staff concept was a new one but had been under development for a few years. When Commodore Bruce Johnston took over as Director General of Military Plans and Operations in 1989, he was concerned about the military's ability to function in times of crisis. He discussed this with the Deputy Chief of the Defence Staff, Lieutenant-General David Huddleston. Johnston wanted to make an effective system his number one priority before a new crisis came along that would push the Department's management capabilities beyond their limits. Huddleston was well aware of the problems. He has since commented that the National Defence Headquarters had "been looked upon by many as an organization which is designed for peace and could not translate to war or to intense operational staffing activity."[5] Johnston's staff, at the time of his takeover, was already on the ninth draft of a new crisis management manual—which, as Johnston says, "the fact that it was a ninth draft was indicative of the fact that they were having some difficulty selling it around the headquarters." Within the ninth draft was the concept of the crisis action team, and the concept of the primacy of operations. Previously any extra effort required by the military in times of crisis had required the authority of the Vice Chief of the Defence Staff; the new plan gave

---

3. The JSTAFF concept used plans formulated around the typical continental command and control structure for CANUS and NATO operations.
4. See Chapter 7.
5. Interview with Sharon Hobson, October 7, 1992.

the Director General of Military Plans and Operations (at this time, Johnston) the authority to call the crisis action team together whenever he felt the need existed. The team itself, however, would be headed by the Deputy Chief of the Defence Staff (Huddleston).

The Joint Staff philosophy recognizes that for operational issues, time is of the essence, and that the usual matrix staffing at headquarters—where any type of request, whether it be policy, materiel, financial or personnel, has to go up, down, and across the various directorate hierarchies—is not appropriate. With the Joint Staff, the senior operational officer—the Deputy Chief of the Defence Staff—heads an organization which contains representatives of all the directorates in headquarters. Using in-house terminology, J1 is personnel, J2 is intelligence, J3 is operations, J4 is logistics, materiel and finance, J5 is policy, public affairs, and legal, and J6 is communications and information systems. Those representatives are responsible for dealing with their own organizations and getting the necessary solutions to whatever problem the Joint Staff is dealing with, within a definite time-frame.

The emerging concept was put into practice in the summer of 1990, when natives at Kanesatake near Oka and Kahnawake near Chateauguay, Quebec, put up road blocks to protest the provincial government's handling of various land claims issues. This domestic crisis, which involved the use of the army in quelling the unrest, was followed in short order by an international crisis when Iraq invaded Kuwait. The latter event resulted in Canada's decision to participate in the multinational action against Iraq. Faced with first one, then two, major military operations, Johnston went ahead and put in place the crisis action team. The team, which incorporated people from personnel, logistics, legal affairs, finance, and medical, was oriented toward the JSTAFF concept. It was just a matter of repackaging the team into the appropriate format. By September, when the naval Task Group was on its way to the Arabian Gulf, the JSTAFF terminology had begun to permeate through headquarters. By the time Summers visited headquarters in early October to discuss the composition of his joint headquarters, JSTAFF was fully formed with Lieutenant-General David Huddleston at its head. Because of the primacy of operations under the Joint concept, his Chief of Staff, Johnston, had the authority to task National Defence Headquarters to meet operational needs.

The Joint Headquarters in the Middle East was an extension of the Joint Staff set-up and was an extremely important element in the success of the Canadian military effort during the crisis. Comprised of army, navy, and air force personnel, the headquarters was responsible for Canada's overall operational plan, handling communications, and intelligence analysis, as well as paying personnel, and bringing in supplies. Summers' official title was Commander Canadian Forces Middle East. As such, he was the Canadian government's military representative in the Middle East and represented the national command authority—the government—over the air and naval forces. Also, the operational command of the Naval Task Force which had been assumed by the Joint Staff was given to Summers as the on-scene Joint commander for the entire time of the Gulf deployment.

After being given his new command, Summers' first job was to set up a headquarters. His first choice was to use PROTECTEUR. The supply ship was already equipped with a comprehensive communications set-up and support staff, and the transition to floating headquarters would be quick and easy. At first glance, this plan seemed sensible—except that it would tie up a valuable asset: PROTECTEUR wouldn't be able to undertake interdiction and resupply duties in the Gulf because she would have to spend most of her time alongside in Bahrain. Moreover, PROTECTEUR's other functions as alternate command ship for the Task Group and helicopter maintenance depot would be severely curtailed. After much discussion amongst National Defence Headquarters in Ottawa, Maritime Command in Halifax, and the squadron staff of the Task Group, Summers agreed to set up a Joint Headquarters in Manamah in what was previously an old warehouse on the shoreline.

When Summers took over his new role in October, he made history by becoming the Commander of the first ever Canadian Forces Joint Headquarters. By having an on-scene Joint Commander, the Department of National Defence had a direct link into all aspects of the conflict, and decisions could be made quickly and with confidence. The benefits of this set up were readily apparent on February 18 when the American cruiser USS PRINCETON hit a mine off the coast of Kuwait, just north of 29 degrees North latitude.[6] U.S. Rear-Admiral Daniel March asked

---

6. The USS PRINCETON (CG-59) "set off an Italian Manta influence mine in less than 20 metres of water, 5 metres away from her side. The blast of the 375lb charge raised the quarterdeck several feet into the air, causing the ship to hinge on her keel. She also whiplashed along the fore-and-aft axis, with the bow and stern suffering the most extreme motions. The superstructure was torn open at the amidships quarterdeck, the I-beams providing internal structural strength were weakened and the high-tensile steel of the main deck was buckled and ripped in several places. The Aegis air defence system immediately went down, and even after all radars and related combat systems were restored, the ship's after battery of VL missiles and 5 inch gun was inoperable." See *NAVINT*, April 11, 1992, p. 4, and *International Defense Review: #7/1991*, pp. 740-741.

Miller, who was commanding the multinational Combat Logistics Force, for help in escorting the damaged ship and its tugboat out of the minefield and into a safe port.

> *When Admiral March called me and said "I need a ship to escort a tug up to extract USS PRINCETON out of the minefield," he specified that he wanted it to have a helicopter and a good anti-mine capability, and he added, "I'd prefer it to have a Canadian flag flying from the stern."*
>
> *There was only one ship that fit that description and I was riding in her!*
>
> *There were two other ships that could have fit that criteria, other than the bit about the Canadian flag—one Italian and one French.[7] But I would have had a hard time ordering either the Italian or the French ship to do it if I wasn't prepared to send a Canadian ship up there, knowing we were about the best prepared of all the ships in the Gulf to handle the mine threat.*
>
> *But to go where Admiral March was asking us to go—and he was asking us, not ordering us—was beyond the limit of the latitude that I had from the national authority. So first of all I talked to the Captain of ATHABASKAN, John Pickford, and said, "here's the job." He said, "Great, let's do it. We're prepared for this. There's no problem."*
>
> *The mission involved leading the tug north around the oil slick and through a couple of mined areas that we knew about, getting to PRINCETON, circling her, and waiting until the tug was attached.[8] Then we had to lead the tug out, towing PRINCETON, back through the mined area, to Bahrain. I called Summers and told him. Because the tasking was beyond our limits, I needed both Summers' and the government's authority to undertake it. The thought did cross my mind to just do it without checking—what's 10 nautical miles between friends?—but only for a nanosecond.*

---

7. In addition to Rear-Admiral March's criteria, there was one other factor that favoured a Canadian response to PRINCETON's distress: ATHABASKAN had on board secure communications equipment that was compatible with the Americans'. The Italian and the French ships did not have that equipment and would have had to use non-secure communication links.

8. The USS BEAUFORT, a salvage and repair vessel, had been in the area when PRINCETON hit the mines, and it took the cruiser under tow. But because the U.S. needed BEAUFORT for other duties, it asked for ATHABASKAN to escort a civilian tugboat to PRINCETON and take over the towing.

Because we were trying to make time, we were actually already heading north when I contacted Summers. He then contacted the Joint Staff in Ottawa who took it to higher levels of the military and political leadership.

The answer to go ahead came back in 29 minutes! It was amazing, especially in contrast to what happened in December 1989 when a Canadian destroyer operating off the east coast of Canada requested permission to forcibly board an illegal fishing vessel which was refusing to stop. It took several hours for the Canadian ship to get the required approval, and by that time the American ship was back in home waters.

The speedy reply to Miller's request was possible because of the Joint Commander and the Joint Staff. If Summers had had to go to Maritime Command first (or Air Command, had it been an air operation), it would have added an extra level of bureaucracy which could have slowed the process. Miller needed to know whether or not he had the authority to go across the 29 degree North Latitude line before he got to it; that meant the approval process had to move fast. Throughout the Gulf deployment, government officials responded quickly to the military's various requests. The Joint Headquarters in Bahrain and in Ottawa had anticipated potential taskings and requests and had, in most cases, briefed the upper levels of the political and military authorities on what might be requested and what the implications might be. Thus, prior approval for many situations and responses had been obtained and handed down through the various levels of leadership. But for those unusual requests that had not received prior approval, decisions were invariably reached quickly because of the previous briefings.

In addition to co-ordinating the Canadian military effort in the Gulf, the Joint Headquarters was also needed to look after the Canadian interests in the region because the Canadian consuls were few and far between. For example, the Canadian embassy in Riyadh, Saudi Arabia, was also responsible for Yemen, and the Canadian Ambassador to Kuwait looked after Canadian interests in Oman, Qatar, Bahrain, and the United Arab Emirates. The effectiveness of the Kuwaiti-based officials was limited after the Iraqis cut off electricity, food and water supplies in September. The Canadian diplomats, acting on instructions from Ottawa, shut the embassy in mid-October.[9] But Ottawa still needed someone on scene

---

9. The Canadian embassy in Kuwait remained officially open, however, in accordance with government policy that Iraq's annexation of Kuwait was illegal.

who could go to officials in the various countries and negotiate on Canada's behalf. Summers' headquarters did that. He was able to steer a way through the red tape to arrange for such things as the delivery of a Phalanx Close-In Weapon System to the dock in Bahrain and subsequent fitting in TERRA NOVA.

The Multinational Conferences

Commodore Summers represented Canada at the multinational conferences set up to co-ordinate the coalition's military efforts to avoid duplication and interference. The allies established the framework for operations in the Gulf at the meeting of coalition navies in Bahrain on September 9-10, 1990, the same meeting at which Summers agreed to consider moving the Canadian ships into the central Gulf. That meeting included representatives from all western nations in or underway to the Gulf, and representatives of the Gulf Co-operation Council (except Iraq and Iran). The meeting was officially hosted by the Chief of Staff of the Bahraini Forces and presided over by the Chief of Staff (in exile) of the Kuwaiti Forces.

The representatives at that meeting selected a commander to co-ordinate the naval enforcement of the U.N. embargo. The U.S. Commander of the Middle East Force, Rear-Admiral William M. Fogarty, was chosen to be the Multinational Interception Force (MIF) co-ordinator on the basis that he controlled the largest permanent force and resided in Bahrain, giving him local knowledge and connections. Moreover, he was already the United States Maritime Interdiction Force Commander. Fogarty arranged for monthly multinational naval conferences to determine the employment and scheduling of the ships in the Gulf. These conferences were chaired on a rotational basis. For example, one naval conference was in Dubai aboard the Australian ship, HMAS SUCCESS, and one was in Abu Dhabi aboard USS LASALLE.

The meetings were attended by the allied naval commanders and their scheduling officers. While their schedulers tackled the next month's tasking, the commanders met to discuss any problems in the embargo enforcement operation and such things as the rules of engagement. The two groups would then get together for a lunch—at which seating was carefully managed. Lieutenant-Commander Greg Romanow, a burly man who can handle himself both physically and verbally, remembers "they always put me between the Argentinians and the Brits, with the French across from me!" In the afternoon, the naval commanders confirmed the schedule worked out by their staff.

Despite whatever differences countries had in their normal day-to-day dealings before the Gulf crisis, Romanow says the monthly conferences were "extremely congenial." There was a sense of purpose that infused the discussions with resolve, allowing for rapid problem-solving, without argument. The allies shared their information and resources, helping out with spare parts, supplies, and technical advice, when and wherever needed.

A couple of the meetings were larger conferences, with representatives of all of the allied navies, not just those from outside the region. Summers hosted and presided over one of these major conferences on December 12 onboard PROTECTEUR, which came alongside in Bahrain. There were 22 navies represented around the table in the wardroom. These meetings dealt with the co-ordination of the interception activities and information exchange, as well as the protection of the various Middle Eastern countries.

> It was at that meeting that I sat across the table from the deputy head of the Kuwaiti navy, Lieutenant-Colonel Ahmed Yousuf Al Mulla.[10] He looked into my eyes and said, "We are very grateful for the Canadians to be here." His words meant a great deal to me; they went beyond the abstract political into the personal. He gave our mission a real, understandable, meaning.

To aid in the co-ordination of Canada's naval efforts with the allies, Summers' staff liaised with the U.S. Navy staffs in USS BLUERIDGE and LASALLE. When, in January, Canada was given command of the Combat Logistics Force, Summers arranged for Lieutenant-Commander Romanow from the naval Task Group and Major Jocelyn Cloutier from the air group in Doha to be sent to USS MIDWAY. They stayed onboard for the duration of the war, providing timely advice on the intentions of the coalition partners and on the integration of the Canadian forces into the overall operation.

Summers requested a dedicated aircraft to be at the disposal of the headquarters staff throughout the Arabian Gulf deployment. It was needed to get the land, sea and air representatives to the monthly conferences held at various locations. Miller attended those conferences with his scheduling officer, (Lieutenant-Commander Greg Romanow before the outbreak of hostilities, Lieutenant-Commander Jim Hayes after the fighting started). When the Canadian ships were operating in the central

---

10. The ranks in the Kuwaiti navy are army ranks.

Gulf, getting to Abu Dhabi could have been a problem since only limited commercial flights were available. Miller would have had to use a Sea King helicopter. But to do that meant taking a ship away from its area of operations to launch the helicopter. And the helicopter itself could face problems at the airport where it landed because there would have to be the right fuel and the right starting equipment for it to make the trip back to the ship after the conference.

To make things easier, the Joint Staff arranged for a Challenger passenger transport aircraft to be based in Bahrain. Prior to its arrival, Summers had hitched a ride with an American commander; when the Canadian plane arrived, he was able to return the favour. Miller and Romanow used the Sea King helicopter just to get to Bahrain where they would then board the aircraft.

> *The Challenger is a military aircraft so it has military identification. It still has to let the co-ordinating agencies know that it's taking off and flying from A to B. When we flew to Abu Dhabi we had U.S. Rear-Admiral Fogarty aboard. We were, of course, not following a normal commercial route, and knowing that there were 90 missile-firing ships out there, all I could think of when we took off from the military airport, was— I hope they filed a flight plan!*

Having a dedicated Command and Liaison aircraft proved to be critical during the fighting portion of the Gulf operation when airlines ceased in-theatre operations. Without the plane, it would have been almost impossible for Summers to visit with his field commanders, attend multinational co-ordination meetings, or to maintain essential face-to-face contact with his coalition counterparts. In addition, the aircraft was available to transport crucial operational material.

Who's on first?...

As Naval Task Group Commander, Miller reported directly to Summers. The Commodore, representing the national command authority, was given a great deal of freedom in his decision-making. For example, the decisions about the area of operations and the functions of the Task Group, were made by Summers and his staff, within the national guidelines provided by National Defence Headquarters in Ottawa.

The decision to keep the three Canadian ships together after the outbreak of hostilities was a particularly important one. Summers and Miller had discussed what would happen in the event of allied military action against Iraq. They agreed that the Canadian contribution to the effort against Iraq should be a clearly identifiable Canadian one. The choice was to be split up and operate screening the carriers in the central-northern Gulf, under another nation's task group's staff, or to remain together and take on a significant task group responsibility. To Miller's way of thinking, "if we'd let them divide us up, we'd have been insignificant."

They knew the ships could not operate in the northern Gulf because they expected a heavy air battle and the ships had only self-defence, not area, air defence systems. But Canada did have a logical and useful role to play—that of combat logistics force co-ordinator.

The role was a natural one for the Canadian Task Group which had a dedicated squadron staff and an excellent communications setup. In addition the Canadian navy has trained extensively in the Naval Control of Shipping role, so the Task Group officers were more than ready to organize the resupply of the allied naval force and the protection of its merchant ships. Finally, the Task Group had outperformed the other allies in the interdiction role in the Gulf, building credibility, trust and respect for its abilities and dedication.

Consequently, while aboard USS MIDWAY with Rear-Admiral March in early January 1991, Summers suggested for Canada the role of co-ordinator for the Combat Logistics Force. The Americans, who were concentrating on their attack role and the protection of their strike force, did not have any extra destroyers for escorting supply ships, and were happy to hand the complex resupply operation over to a trusted ally.

In addition to the freedom of action Summers enjoyed in defining Canada's role in the Gulf, he was fully prepared and able to act quickly when the predicted actually happened, such as the start of hostilities or an Iraqi attack on a ship. Commodore Bruce Johnston explained, "It was very, very carefully calculated as to the amount of time in certain situations that might be available for consultation. In other words, when might it be reasonable for the Commodore to come back to National Defence Headquarters if not necessarily for guidance, then for concurrence, and when might it be unreasonable for him to do that." In order to give Summers as much freedom as possible, Ottawa provided him with very detailed guidance for various situations. Johnston says, "The emphasis was on making sure that he had the latitude to make the decisions for the effective and safe deployment of the forces without consultation if time was short."

To make sure that there were no small problems that could snowball into bigger ones, Johnston spoke with Summers every day. If Summers had any questions arising from events, Johnston would clear them up. Both men were naval officers and good friends, who had worked together previously. They were relaxed and clear in their dealings with each other.

Anytime Miller wanted to do something unusual, he would check with Commodore Summers. Each country had determined its geographical national restrictions. Canada was no different. Between 27 and 28 degrees North Latitude, Miller was free to act as he saw fit; between 28 and 29 degrees, he had to inform Summers of his movements and activites; anything beyond 29 degrees he had to call Summers for authorization.

Occasionally, Miller had to let Summers know after the fact because there was not time to do so beforehand. For example, when a hailed ship refused to stop and the Canadian ship had to fire a warning shot across the bow. Although such action was entirely within Miller's mandate—and strictly speaking, at his discretion—it was an unusual event and as such, would undoubtedly make its way into the news. It was only proper that Summers should be told of the action before reading about it. Fortunately, shooting across the bows of ships was a rare occurence. When it was called for, the ship or helicopter used its machine guns, which were accurate and made an effective splash in front of the unco-operative vessel.

Although Summers retained operational command of the Canadian Task Group throughout the Gulf deployment, he delegated operational control to the Americans. Operational control is "the authority delegated to a commander to direct forces to achieve the tasks (usually limited by function, time or place) laid down by the Command (either Full or Operational). It does not include the authority to change the task."[11]

For example, in mid-November, the Task Group participated in an amphibious exercise, "Imminent Thunder," in which American and Saudi forces practised invasion techniques near the coast of Kuwait. During the exercise, ATHABASKAN and TERRA NOVA, which were providing escort to the American hospital ships USNS MERCY and COMFORT, were under the operational control of the U.S. commander. In this way, he directed exactly how he wanted the Canadian ships to be used.

11. Capt Richard Sharpe, RN, ed., *Jane's Fighting Ships, 1991-92*, pp. 61-62.

.... What's on Second?

Vice-Admiral Henry H. Mauz, Jr., Commander U.S. Naval Forces Central Region (COMUSNAVCENT), was in charge of the overall multinational naval operation in the Red Sea and the Arabian Gulf.[12] He held that post until December when he was relieved by Vice-Admiral Stanley R. Arthur. Both Mauz and Arthur were embarked in USS BLUERIDGE.

The Canadian Task Group, while not directly commanded by Vice-Admiral Mauz, still had to co-ordinate its activities with the allied operations in the physically confined space of the Gulf. Throughout the six-month deployment, that meant staying in touch with Rear-Admiral Fogarty, embarked in USS LASALLE who was co-ordinating the embargo enforcement operations.

Once hostilities between Iraq and the allies began, Fogarty was also responsible for co-ordinating the Tomahawk missile attacks on land targets. Although Canada had no role in this, the Task Group continued with its interception of shipping role throughout the six weeks of hostilities, and thus continued to report back to Fogarty.

The U.S. also had a naval strike force under Rear-Admiral Daniel P. March, embarked in the American carrier USS MIDWAY. As the Commander of the Joint Battle Force known as Battle Force ZULU, March had under him 4 carriers (USS MIDWAY, RANGER, THEODORE ROOSEVELT, and AMERICA), 33 logistics ships, 20 escorts and 6 other ships. Of those 63 ships, 23 were from navies other than the U.S.[13] All of them had to be kept supplied with food, fuel and spares.

That's where the Canadian Task Group came in. The third major naval command was that of Combat Logistics Co-ordinator, and it was given to Canada's Captain Miller. It was the only major naval responsibility during the war not commanded by the U.S. Navy. In order to give command of the Logistics Force to Miller, the Canadian Task Group had to first become a part of Rear-Admiral March's organization.

12. General Norman Schwarzkopf, Commander-in-Chief, U.S. Central Command (CENTCOM) was the supreme commander throughout the Arabian Gulf crisis. He had overall operational command of all the forces in the Gulf region, which gave him responsibility for designing and co-ordinating the battle plan, orders, and actions, as well as administrative and logistics plans. However, Vice-Adm Mauz handled the naval side of the multinational operation. See, "Command and Control" by Joel H. Nadel, in Watson, Bruce W., Bruce George, M.P., Peter Tsouras, and B.L. Cyr, *Military Lessons of the Gulf War* (Greenhill Books, London, and Presidio Press, Calif: Bruce W. Watson 1991), p. 135.

13. Commodore D.E. Miller, Presentation to "Wargames of the Americas," in Rio de Janeiro, Fall 1992.

Once that was done, the chain of command on logistics issues, went from March to Miller. On deployment issues, the chain of command went from Summers to Miller.

Summers discussed this new set up with Miller. As the ships were now placed under the tactical control of the U.S. Admiral, Summers noted that "we're going to have to keep in touch when you're asked to do things that you may disagree with or may be outside our national authority. If there comes a conflict, you'll have to bring me in from a national command perspective." That is what happened, on February 18, when the U.S. asked for a Canadian ship to escort the crippled USS PRINCETON out of a minefield off the coast of Kuwait.

In practice, the loose command and control arrangements set up by the allies meant that any navy could object to its tasking. To avoid this, the White House would clear major strategic decisions with the various governments, and then issue military directives to General Norman Schwarzkopf.[14] Consequently there were no embarrassing situations where an ally had to refuse an American request. Miller, as Commander of the Combat Logistics Force, used the same technique in order to assign taskings to escorts of other countries. Miller invited each of the commanders over to ATHABASKAN before the allied action against Iraq began, and he asked them what their national parameters were, and how they wanted to be employed. With that information and the commanders' agreement, Miller was able to task the allied ships without worrying that his request for action might be refused.

Back in Canada, the pundits were confounded because the command and control arrangements that were used in the Gulf did not correspond to the usual definition and interpretation of those terms. Instead, the navies of the coalition used the definitions as guidelines while discussing what needed to be done and how they would do it. Instead of "command and control," they had in effect adopted a system of "co-ordination and co-operation." Individual ships could—and did—volunteer for roles that best suited their capabilities. It was a looser arrangement than would be the case, in for example, NATO exercises, where there are hard and fast rules about who commands what, when. But in the case of the Arabian Gulf deployment, where ships from NATO, the Arab world, and the non-aligned movement, were coming together for a common goal, it was the only arrangement that could work. It allowed the individual nations to do what they did best, and to be tasked according to their own strengths

14. Watson et al, p. 144.

and restrictions. It also provided the navies with independence of action—something that Miller found necessary to exercise on occasion.

For example, during the run-up to the January action, the U.S. sometimes ordered a higher state of readiness and the Canadian ships were expected to respond. When this happened, Miller would immediately order the Task Group to adopt that state of readiness, which includes everything from changing the watch system[15] to shifting the Phalanx Close-In Weapon System from a standby to manual operation mode. This caused a few problems. Every piece of equipment has an operational life expectancy before needing maintenance and because the Canadians had no idea how long they would be in the Gulf, or if hostilities would start, the Task Group wanted to conserve its weapons systems. Putting the Phalanx on manual meant it was using up its precious maintenance-free hours—months before anyone expected fighting to start. The first time it happened, Miller queried the rationale for the alert, and found out that it was because there was an incident in the Gulf of Oman where a merchant vessel was opposing a boarding and was in communication with its base in Iraq. The Americans were concerned that Iraq might launch an attack in support of its merchant ship. But because there was no corroborating evidence of an attack—such as aircraft scrambling on Iraqi airfields or fast patrol boats heading out into the Gulf—Miller decided the threat to Canadians in the central Gulf was minimal. He returned the ships to their previous readiness level. As it turned out, the Americans kept that higher state of alert going for three days; the Canadian Task Group kept it for two hours. For future alerts, the Canadian Task Group followed the same process: the ships' readiness level was immediately raised, the squadron staff evaluated the threat, and the readiness level was either maintained or returned to normal. The Americans may have been the overall co-ordinating authority for the deployment, but the Canadians could still decide what was their most appropriate tactical action.

⌘ ⌘ ⌘

Keeping track of the command and control arrangements was tough enough, but for Yeoman Serge Joncas, keeping track of his commanding officer, was tougher.

---

15. The length of watches on board ship varies from department to department. But generally, Canadian ships involved in actual operations change from a 3-watch to a 2-watch system: 50 per cent of the crew is always on duty. Some other countries continue to use a 3-watch system, so that only 33 per cent of their crew is on duty at any one time. The Canadian navy prides itself on being able to get to a full alert status, with all crew members on duty, in less than six minutes.

Joncas travelled everywhere with the Commander of the Task Group, which en route to Bahrain, was Commodore Summers. Just after leaving Djibouti, Summers wanted to go over to PROTECTEUR and then over to TERRA NOVA for a quick visit. Joncas accompanied the Commodore, to be there if he wanted to send messages. After a day's visit, two simultaneous jackstays were set up to get Summers and Joncas back. The first one went from TERRA NOVA to PROTECTEUR, and the second one from PROTECTEUR to ATHABASKAN. Joncas arrived back on board ATHABASKAN first, but he wasn't followed by the Commodore. I knew that Summers would probably stay an extra day in PROTECTEUR, so when Joncas came up to the bridge, I said, "What are you doing here?"

He was surprised and said, "What do you mean, what am I doing here? I've come back."

"Yeah, but what about the Commodore? Is he coming back?"

Joncas went white as a sheet. He had not realized that the Commodore was staying in PROTECTEUR, and had just continued his transit from her to ATHABASKAN. He began running back to the deck, yelling, "I've got to go back. I've lost the Commodore!" Everyone was laughing, while poor Serge was desperately trying to get back to Summers. But it was too late, they'd disconnected all the jackstays. We phoned Summers and said, "We need to report your Chief Yeoman has lost you!" And then we continued to make Serge feel worse by telling him, "That's the last time we send you to keep tabs on the Commodore. You can't even stay by his side!" It took a long time for him to live that down.

The Rules of Engagement and Weapons Control

Military forces operate under strict rules of engagement that specify exactly how they should act when coming into contact with a potential enemy. Those rules vary depending on whether operations and exercises are taking place in times of peace or tension or war. It's very important that these rules be clear to everyone at all times, because when things are tense, a wrong move can start a war. While rules of engagement drafted for peace or tension can still apply during hostilities they are not designed with hostilities in mind, given that in war one engages the enemy anywhere and at anytime. Once war has begun, the operations of a military force have to comply with the international laws of armed conflict, including the Geneva Convention. Constraints can be placed on the roles and missions of such operations by both political and military authorities. In the case of the naval Task Group in the Arabian Gulf, only geographic limitations were issued.

At all times—whether at peace, in war, or during times of tension—a ship's captain has the responsibility to defend his ship against an attack. Defence Minister Bill McKnight explained this right of self defence to a parliamentary committee conducting hearings on the Iraq-Kuwait crisis:

> An essential premise in the rules of engagement framework is the right of self-defence. The commander has the inherent right to employ such force as may be necessary to protect his command and the lives of his crew. Nothing in the rules of engagement—nothing—can be construed as limiting a commanding officer's basic right to exercise his judgement and initiative when immediate action is required for self-defence.[16]

The ships deployed to the Arabian Gulf formed a Task Group and as such, had a Task Group Commander—initially Summers, then Miller. While each ship's captain in the Group had the responsibility for his ship's defence, the commander of the Task Group had a greater responsibility: if an attack on one ship occurred, he would have to determine whether or not it was the beginning of an attack on the whole group and the start of a war.

The decision to activate a ship's defences and fire at a perceived threat is not always a clearcut one. Sometimes a ship will think it is being attacked, but it isn't. It is merely being harassed. Aircraft do this by making high-speed runs at enemy ships, hoping to evoke a response. If the ship shoots down the aircraft, then it has committed an act of war. Few commanders would want to be responsible for that escalation from tension to fighting. Thus, it is absolutely necessary that the ships in a crisis zone establish clear rules of engagement, and know exactly what line has to be crossed before a shooting match starts.

En route to the Arabian Gulf, the three Canadian ships' captains met with Summers and Miller in PROTECTEUR and went over the rules of engagement. They decided that the Canadian ships could only fire their

---

16. Standing Committee on External Affairs and International Trade, *Minutes*, Issue No. 67, October 15, 1990, p. 12.

On the jetty alongside HMCS ATHABASKAN just prior to departure, August 24, 1990

In Front: Commodore Ken Summers
From Left to Right: Maj Pete Nordlund, Maj Dan T. Cook, Cdr J.Y. Forcier, CPO1 Childs,
Cdr Stu Andrews, CPO1 Don Sanford, Cdr John Pickford, Capt Duncan (Dusty) E. Miller,
CPO1 John Auld, Capt Doug McClean

HMCS TERRA NOVA leaving Halifax, August 24, 1990 as thousands of people gathered to say goodbye.

Photographs from the Department of National Defence and personal collections.

The squadron staff dressed in nuclear-biological-chemical warfare defence suits.

The squadron staff unmasked:

From Left to Right
Back row: PO1 Jim Hawkins, Maj Pete Nordlund, CPO2 Serge Joncas, LCdr Greg Romanow,
CPO2 Al Dunn, LCdr Jim Hayes, Front row, seated: LCdr Greg Hannah, Capt Duncan (Dusty) Miller,
PO2 Buck Taylor

A refitted Sea King with its Forward-Looking Infrared (FLIR) system fitted at the nose of the aircraft.

A Sea King helicopter releasing its flares for missile defence.

The Gulli Gulli man in Port Said, entertaining members of PROTECTEUR's crew.

The ship's company of HMCS TERRA NOVA.

Two soldiers (M/Bdr Brad Redding on left, Gnr Paul Martin on right) dressed in nuclear-biological-warfare defence suits, practicing with their Javelin close air defence weapon.

Petty Officer, 2nd Class Haines and Master Seaman Sawicki preparing the Phalanx gun for firing.

Sea Sparrow missiles
aboard HMCS ATHABASKAN.

The Bofors 40 mm gun in a live
firing exercise.

HMCS PROTECTEUR refuelling two ships in the Arabian Gulf.

Replenishment while underway of HMCS TERRA NOVA (with Harpoon Missile System in centre of photograph).

Air Force Lieutenant Steve McLean outside his Sea King helicopter following a chemical warfare environment exercise.

A boarding party from HMCS ATHABASKAN (in background) races, in a rigid inflatable boat (RIB), towards HMCS PROTECTEUR during a boarding exercise in the Arabian Sea.

A crew member practicing the Vertical Insertion Search and Inspection Team (VISIT) method of boarding a ship.

The unofficial Task Group crest showing the Arabian Gulf and the ubiquitous sea snake.

A boarding party from HMCS TERRA NOVA takes charge of the bridge of HMCS PROTECTEUR during a boarding exercise.

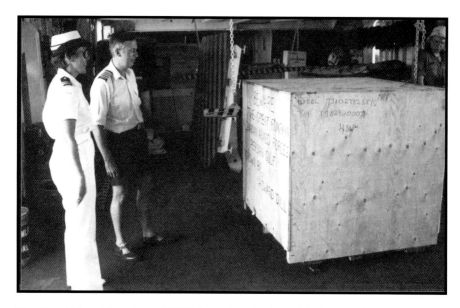

The Great Pumpkin arrives. LCDR Anne Gourlay-Langlois Supply Officer HMCS PROTECTEUR supervises.

Miller with Santa Claus about to board his Sea King helicopter.

Chief Petty Officer 2nd Class Dave Ashley.

HMCS PROTECTEUR's team, with ringer Marcel Dionne, in the First Annual Desert Sand Hockey Tournament in Bahrain.

Captain Duncan (Dusty) Miller and Commander John Pickford decorating the "wrong" Christmas Tree.

The Squadron Staff's Christmas Card.

From Left to Right:
In rear: Capt Dusty Miller, Middle row: Lt Geoff Frusher, LCdr Kevin Laing, CPO2 Melvin Antle, LCdr Greg Romanow, LCdr Jim Hayes, CPO2 Dave Ashley, CPO2 Al Dunn, Maj Pete Nordlund
Front row: PO1 Jim Hawkins, PO2 Buck Taylor, CPO2 Paul Barry, CPO2 Serge Joncas

Leaving the ship for a New Year's Eve Barbeque in the desert.

From left to right:
Back row: CPO2 Al Dunn, CPO2 Mel Antle, LCdr Greg Romanow, Cdr John Pickford, CPO2 Dave Ashley, LCdr Greg Hannah, Capt Doug McClean
Front row: PO2 Buck Taylor, LS Gerry Doucet, Capt Dusty Miller, PO1 Jimmy Hawkins, LCdr Jim Hayes

Commander Mike Pulchny (left) and Captain Doug McClean, discussing operations on board HMCS PROTECTEUR.

A flight crew member with .50 calibre machine gun in doorway of Sea King helicopter.

Tug and crippled USS PRINCETON after hitting a mine. Photo taken from
ATHABASKAN while circling and checking for mines in the minefield.

Kuwait after the ceasefire.

Burning oil wells in Kuwait.

Iraqi beach defences
in Kuwait.

Fake Iraqi Scuds.

weapons at a high speed aircraft carrying missiles which were *seen to be physically separating from the aircraft.* The ship also had to have some indication that it was being targetted by fire control radar.

The officers knew they were asking their ships' crews to operate under exceedingly difficult guidelines. After all, there would be very few seconds in which to react once the missiles separated from an aircraft. But the Canadians felt that, ethically, there was no other course: Canada was not at war and its naval forces could not be the first to attack.

The other countries in the coalition were operating under similiar rules but there were some differences. For example, any of the countries could opt for a more aggressive interpretation of self-defence. Because of the fragile situation in the Gulf, the Canadians were very conscientious in providing information to coalition ships—especially those operating under more aggressive rules of engagement—in order that they would make the "right" decision in tight situations. There was a constant flow of information among the members in the coalition on which ships were where, who was doing what, and which aircraft had been identified.

Major Pete Nordlund says "Canada had probably the most autonomy in its rules of engagement of any of the nations in the Gulf, including the Americans. In fact the Americans envied us quite a bit for what we were able to do in certain circumstances." The Canadians were well prepared for most eventualities and their rules of engagement reflected that, in exquisite detail. Consequently, they did not have to seek further authority for every move they made. For example, if a ship did not stop when requested, the Canadians had the authority to warn the ship that, if a warning shot across the bow did not work, they would fire into the ship's engine room or the ship's screws in order to stop it. Fortunately, the Task Group never had to exercise that kind of authority, but having it was an important symbol of confidence from their political and military masters back home.

It was necessary to establish the rules of engagement early on, because right from the beginning of the international maritime force's deployment up to the start of the war, the Iraqis flew daily missions, practicing their air-to-surface targeting techniques. Five or six Mirage aircraft would take off at the same time and would fly slowly south until they were just outside the weapons range of the ships in the northern Gulf. The Iraqis guessed where the invisible line was, that if crossed, risked their being shot out of the sky by the members of the coalition who had a more liberal interpretation of self-defence.

During the Atlantic crossing, one of Summers' top priorities was weapons control. He was keenly aware that the rapid fitting of new weapons systems in the ships had created a situation which had the potential for confusion, accidents, or disasters. To avoid any of this, he had his Weapons Officer, Lieutenant-Commander Kevin Laing, put together a weapons policy that would help the ships' captains establish absolute control over their weapons by ensuring that everyone had the same response to an unusual event. Laing used the navy's system which classified the threat status at different levels, and he defined what equipment should be up and running for each of those levels. The first level indicated there was no attack expected without adequate warning and the weapons technicians did not have to have their communication headsets on and the ammunition did not have to be sitting right at the weapons mount, but could be kept under cover out of the sun. The next level indicated there was a probability of an attack and the technicians should be wearing their headsets with the ammunition brought up and put beside their weapon. At the highest level everyone knew an attack was imminent, and that all weapons should be loaded and ready to fire. To refine further the threat status, each of the levels was broken down into degrees of readiness. These referred to the manning of the ship and its equipment, how many people should be at their posts.

The system, with its very clearly defined manning and equipment specifications, was tested extensively during the Gibraltar exercise and its success left Summers feeling confident that each "captain had iron-clad control over every weapon in his ship."

But that was only one aspect of the complex issue of weapons control. Whether or not to fire, would depend on the interpretation of the information being provided by sensors and lookouts to the officers in the operations room. The squadron staff did not want a repeat of the 1988 USS VINCENNES incident—in which an American warship shot down an Iranian airliner—so they established a method of confirming and analysing an abnormal contact.

Figuring out what was "normal" and "abnormal" in the congested airspace of the Gulf, was in itself a feat: on an average day there were about 30 aircraft at any one time in the air around the Canadian ships—commercial airlines, allied air patrols, and Iraqi fighters practising tactics. Everything in the air was suspect until proved otherwise. Once a contact was determined by any of the sensor operators or officers to be "abnormal," the newly-devised "Resolve" procedure went into effect.

The use of the code word "Resolve" by anyone alerted everyone else in the operations room that they should stop what they were doing to concentrate on that contact. Using all the tools at their disposal—radar and electronic support measures equipment, as well as an air traffic controller, and a lookout on the bridge with high-powered binoculars—the operations team would go into high gear, comparing and assessing the information to determine the nationality and intent of the aircraft. If the plane was not following commercial air lanes, the team would contact it on a commercial distress frequency, tell it to identify itself immediately, and warn it that it was in the vicinity of a Canadian warship which would take defensive action if necessary. At the same time, the team would request a fighter aircraft to fly at the contact and determine if the aircraft was equipped with missiles—i.e., if it was a Mirage fighter-bomber with Exocet missiles slung underneath.[17]

The work put into establishing and exercising this procedure paid off very quickly once the ships began their embargo enforcement patrols in the central Gulf. It was just after dawn, and ATHABASKAN was sailing along the Iranian side of its patrol area. An American Seahawk helicopter was reported to be approaching the ship from her north. Lieutenant-Commander Jim "Tilley" Hayes, who was the Squadron Watch Officer at the time, wondered where the helicopter had come from. As the aircraft approached, the operations room implemented the "Resolve" procedure. The aircraft controller, Petty Officer Jimmy Hawkins, used both military and civilian frequencies to ask the aircraft for identification. There was no reply and the aircraft just kept on coming towards the ship. Hawkins tried again. No reply. Then the high-powered binocular lookout on deck reported, "Hey, that's not an American aircraft, it's Iranian. It's got Iranian markings on it." Suddenly, the situation looked very serious. ATHABASKAN's Operations Room Officer ordered the fire control radar to lock on to the aircraft and the missile launchers to be extended. Hawkins called the aircraft for a third time, and finally, just moments before the command to shoot would have been issued, the helicopter pilot responded by identifying himself as an Iranian who was just undertaking an ordinary maritime surveillance mission in the international waters of the Gulf.

---

17. This was an unusual procedure for the Canadian navy which has traditionally focused on ASW and has relied on its NATO allies to cover off the air threat. Not only did this relatively new task require new skills, but it required a different mentality. As opposed to the slow process of submarine identification—something that could take several hours of patiently following a contact and listening intently—air defence required analysis and reaction in a matter of seconds.

That incident, while not a common occurrence, typified the type of tension under which the ships operated in the Gulf. Yet, in the high-pressure atmosphere of the operations room, the staff of the Canadian ships were surprisingly relaxed. Miller told each of his officers and the three ships' crews that he expected a relaxed professionalism to prevail. He stressed that that did not mean being slack, but rather that the men and women be able to handle a great amount of tension because they knew their jobs. Miller believed a thorough knowledge would give them the confidence they needed to deal with the everyday tensions in a relaxed fashion.

Of course, there were times when the cool professionalism went out the porthole. For instance, during the very first perceived attack of a SCUD missile on ATHABASKAN.

It was before the war started and ATHABASKAN was on patrol in the central Gulf. Hayes, who as a Duty Officer was Miller's representative when Miller was not in the operations centre, had been thinking about the Iraqis and their SCUD missiles. He wondered, if the Iraqis launched a pre-emptive attack on the allies and, for example, sunk a Canadian ship, would the other countries in the coalition view that as sufficient cause to start a war? Or would Hussein get away with a freebie? Would the Iraqi leader gamble that he could? Would such an act scare away some of the members of the coalition? Hayes didn't know the answers to these questions and he didn't want to find out.

Unfortunately, Hayes, with his head still full of questions, was on duty in the operations room the time the intelligence officers announced that there had been a SCUD launch and the missile was heading south. Hayes decided immediately that Miller should be informed and he ran from the room to the Task Group Commander's cabin, making it in less time than it would have taken for the Operations Room Officer to put through a phone call. Miller and Commander Pickford were having breakfast when Hayes burst in, eyes like saucers, and screamed, "SCUUUUDDDD! SCUD attack!" Then he flew back to the operations room. Miller and Pickford leapt up, both trying to make it through the cabin door at once. After sorting themselves out they raced to the ops room, only to find out that the SCUD was just being tested over Iraqi territory and was not bearing down on the Canadian ship.

If a SCUD or other missile actually had been fired at the Task Group, the ships would have responded by taking evasive manoeuvres and possibly firing back. The Phalanx Close-In Weapon Systems on board the ships could be set for automatic firing. In order to decrease the possibility of firing at something by mistake, the weapon's computer could be set to respond to a certain size and speed of aircraft or missile. For example, the system could be programmed to fire at aircraft only flying *faster* than 140 knots—the top speed of a Sea King helicopter, thus protecting the Task Group's own aircraft.

Another safety precaution was to set the weapons systems in a semi-automatic mode. That way, the equipment could pick up the target and do the necessary calculations for firing, but would be unable to release its weapons without someone actually flicking a switch.

This was important because of the number of friendly aircraft flying in the region. The first line of defence in the northern Gulf was the combat air patrols (CAPs) by fighter aircraft. They watched the Iraqi aircraft closely, checking both their apparent destination and their weapons load. The patrols by the various coalition forces were controlled by the U.S. which scheduled the flights and made the schedules known to the ships. The aircraft were also assigned very specific operating areas, so that they did not stray near the naval forces where they could be mistaken for Iraqi aircraft and possibly shot down.

The eight nations of the Gulf Co-operation Council, however, were not a direct part of the organization, although they were operating aircraft in the Arabian Gulf. To complicate matters, the Qataris were flying Mirage aircraft the same as the Iraqis. After the fighting started in January, the Gulf Co-operation Council offered to fly combat air patrols for the Combat Logistics Force in the southern Gulf. This offer concerned the ships' captains, who feared they would suddenly see a Mirage coming out of the clouds, and the weapons systems—on automatic during that period—would shoot it down. Although the Combat Logistics Force was nervous about this, the commanders appreciated that the Arab countries wanted to help, and therefore set up a couple of these high-speed air patrols. They were scheduled precisely, with the ships knowing exactly when the aircraft were coming, and that the Mirage aircraft was an allied sortie. Other times, however, Arab air forces, in their enthusiasm, scheduled their own combat air patrols. Those flights kept everyone on their toes.

Having established the rules of engagement and the weapons policy to avoid any accidental firing of shipboard weapons, there was only one more area in which to establish firm control: firing orders. The navy follows a specific sequence of orders for firing a weapon. Each gun system in a ship is given a letter, such as A system, B system, etc. When preparing

104 The Persian Excursion

to fire the 3"/50 gun system, for example, the operator reports that "B system is loaded."[18] When the system's radar, the ship's radar, and a lookout all confirm that the target has been acquired, the operator states "B system on target". The Weapons Officer on the bridge then tells the operators, "B system engage," followed by the operator turning the necessary keys to complete an electronic circuit to make the system operable. The technician in the gun control room then says "B system shoot" and the operator in effect pulls the trigger.[19] Each of the people involved in the sequence is responsible for a set of checkpoints before giving the order. As soon as the operator hears the Weapons Officer say "Stop Loading," he lets go of the shoot trigger and the technician in the gun control room breaks his switch as well so that the gun stops firing.

That's the navy way of operating its weapons systems. But its not the army way.

Lieutenant-Commander Kevin Laing had to put together new instructions for the air defence personnel on the upper decks who were armed with Javelin low-level air defence weapon systems.

> *Laing went to the army fellows and asked, "What orders do you have to make you shoot at something?"*
>
> *One of the soldiers answered, "'FIRE' is one of them."*
>
> *"Yeah, well, don't use that word onboard ship unless you want 200 sailors with firehoses bearing down on you!"*
>
> *The navy uses the order "engage." But when the soldiers heard that, they looked at each other and said, "engage what?"*
>
> *It was through those kind of discussions that Laing was able to sort it out so that everyone on board—army, navy, and air force—was speaking the same language.*

It was another example of heading off problems before they occurred and not waiting until the shooting started to find out what could go wrong. What the navy was assigned to do in the Gulf, it had never done before. There were bound to be problems crop up as the ships set about their mission. But the command and control arrangements worked out during the Atlantic crossing and in the early days of the Gulf deployment were comprehensive and sensible, so that no problem was insurmountable.

---

18. This example indicates some of the key orders, not the exact sequence. The quotes are a paraphrase of the actual drill manual instruction and vocabulary.

19. The 3"50 gun fires at about 120 rounds per minute which tends to overheat the barrel. So the navy operates it at a slower rate, about 60-90 rounds per minute.

Chapter Six

Reach Out and Touch Someone

At 1:00 p.m. on August 9, Chief Petty Officer 2nd Class Dave Ashley was getting on with his job as senior radioman for the 1st Destroyer Squadron when he was approached by the squadron's Technical Officer. Commander John Meehan had a question. "If I was to send three ships away on a major deployment, what would you need in the way of communications to have it work?"

Ashley, used to hypothetical questions, was only slightly curious. He replied with a question of his own—"Where am I going?"

"I can't tell you."

This wasn't the usual answer he got to questions about exercises and training, so Ashley knew he was being asked about a real operation. He gave his full attention to the problem being put to him by his senior officer.

"That doesn't do me any good because I've got to know." Ashley pressed further. "What three ships am I taking?"

"I can't tell you that either."

This was getting worse. Ashley insisted he had to know some details before he could design a communications setup. Meehan, sworn to secrecy, could only give clues.

"It would probably be an AOR, a 280 and an IRE.[1]"

Knowing which ships were in Halifax, that's all Ashley needed to figure out the ships were PROTECTEUR, ATHABASKAN, and

---

1. An Auxilary Oiler Replenishment ship (or tanker), a DDH-280 Tribal class destroyer, and an Improved Restigouche class destroyer.

TERRA NOVA. But he still needed to know to what part of the world the ships would be deploying.

Trying to help Ashley without betraying his oath, Meehan said, "Without saying anything, look at the front page of the paper."

On that Thursday, the front page of the paper was covered with the Iraq-Kuwait crisis and the fact that the Americans had U.N. approval to send a military force to the Arabian Gulf. As Ashley says, with those clues, "you didn't need to be a rocket scientist to figure out that the Canadians were going to the Gulf and they were taking three ships with them."

Having obliquely defined the mission, Meehan now asked Ashley for a list of the equipment needed on each ship in order to cover the necessary communications links. Oh, and one other thing—he wanted it within two hours.

That request was just the beginning. Ashley's wife saw very little of him over the next 10 days; many nights he stayed in his office, using his desk as a bed.

⌘   ⌘   ⌘

The world is divided into communications regions, with the plans and procedures for operating in each region contained in books and publications distributed by various civil and military authorities. However, overall control of commercial and military radio frequencies is exercised by the International Telecommunications Union (ITU). If the navy wants to be able to do long-range or tactical communications on a frequency that it doesn't normally use, the Defence Department's Director of Frequency Spectrum Management approaches the ITU for both permission and procedures. However, if the navy wanted to use frequencies that were controlled by, for example, NATO or the U.S. in its Pacific area of operations, the Director would seek permission from that particular agency rather than the ITU.

For its journey, the Task Group would have to get clearance from the authorities to use various frequencies in the different regions of the world. The trans-Atlantic crossing was not a problem for the Canadian Task Group, because they would use the communications setup Canada always uses during NATO exercises—those authorized by CincEastlant and CincWestlant.[2] But in Gibraltar, the plan had to be completely

---

2. Command-in-Chief, Eastern Atlantic, and Commander-in-Chief, Western Atlantic.

changed to that of the Mediterranean commander's. And from the Suez Canal, Ashley would have to set up an interim plan until the Task Group could make contact with the multinational forces and discover what they were using locally. The east coast fleet, which had never before operated in the Indian Ocean and the Red Sea, did not hold the communications book for that region of the world.[3]

The east coast fleet, which works mainly with NATO, uses NATO procedures and publications. On the west coast, the Canadian fleet works mainly with the Americans and thus is familiar with, and uses, U.S. procedures and publications. Over the years, however, Canada, the U.S., and other Pacific Rim navies have put together a book called "The Combined Exercise Agreement," which is a compendium of the U.S. and NATO publications. It is used by countries participating in Pacific Ocean tactical exercises.

Ashley contacted a friend in the U.S. Navy who figured out what equipment, circuits, and communications plan the American forces were using in the Gulf. He reported back to Ashley that the U.S. was using the Pacific Fleet communications plan. Ashley then tracked down a copy of the book within the Canadian navy. The only problem was the book was on the west coast, and Ashley, on the east coast, needed it immediately.

Ashley's main contacts within Maritime Command were Lieutenant-Commander John Gardam and Major J.R. (Bob) Ruohoniemi. When the Chief told Ruohoniemi his problem, the Major moved quickly. Because the normal military courier service was stretched to the limit and the book was needed immediately, Ruohoniemi arranged for a CT-133 Silver Star to fly to Esquimalt to get it.

Once Ashley had the book he told Maritime Command the Task Group would need to use the U.S. Navy's Pacific Fleet communication plan in the Gulf. The Director of Frequency Spectrum Management made the necessary arrangements with the Americans.

Reliable and secure communications were essential to the success of the operation in the Gulf. When the Canadian ships sailed, Ashley believes they had the best allied communications package in the Gulf for embargo enforcement and wartime operations. All three of the ships were fitted with satellite communications, radio teletype, fax machines, secure

---

3.   The last time a Canadian ship was in that area was in 1964 when HMCS ST. LAURENT sailed through the Suez Canal.

telephone units compatible with both U.S. and British forces, as well as a full communications fit of HF, UHF, and VHF transceivers.[4]

Ashley had designed the setup based on Murphy's Law—everything that could go wrong, would go wrong—in order to be prepared for every eventuality. And it was thanks to Ashley's knowledge and foresight that the Canadians had the communications capabilities to co-ordinate the Combat Logistics Force.

Long-Range Communications

Canada does not have a military satellite communications system. The navy normally uses High Frequency (HF) waves, which bounce off the ionosphere[5] and can travel long distances, to pass messages between its deployed ships and Mill Cove where Maritime Command has its 24 hours-a-day/365 days-a-year communications facility. But Canadian east coast ships are not ordinarily deployed on the other side of the world; they are usually in the North Atlantic or down south in the Caribbean. The west coast ships, which operate in the Pacific, pass their messages back to Maritime Pacific Command headquarters via Aldergrove.

In addition to the problem of setting up communications over a 13,000-kilometre distance, there was the problem of wave propagation in the Gulf: it was not like anything that Ashley had ever seen before. It was as if the laws of physics did not apply. When the Task Group first arrived in the Gulf, Ashley did trials using HF waves taking various routes back to Canada. Neither going through Aldergrove on the West Coast, nor through Australia or New Zealand worked. Going through Mill Cove only worked occasionally. That meant there could be no guarantees attached to the use of HF waves as the main mode of message transmission. In anticipation of such problems, the Department of National Defence had arranged for the Canadian Forces to use American satellites for both global and regional communications.

Maritime Command sent a Hercules transport aircraft to Houston to pick up four Demand Assigned Multiple Access Satellite Communications (DAMA/SATCOM) and 12 civilian technicians to install them in the three ships and the shore facility at Mill Cove. The American civilians also trained the navy's technicians to use the equipment. One civilian,

---

4. In the military, HF (High Frequency) waves occupy the 2-30 MegaHertz part of the radio wave spectrum; VHF (Very High Frequency) are the 100-156 MHz waves; and UHF (Ultra High Frequency) are 225-400 MHz waves.
5. The ionosphere is the outermost layer of the earth's atmosphere. It is characterized by the presence of a large number of electrically charged particles.

Mr. Richard Twigg, went with the ships as far as Gibraltar. He had only limited experience at sea, but soon became an old hand at transferring between ships by jackstay and helicopter, as he checked the equipment and made sure it was working properly.

PROTECTEUR was tied into the Fleet Satellite (FLTSAT) over the Atlantic Ocean which connected her directly to Mill Cove in Nova Scotia.[6] ATHABASKAN and TERRA NOVA were tied into the LEASAT Communications Satellite System over the Indian Ocean because that's where the command circuits were that the Americans were using. If ATHABASKAN or TERRA NOVA wanted to use the Atlantic satellite, they would have to change their antenna direction; they could not use both satellites simultaneously. Because it was important to have the two destroyers, which were operating as escorts during the war, on the command circuit of the Indian Ocean satellite, Ashley had PROTECTEUR take care of the Canada connection. If ATHABASKAN was unable to get its message traffic to PROTECTEUR for relay back to Canada—for example, if the supply ship had gone south to refuel and had had to shut down while it was alongside[7]—then Ashley would get TERRA NOVA to change her antenna over to the Atlantic satellite. He tried to keep ATHABASKAN, as command ship, on the Indian Ocean satellite all the time.

That the Task Group was even able to use the Atlantic satellite was a fluke. A satellite has a "footprint" which is the area that it looks at on the face of the earth. The Atlantic satellite's footprint was not supposed to cover the Arabian Gulf, but it did. Ashley found out about it by mistake. Coming through the Red Sea, the Canadian Task Group was scheduled to change its satellite dishes over from the Atlantic satellite to the Indian Ocean satellite, the same as the Americans. The ships made the change, but they were unable to get any messages through. The relay station on Guam was not answering the Canadian calls. By the time the ships arrived in Djibouti, Ashley was getting desperate. He was trying to pass the traffic through the French or anyone that he could raise on the radio, to get messages back to Canada. He wasn't having any luck. So he used the INMARSAT to get hold of John Gardam and told him the Task Group

---

6. The rate of transmission was 300 baud or approximately 400 words per minute.
7. For safety reasons, when a ship is taking on fuel or stores, it turns off its antennae because static builds up in the communication system which can produce a spark. Therefore, the Officer of the Watch collects the keys from all transmitters before the ship can refuel. The antennae are also shut down during rest or maintenance periods. During these down times, the ship can receive but cannot transmit messages.

had to have the use of the Atlantic satellite for at least a couple more days until it entered the Gulf of Oman. Gardam called U.S. Navy headquarters in Norfolk and arranged for a channel that the Task Group could use 24 hours a day. Both Gardam and Ashley expected that the Atlantic satellite channel would only be good for about another day and then the ships would be out of range. But when the ships steamed through the Strait of Hormuz and the Atlantic connection was still working, Ashley knew they had it made. The Strait was the furthest point from the satellite; from there on, ships would be steaming northwest, bringing them more within the satellite's footprint.

The Americans, meanwhile, were passing their message traffic through the Indian Ocean LEASAT because they believed that the Atlantic satellite did not cover the Arabian Gulf. The messages sent via LEASAT bounced up and down around the globe—from the Arabian Gulf to Guam to Hawaii to California. But Guam was only a minor radio station and all the American ships were on that circuit. To top it off, the island was hit by a typhoon during the war, really fouling up communications. At one point Ashley was talking with the radioman in USS BLUERIDGE, the American command ship, and the American asked, "how's your backlog?" Surprised, Ashley said, "What backlog? I don't have a backlog." The American asked if the Canadian Task Group was going through Guam, and Ashley told him, "No, I'm going through Mill Cove in Nova Scotia." The American couldn't believe it. He said, "Come with me, I want to show you something." He took Ashley to the main control room and to a crewman who was handling the message traffic. "What's your backlog right now?" he asked. Pointing to the output queue of the operator's Visual Display Unit, which contained the "flashes" (top priority messages to be sent by teletype "as fast as humanly possible"), and the "immediates" (teletype messages to be sent "within the hour"), the crewman replied, "Flashes and immediates are getting out with probably about six hours delay, maybe seven hours. Priority on backlog, three days."

If Halifax wanted to contact Miller directly in ATHABASKAN, rather than go through PROTECTEUR, it could use the HF system providing the conditions for receiving were good, but usually relied on the Indian Ocean satellite. The message had to be patched through from Mill Cove to Argentia to Norfolk to Stockton, California to Hawaii to Guam and then onto the LEASAT from which ATHABASKAN was able to copy the broadcast. The traffic load from Mill Cove via this "Snake," was such that the navy instituted a two-broadcast system: one for immediate and flash traffic and one for priority and routine traffic. "The traffic load for these two broadcasts was normally between 600-700 messages a day, per broadcast (1200-1400 messages total, each message six to eight pages long)," according to Ashley. "Added to this was the 100-200 messages a day that was being transmitted into Mill Cove via PROTECTEUR, and it is very easy to see that the operations people at Mill Cove were very busy people. They operated four shifts of people, 20-25 people per shift, working 12 hour shifts, supplemented by 30-35 day staff." Ashley was impressed with their dedication and professionalism. "I feel that these people provided us with a service that bridged on continuous excellence, and they have received very little recognition for this service and all their hard work. Without them we would never have been able to operate as well as we did."

A relay failure could occur at any point in the "Snake," requiring Ashley and Mill Cove to start at their respective ends of the relay, looking for the problem. Ashley says 90 per cent of the time, the problem was in Guam because all the senior people there had been sent to the Gulf, leaving junior people and reserves to handle an enormously expanded workload. It happened so often, that the watch officers on Guam began to recognize Ashley's voice. One night he heard the officer saying to a colleague, "It's that Canadian Chief in the Gulf again!"

For using the commercial INMARSAT, Gardam and Ashley made sure that the three Canadian ships were equipped with both the British secure voice system, the Brahms,[8] as well as the American Secure Telephone Unit (STU III) system. Because Canada normally uses the same equipment as the Americans, the STU III equipment was already on board. But aware of the importance of being able to communicate with more than just the Americans in this multi-national operation, Ashley had arranged for the installation of British equipment on board all three ships. However, even without the British equipment, Canada would have been in a good position because the Americans had the most ships and aircraft in the Gulf, and the Canadian Task Group could talk to all of them.

Amazingly, neither the British nor the Americans had the other's system. Canada was the only ally who could communicate with both.

In addition to having the secure systems in the communications room of ATHABASKAN, Miller had a Secure Telephone Unit line in his cabin, giving him easy access to not only the American commanders, but also

---

8. The Dutch and Germans also use the Brahms system, so Canada was also able to use it for secure traffic to those navies.

the Canadian liaison in USS MIDWAY (Lieutenant-Commander Greg Romanow), Commodore Summers in Bahrain, Maritime Command in Halifax, and National Defence Headquarters in Ottawa.

The Land Link: Ottawa to Bahrain

Sending three ships to the Gulf was not just another routine deployment. The decision had been made at the highest political level and it was involving Canada in the complicated politics of the Middle East. With such a high-profile action in a volatile region, it was absolutely necessary that the deployment be directly overseen by the Prime Minister and his war cabinet. That required an instantaneous and assured communications system between Ottawa and Summers as the Joint Commander.

The Joint Staff came up with a communications plan for the Ottawa to Bahrain link which used the army's long-range communications terminals. But that had its disadvantages. First of all, the speed of transmission was restricted on the teletype to about 75 words per minute. Second, the army could not guarantee 24 hour-a-day availability. Third, there would be no voice transmission. The army's terminals would be supplemented by the commercial INMARSAT, but it also came without a 24 hour-a-day availability guarantee.

Summers and Commodore Bruce Johnston of the Joint Staff worked together to find a solution to the communications problem. Johnston directed his crisis team to look for some other system to meet the long-distance requirements. Summers looked to what the navy had so that it could also be put in the Joint Headquarters.

Maritime Command took a satellite communications system out of a ship in Halifax and flew it to Bahrain where it was installed in the headquarters. The satellite system gave the Joint Staff the capability to send hard copy message traffic very quickly from Ottawa to Maritime Command, through Mill Cove and then into the American satellite and over to the Gulf. That was important because it carried the intelligence summaries as well as other messages.

What was still needed was a voice connection. The Joint Staff finally settled on using an Intelsat[9] Canada system to meet that need. Intelsat

9. The International Telecommunication Satellite Organization (Intelsat) is the principal provider of international satellite capacity, providing voice, data, and television transmission services. The organization has more than 100 member countries, and access to the Intelsat satellites is controlled by their national telecommunication authorities.

systems were installed in Doha and Bahrain, to provide a telephone line between the Gulf and Ottawa for both voice and fax transmissions. The system was expensive but its value was immense. Johnston says, "this provided the capability to have discussions on future decisions. When that was in place, I could pick up my phone, dial three digits and either get the ops centre or the Commodore's office, in a flash."

Summers could—and did—phone the Joint Staff any time of the day or night, but he made a point of always calling first thing in the morning in Ottawa, to update them for their morning briefing with General de Chastelain.

Gulf Communications

During the Gulf deployment, High Frequency (HF) waves were used for regional communications, as well as communications amongst the three ships of the Task Group. Very-high frequency (VHF) and ultra-high frequency (UHF) radio waves, which only travel along the line-of-sight, were used for communicating locally with ships and aircraft from other countries.[10]

Because all commercial ships monitor Channel 16, a VHF distress and hailing frequency, it was used by the interdiction force to hail a vessel before switching to a mutually accessible channel for the questioning. Similarly, to talk to commercial aircraft, the ships carried a VHF AM transceiver and used the Civilian Emergency frequency of 121.5 Mhz.

But the unreliable wave propagation in the Gulf caused message traffic to be a hit or miss affair. At times neither end could be sure that the whole message had been received.

In the northern regions of the world, such as the Atlantic Ocean, UHF communications are good for about 20-30 miles or line-of-sight. In the southern regions, however, there is a phenomenom called tropospheric[11] ducting. A very dense layer of air deflects the radio waves rather than allowing them to pass through. In effect, the troposhphere acts as a tube, relaying the radio waves over the horizon out to ranges of 200 miles. Ashley says "the Arabian Gulf was one great big tropospheric duct. The only difference was that, down south these ducts come and go, but in the Gulf, they never left."

---

10. The satellite channels were also UHF.

11. The troposphere is the lower layer of the earth's atmosphere, and is characterized by air turbulence.

This created a problem. In the North Atlantic, ships in a 20-mile area can all talk to each other, and ships outside that range will not be able to hear, and will not interfere in the communciation. In the Gulf, which is only about 300 miles long, there could be ships talking to each other in the southern Gulf, unknowingly interfering with the communications of ships that were conducting an operation in the northern Gulf. (It would be rather like having four people in a room all talking about different subjects at the same time, making it very difficult to follow any one conversation.)

The tropospheric ducts also affected the High Frequency waves, but ATHABASKAN had a piece of equipment which could indicate the best frequency for transmitting on at any given time. A "chirpsounder" checking system used shore-based transmitters which sent out a tone every hour. The tone was not a steady one, but ran across the 2 and 30 Megahertz frequency bands of the High Frequency spectrum. A receiver in the ship ran the spectrum at the same time and a display would show which were the best frequencies for receiving the transmitted tone. Generally, the atmospheric conditions so restricted these communications that they never got above 3 Megahertz.

Not all the navies had a chirpsounder. The Americans had them in a couple of their ships which were up north with the carriers. By combining results with the information from the chirpsounder in the more southerly-based ATHABASKAN, the Americans were able to establish which frequencies throughout the Gulf were best for distributing tactical information among the ships and aircraft.

In the areas where the troposphere behaved normally, where there were no tropospheric ducts, there were "black holes." In certain areas, especially the area off Qatar and Bahrain, a ship would not be able to receive any UHF communications, although HF and VHF communications would not be affected. Ten miles to the south, UHF communications would be crystal clear. When a ship found itself in a "black hole" it would call a nearby ship and ask what she was getting. If the neighbouring ship was receiving communications with no problems, she would relay the information to the ship in the "black hole" on a different frequency.

The navies operating in the Gulf were working with different communications capabilities. Everyone was able to use the main tactical and warfighting frequencies, but it depended on their equipment what other frequencies they could use. For example, communication with the

Argentinian and Arab navies was limited to VHF and signalling.[12] Canada had no such problem. Prior to leaving Halifax, Ashley had put together an incredibly comprehensive and flexible communications package which enabled the Canadian ships to talk to everyone as well as come up on the main American command nets. ATHABASKAN could monitor 35 frequencies but some of the allied ships could only monitor five or six.

There was an initial problem with the different codes which have to be programmed into the cryptographic equipment used by the various navies in the multinational force. Cryptographic equipment scrambles communications into a code so that only a decoder keyed with the same code can read the message. "The codes, which have to be programmed into the equipment, either once daily, weekly, bi-monthly or monthly are produced by National, NATO and Allied authorities; the National codes all being different from the NATO codes, and both being different again from the Allied codes. They also differ from one piece of equipment to another," says Ashley.

> This means that the Allied codes used for a UHF Secure Voice device is different from the code that is used for an HF Secure Voice device, and different again for a secure radio teletype device. Compounded further is the problem that a National/NATO/Allied Code for one geographical location is different from that for another location (i.e. the Allied codes for the Atlantic are different from those for the Pacific, and different still for the Indian Ocean). The U.S. Commander Far East's staff finally produced a working Communications Plan which employed maximum use of common Allied Keymat Codes for all encrypted circuits. They also received authority to provide copies of the required codes for anyone who didn't hold them and was unable to receive them from National Sources.

The multinational naval forces had a co-ordinator to sort out the tangle of communications at the local level in the Gulf. There were three operational sectors—northern, central and southern. In addition there were the coastal areas which were patrolled by the Saudis. Each region had a different communications set-up. Only the main tactical frequencies such as the anti-air warfare circuit, and the "navy red" circuit—a

12. B.L. Cyr, Bruce W. Watson, Raimondo Luraghi, Bruce George, M., Tim Lister, and James Piriou, "Naval Operations" in *Military Lessons of the Gulf War*, ed. Bruce W. Watson, Bruce George, Peter Tsouras, and B.L. Cyr, (Greenhill Books, London, and Presidio Press, Calif: Bruce W. Watson 1991), p. 124.

warfighting frequency—never changed. Any ship changing from one operational sector to another had to change its communications so that it could talk to the sector commanders.

Different sectors used the same frequencies for different subjects. For example, the frequency that was being used to talk among ships in the southern Gulf, might be the same frequency that the ships in the northern Gulf would use to talk to aircraft.

In addition to the sector communications arrangements, each carrier battle group had to have its own set of frequencies, which could be meshed so that they could work together. Solving the problem was not just a matter of putting the carriers on the same frequency. For example, USS MIDWAY's land/launch frequency had to be for its aircraft only; it couldn't launch and land aircraft using USS THEODORE ROOSEVELT's frequency. The whole thing was made more difficult because the carriers were operating at such close quarters.

There were not enough frequencies for the size of the Gulf operation. With that many ships, and that many jobs, the frequency spectrum was rapidly used up as the operators tried to avoid the problem of mutual interference.[13] The Canadian Task Group got clearance for a Canadian command circuit, a UHF secure voice circuit which ran among the three ships. Permission to use the various frequencies came from the Americans—the U.S. Military Installation in St. Petersburg, Florida, which set up the communications and frequency clearances and is the American counterpart to Canada's Director of Frequency Spectrum Management. According to Ashley, it was not a very good system. "It didn't work worth a darn. It seemed like everytime another aircraft carrier came into the Gulf, he was sitting damn smack on one of my frequencies." Because Ashley had clearance for Canada to be using that frequency, protocol called for the aircraft carrier to vacate it. But, as Ashley says, "Rather than me turn around and tell an aircraft carrier to get off my frequency, especially when he's trying to talk to a bunch of fighters, I used my scope." This was a UHF Frequency Spectrum Analyzer which had been installed in ATHABASKAN, thanks to the foresight of John Gardam. The picture on the scope consisted of a straight line across the center. One end of the line was 225 Mhz, the other end was 400 Mhz. The scope was hooked into one of the ship's UHF antennae so that anytime someone

13. Mutual interference stems from assigning two frequencies too close together. It involves static or bits of conversations from one frequency spilling over into another. To avoid that, the frequencies have to be several hertz apart. Because of that requirement, it doesn't take long to fill up the usable spectrum in a complex operation.

transmitted on UHF, a "spike" or vertical line would appear. By using an adjustment dial and an LED display screen, the operator would find out exactly what frequency was being used. Ashley says,

> I would stand in front of this thing, looking at the spikes. Where I saw a clearance, I would dial in on that frequency and I would stand there and I would watch that frequency for about five or six minutes to see if anybody talked on it. If nobody talked on it, then I would get back on the air and I'd tell TERRA NOVA and PROTECTEUR to shift to this frequency on that particular circuit.

This didn't only happen when an aircraft carrier arrived in the Gulf. It happened constantly during the Task Group's six-month operation there.

> Two o'clock in the morning I'd be standing up there looking at this damn scope, simply because all of a sudden an aircraft carrier did a shift in its frequencies because the frequency they were working their aircraft on, wasn't that good, it was noisy or something. So they'd shifted over to another frequency before checking with anybody.

The Task Group ships used two 2MHz radio teletype (RATT) circuits[14] to communicate among themselves.[15] One was an internal Task Group administration circuit used to pass both classified and unclassified traffic, either among the three ships, or from ATHABASKAN and TERRA NOVA to PROTECTEUR for relay via satellite to Mill Cove. The other 2MHz circuit was a naval rear link circuit in ATHABASKAN. It linked the ship with the long-range communication transmitters set up at Joint Headquarters in Bahrain and in Doha where the CF-18 squadron was based. Without that linkup, the command ship would have had to take the long way around to get its messages to Commodore Summers: transmit to PROTECTEUR, which would have had to send the message via satellite to Mill Cove, and then back again to Bahrain.

War made the complicated communications arrangements even more complex. In addition to United Nations interdiction operations circuits, and national circuits, the Canadian command ship ATHABASKAN had to maintain warfighting circuits. These included a Force Commanders Satellite Radio Teletype, a Battle force Commanders Voice Net, and a Maritime Rear Link. Furthermore, with Miller in command of up to 60 allied ships spread throughout the Gulf, the High Frequency circuits

---

14. The 2MHz frequency runs from 2000KHz to 2999KHz.

15. The transmission rate alternated between 600 and 1200 baud or 800 and 1600 words per minute.

were in demand. Under normal circumstances, having more than four or five ships talking on one circuit creates problems with getting messages through because the frequency is constantly occupied. But in the Gulf, Miller's staff were trying to co-ordinate 20-30 ships using one circuit. To alleviate the problem, messages were kept extremely short, with any lengthy ones being flown over to the ships.

With the coalition's entry into the war, Ashley's life became even more hectic. He remembers that a few days after the fighting started, air controller Jimmy Hawkins came up to him in the ops room and said, "Geez Dave, you look like shit; when was the last time you got some sleep?" Ashley looked puzzled. "Sleep? What day is it?" It was the 19th of January—Ashley had not been to bed for three days. He was surviving on cat naps, jealously guarded moments of peace grabbed in corners, that lasted as long as it took for someone to shake him and say, "You're needed."

Tactical Data Links

The Canadian ships were also equipped with an export-version of the U.S.-built Joint Operational Tactical System (JOTS), a worldwide tactical system that gave a video display of the disposition of all of the ships in the Arabian Gulf. The JOTS operator—in ATHABASKAN Chief Petty Officer Al Dunn was the key person—could point to one particular ship on the display and ask for more information. The computer would then supply the name of the ship, its speed and heading. During the Gulf crisis, all the merchant ships were put into the system, so that the allies would know who had been challenged and in which area. But the system relies on each ship to put the correct information into the system in the first place. Also, the information is only as current as the latest update from that ship. For example, if the computer said the ship is heading northwest at 20 knots, the JOTS operator had to ask when did the ship log in that information. If it was two days ago, then the information was no longer valid, and the Canadians would not really know where that ship was. However, when a crisis occurs, ships tend to update their information on a much more frequent basis, giving a more accurate picture of what is happening.

But the system wasn't foolproof. Occasionally it would happen that a Canadian ship would be asked to board a vessel that was supposedly five miles away. But when the staff checked the radar screen, the ship wasn't there. Hayes says at those times the ships relied on voice information to update the general operation plots. "What you'd do is you'd get up on the circuit and ask if anyone had seen this guy? An Italian ship may reply, 'yeah, he's in our sector'."

The JOTS picture was transmitted to ATHABASKAN from the American battleships WISCONSIN and MISSOURI. The system was not without its glitches. Ashley says

> We'd have periods of time where we'd have nothing coming across the JOTS circuit. We'd be checking out, and making plugs, and other things, and what we discovered was when they fired their Tomahawk cruise missiles, sometimes they shut down the JOTS because of mutual interference. The idea was that if WISCONSIN was firing her Tomahawks, MISSOURI was supposed to take over the JOTS circuit. But sometimes they did, and sometimes they didn't.

So whenever there was an interruption in the JOTS information, Ashley would check to see if the battleships were firing their cruise missiles.

The Department of National Defence also purchased a Joint Operational Tactical System from the U.S. and installed it in the Joint Command Headquarters in Bahrain. That gave Summers the capability to understand better what the ships were telling him about the tactical picture because he could then look at the same display that Miller and his staff were studying.

In addition to JOTS, the Task Group received a local picture, on a real time system, of all of the aircraft, missiles and ships in the area. An airborne warning and control system (AWACS) aircraft flying overhead sent its radar picture by UHF data link (Link 11) to a shore station in the Gulf. There, the air picture would be superimposed onto a radar picture of the same sector taken by a shore station, and the composite view would be sent via HF to the USS ANTIETAM Aegis cruiser. The ship's radar picture was co-ordinated and superimposed on the air/ground picture, and then the whole thing was sent out to the rest of the multinational naval force. Not all ships were able to receive that information, but the Canadians were. They could also take data from the AWACS aircraft directly by UHF rather than wait for the add-ons from the other radars. This was particularly useful for those times when the HF picture was not transmitting very well.

It was during these times that the Canadian radar plotters earned tremendous respect from the allies. Professional and helpful to a fault, the Canadians willingly passed along any information they had to the other ships that didn't have the same wide-ranging communication capabilities.

Both the Joint Operational Tactical System and the Link 11 were vital to the confidence and smooth operation of the Canadian Task Group. However, each system had its advantages and disadvantages. The JOTS proved most useful in the interdiction phase before the war, giving the Canadian Task Group information on where merchant ships were coming from and going to. However, because JOTS operated with a time delay caused by having to have the information manually entered, during the war, the Link system proved more critical. It provided the information in real time. However, JOTS gave a wider picture, including in its display the Gulf of Oman. Link, being a real time system, provided only a local picture.

The Task Group could not have done without either system. What it got by using both was a bird's eye view of the Gulf in which the movement of every ship, aircraft and missile was clearly discernible.

The 1900 Brief

Each evening at 1900 (7:00 p.m.), Miller held a briefing at which the schedule and other important matters were discussed. Miller's briefing sessions were unlike just about any other. Normally military briefings are very sombre, disciplined affairs, at which there is a great deal of tension in the air. At Miller's briefings, officers were encouraged to participate in freewheeling discussions conducted in an extremely relaxed atmosphere. This was where the staff would air their concerns and their disagreements. Intelligence reports were a frequent topic, and were not always discussed favourably.

> *Intelligence would say, "Here's what's happening," and everybody would say, "That's ridiculous. That's not what's happening." And the intelligence officer would say, "you know, you're absolutely right." He'd be getting his information from several good sources, but it would be wrong. It didn't happen often, but it did happen, and we would say "where'd you get that from? That's stupid. That's not the way it is at all. Send a message back and let them know."*

This was the first time in many years that the Canadian intelligence community had received direct feedback on the information they were putting out.

> *Normally they just pump out information and they never get any feedback as to whether its either no good or extremely useful. So we consistently would send feedback to them. I think they just couldn't believe that somebody was actually talking back,*

and that we were actually using the information they were sending us, and not just using it, but thinking about it. And sometimes we were thinking, "Hey, you've got this all wrong."

Telling them this was very useful from their point of view, because they would go back and check their source, its credibility and validity. Finding out that their source was wrong allowed them to improve their system. They certainly didn't take it as an affront for us to tell them when we considered they were wrong.

In the informal atmosphere of the 1900 Brief, nothing was sacred.

One evening, Chief Ashley, who had done just an incredible job with communications and keeping in touch with back home and the world—not a small task with ATHABASKAN having 35 different frequencies that were constantly changing and had to be listened to, or transmitted on, all the time—came in wearing glasses that had a funny nose attached, and he used his comb as a kazoo, to give his report as a rap.

> Good evening sir, I'm the SCRM[16]
> And this is how your comms were run
> Circuits have been up, circuits have been down,
> Which is nothing new, since we hit this town
> Got comms with the Yanks, 'cos we're no fool,
> They gave us DAMA, and that's been cool.
> Talked to the Italians, and to the Brits
> But Gulf info on JOTS has been the shits.
> Incoming messages, there's been a few,
> You've got the numbers in front of you.
> So good evening sir, I'm your SCRM,
> That's your comms, and I'm all done.

Other nights, Ashley did communications briefings as Groucho Marx. Holding a pen like a cigar, wriggling his eyebrows, and talking out the side of his mouth with a Brooklyn twang, he would have the squadron staff, especially Miller, in stitches. It was an unusual approach to a serious subject—but it was Ashley's way of keeping an important promise.

---

16. Squadron Chief Radio Man, pronounced "scrum".

CHAPTER SEVEN

"Okay, he wants the missiles—Take Off!"

The task of moving people around and supplying fuel, food, ammunition, spares and other consumable items to a combat unit is called logistics. It is an unglamourous task that is absolutely essential to the success of any mission. Military history is full of examples to prove that neglecting any aspect of a supply line is a sure route to disaster.[1]

Maritime Command (MARCOM) was the naval Task Group's umbilical chord. As the support command, MARCOM obtained the necessary supplies and spare parts for the Canadian ships and helicopters. It also was responsible for maintaining the group's combat capability—arranging for repair or replacement if a weapon system broke. MARCOM's control over the equipment and what happened to it, was absolute. Not even the Joint Commander could change the process. Although he tried. At one point, Summers needed satellite communications for his shore facility in Bahrain. The quickest and easiest way to get the equipment was to take one of the two systems off ATHABASKAN. There was only one problem—Miller needed both systems to guarantee his communications. He spoke with Summers, pointing out, "I'm using both systems for the co-ordination that is going on out here, and to keep in touch with you. Taking my second set away is going to hamper our operational capability considerably." While Summers understood Miller's need, the Commodore was unmoved, and emphasized his pressing requirement to be able to talk to headquarters in Ottawa. But Miller was not able simply to hand over a piece of MARCOM's

---

1. James F. Dunnigan, *How To Make War* (William Morrow and Company, Inc., New York: 1988), p. 451. Perhaps the most famous example is that of Napoleon's march into Russia. The speed of his advance quickly outstripped his army's resupply capabilities, substantially reducing the size of the spearhead that eventually captured Moscow. During the retreat back to France, the logistics problems left Napoleon's men vulnerable not only to the Russians but also to starvation and hypothermia.

equipment. As Joint Commander, Summer's support requests had to go through National Defence headquarters which would then process them through the relevant command—in the case of satellite communications gear, the request was forwarded to Communications Command. By following the official procedure, Summers eventually got the equipment he needed from Maritime Command in the form of a complete system from one of the other ships in Halifax.

The navy set up a specific organization in the Arabian Gulf region to support the ships. The Canadian Maritime Logistics Detachment, located in Manamah, Bahrain, in the Joint Headquarters, worked for Maritime Command, and was the first step in requesting spares, supplies and other consumables. This detachment would either supply the Task Group from the items it had on hand, or request them from Maritime Command in Halifax. All the supplies arriving in Bahrain for the ships and the Sea King helicopters went through the Logistics Detachment.

For Maritime Air Group, the big concern with the Gulf deployment was supportability. It was the reason that the ships took with them five helicopters instead of four, the usual complement for a task group of this size. Lieutenant-Colonel Larry McWha felt that in order to guarantee that the Task Group would have operational helicopters available throughout its deployment in the Gulf, it was necessary to take an extra aircraft. The air group also took as many equipment spare parts with it as there was room for, including extra rotor heads, blades and gear boxes. For the rest of the supplies and spares, the air group had to depend on the navy's supply line.

The decision to handle support of the Sea King detachment through a central naval supply system seemed like a good idea but it caused some problems. First of all, there was the time factor. The air departments on board Canadian ships are used to getting their operational supplies within 72 hours, no matter where they are in the world. This has been made possible because of the rapid reaction logistic support system developed by Maritime Air Group. In the Gulf, that system was not used. All supplies and spares for the Sea King had to be sent from Shearwater to Halifax for documenting and processing before being consolidated with the rest of the navy's requirements, packed into large containers, and shipped back to Shearwater for air transport to the Middle East.

The second problem arose from the processing in Halifax. Many of the parts packed into the containers were new and did not yet have stock numbers, making it very difficult to identify what was where when the containers arrived in Bahrain. There was also a problem with unfamiliarity of equipment. For example, McWha says the air departments were supposed to receive laser warning receivers. This is a plastic box about the size of a cigarette package with suction cups on it so that it can be stuck to a window. It flashes to warn the pilot when he has been targetted by a laser targetting device. McWha says,

> We only had a limited number of these so they were spread fairly thinly. There was a back order of them and we were supposed to get enough sent over so that we could stick one in every window [in the Sea Kings]. One day I was on the bridge of ATHABASKAN and I saw these things stuck all over the window. I asked 'Where the heck did you get all these?' Well, it turns out they were sent for the air department, but the ship received them, read the instructions about sticking them on the window, and put them up!

A third problem became apparent after a few weeks in theatre, when the Sea King technicians became increasingly concerned about not receiving any spares or items that had been sent back to Shearwater for repair. It turned out that the repairables had not been returned to Canada, because the ships' supply departments had been holding onto them, waiting until they could offload them during a maintenance period in Bahrain. When McWha pointed out the hold-up to Miller, the Captain changed the procedures to reflect the importance of maintaining a constant flow of parts along the Sea King supply line. He ordered all the Sea King repairables to be sent immediately to the Logistics Detachment, and he told that Detachment to ensure that it always had 1,000 lbs of aircraft spares ready for transport to the ships anytime a Sea King made the journey to Manamah.[2]

Many of the Task Group's supplies, such as fresh food and fuel, were acquired from local merchants. Everything else came in by air and by sea. The ships, chartered merchant vessels, took about a month to make the 9,000-mile journey from Halifax to Bahrain. More urgently needed supplies were flown in on Boeing 707 and CC-130 Hercules aircraft from Trenton, Ontario, through Lahr, Germany, to the international airport just outside Manamah.

---

2. There was a further problem, however, that cropped up back in Canada. The repairables sent by Hercules aircraft made it to Halifax, but no further, having been left in the navy's warehouses awaiting delivery to Shearwater. The problem was discovered and rectified by air force Captain Don Feltmate when he returned to Canada from the Gulf in early November.

These flights brought in everything from people to pizzas. They also brought in the most important cargo of all—the mail.

> *The first load of mail got lost. We had just arrived in the Gulf and we were waiting for the mail and it didn't arrive. They sent it down to an American airport—not an unusual route, but there was no special attention paid to it, and it ended up getting sent to a U.S. carrier which was not in the Arabian Gulf. It was just a nightmare. Admiral George personally got involved. He went to the post office and had words with those responsible. He then called me and said, "You can rest assured— and tell all the sailors—that the next bag of mail is going to have someone handcuffed to it. And they will both show up!"*

The first load of mail eventually appeared, but not until much later in the deployment. Losing the mail—the sailors' lifeline—so early on, forced the navy to revise its handling of this special cargo. A regular distribution system was set up, and Hercules flights came in every four days with supplies, but most importantly, with the mail, on board.

Having supplies flown in every four days was fairly demanding on the Logistics Detachment and the ships' supply departments. To ease the strain on both, the Sea Kings picked up the mail as it came in, but left the stores with the Maritime Logistics Detachment in Bahrain. This provided time to process the inventory before the ships came into port for rest, maintenance, and resupply.

Ships did not have to come into port, however, for all their supplies. They could take on fuel and provisions from PROTECTEUR while on patrol in the central Gulf. Replenishment at sea (RAS), involves the transfer of fuel, ammunition, food, spares, clothing, and mail from a supply ship to another ship, while both continue to steam forward. The transfer is accomplished by the use of cables and hoses.

Canada uses a different replenishment system than most other nations. It has all its supplies—fuel, food, and ammunition—plus maintenance facilities for helicopters aboard one ship, an auxiliary oiler replenishment vessel, or AOR. It's a very economical way to supply a task group, but it is also risky. Because of the importance of the supply ship it is a prime target for enemy forces. And in Canada's case, if that ship is lost, all three types of supplies are lost. Because of that, other navies—for example, the British—have continued to use three separate types of ships to handle each of the different types of cargoes.

PROTECTEUR was the only tanker in the Central Gulf and so was refuelling all the ships in the area, not just the Canadian vessels. Any allied ships needing fuel could make their way to PROTECTEUR, nicknamed "Chuckwagon" by Captain Doug McClean (who was born in Calgary).

To keep the combat vessels resupplied, PROTECTEUR needed a nearby port where she could fill up her storage tanks easily and quickly. But the AOR was having great difficulty getting into the port at Bahrain,[3] and the Bahraini authorities wanted cash (in U.S. dollars) in advance of refuelling—a transaction which totalled $1.7 million. The one time PROTECTEUR did pick up fuel in Bahrain, the crew underestimated how much would be needed. They said they needed 60,000 barrels and after paying for it, while taking that much on board—a process that took 12-14 hours—they realized that they had room for more. So McClean asked for an additional 500 barrels and the authorities said no. Even though McClean said he had the money and would give it to them immediately, the Bahrainis said no. The ship had only asked for 60,000 initially and that's all it would get.

McClean decided to look for a more flexible refuelling port and he picked Jebel Ali in the United Arab Emirates. The Americans had a fuel storage depot there and because the majority of PROTECTEUR's fuel was being given to American ships, they were willing to work out a deal. Not only was the new refuelling stop relatively hassle-free and fast (8-10 hours for a full load), but the fuel was cheaper as well. McClean could also have refuelled at Dubai but the pumping rate was much slower—the one time he used that port it took two days to take on the fuel.

In addition to the tonnes of food and ammunition, PROTECTEUR's dry holds were filled with crates and crates of spare parts for the Task Group's ships and helicopters. Normally all the spares and supplies in the holds are precisely catalogued so that any item, no matter how small, can be found easily. But in the haste to get the ships and Sea Kings ready for their mission in the Gulf, the various bits and parts had been packed in no particular order, and with no catalogued list. So the supply technician looking for that one gearbox or that one computer card had to physically open the various boxes and look inside. It was a tedious and daunting task considering the ship's holds were built to carry enough dry cargo, spare parts, and refrigerated and frozen food to supply four ships for three to four months.

---

3. See Chapter 3, pp. 67-68. PROTECTEUR took on fuel at Bahrain only once because it took a couple of extra days of navigating the bureaucratic morass to get into the harbour.

Because of PROTECTEUR's importance and vulnerability, the Task Group had decided to give her a patrol sector out of the range of Iraq's Exocet missiles. But she was still expected to carry out patrols the same as the two destroyers. Using a supply ship in the role of a destroyer created problems.

First of all, McClean was under great pressure from the ship's crew, especially the engineers, to get some time ashore for routine maintenance and resupply. During enforcement operations, the schedule was eight to ten days on patrol and three to four days in port at Manamah, Abu Dhabi or Dubai. Two ships were continuously on-station in the Gulf while the third was alongside in port undergoing maintenance, taking on supplies, and giving the crew a breather from the tension of being on patrol. During that down time, the crew took on supplies and after shutting down some of the electrical and engineering equipment, also did routine maintenance. The heat and the water was demanding on all of the ships but they especially took their toll on PROTECTEUR— early in the deployment one of her high pressure steam valves in the boiler room sprang a leak. The pipes carry extremely high pressure, superheated steam, so any leak is a danger to the crew. A blown pipe would also leave the ship dead in the water. The crew acted quickly to fix the problem and thought they had done so, but a short while later, it blew again. With equal helpings of determination, elbow grease and ingenuity, the second fix held.

> *The maintenance side of things in the Gulf was the thorn in our side. The engineers tended to make sure they got all their maintenance done, and we kept reminding them that this was not a NATO exercise. We had to do the minimum amount of maintenance to keep the ship going, but they wanted to have extended maintenance periods.*

> *We compromised and gave them reduced extended maintenance periods on a regular basis. But after the first couple of months, they found that four days in port wasn't enough. The engineers didn't get any rest because they were tearing their pumps apart and putting them together again, and the other members of the crew were busy taking on supplies. (The other ships could do their storing in half a day, but the amount of stores for PROTECTEUR were so significant it would take 2-3 days.) So no one got a break.*

A second problem was the inherent conflict between the roles of supply ship and interdiction vessel. As a supply ship, PROTECTEUR felt that every time stores came in, she should go and get them. But she couldn't do that if Canada was to keep two ships on station conducting the interdiction mission. So a conflict arose between what PROTECTEUR is—a supply ship—and what the navy was using her for in the Gulf—a destroyer with an operations room. Captain McClean felt loyal to the ship, that it was a supply ship and its job was to supply, and yet he, himself, was a destroyer graduate, and could see the other side of the issue. Finally, Miller and McClean struck a happy medium: they devised a longer maintenance period for all the ships. This would allow PROTECTEUR time to take on supplies, do her routine maintenance, and give the crew a well-deserved rest.

Initially, PROTECTEUR wanted to go in for about 12 days, but that was too long a time to send one ship into port and have the other two cover off in the Gulf. So the ships were put on a new schedule which included an extended maintenance period of eight days every couple of months. During these routine assisted maintenance periods (RAMPS) one ship would go alongside at a dockyard where her mechanical systems and on-board electronics as well as underwater fittings could be inspected and maintained. The other two ships would extend their patrol time by two days each—increasing their time on station from eight to ten days— to cover the extra four days for the ship undergoing a RAMPS.

When it was ATHABASKAN's turn to head into port after its normal patrol period of eight to ten days at sea, a small corps of the squadron staff[4] would transfer over to PROTECTEUR and continue co-ordination of the embargo enforcement operations from there. To lessen the difficulty of this changeover, Miller kept two of his staff members in PROTECTEUR on a permanent basis: Master Seaman Peter Nowlan, the signalman who looked after all of Miller's message traffic, and Master Warrant Officer Rick Lavalee, who kept the intelligence and scheduling stateboards up-to-date. They had a dedicated communications link with ATHABASKAN which kept them constantly abreast of any new developments. Thus when Miller and his staff made the transfer to PROTECTEUR, everything was ready for them and there was minimal disruption to the daily operations.[5]

---

4. Miller, his yeoman Serge Joncas, two Lieutenant-Commanders, and Chief Petty Officers Dave Ashley and Al Dunn.

5. Throughout the entire Gulf deployment, Miller went ashore only three times: a total of 17 days in which he either attended conferences or took a few days leave. During those times, Captain Doug McClean of PROTECTEUR took command of the Task Group.

Miller had set up the ship patrol schedule so that either PROTECTEUR or ATHABASKAN was on patrol at all times, because they were the two ships that carried Sea King helicopters. The five aircraft were regularly swapped between the two ships as the flying hours were juggled to make sure that not all the Sea Kings came due for their in-depth maintenance at the same time. The juggling of flight hours also had to take into account Miller's requirement that all five aircraft be available for the crucial months of January and February.

The Sea King technicians were on a two-watch system—eight hours on and eight hours off—that was hard on their bodies and their psyches, but they rose to the challenge. Moreover, it was their determination, hard work and innovative ideas which kept the aircraft flying. In November, these dedicated professionals achieved a maintenance "first": they completed an at-sea major inspection of a Sea King helicopter. These inspections, called "periodics," are undertaken after 500 hours of flying time and usually take three months to complete. The aircraft are stripped down, with every part inspected and repaired or replaced if needed. Until the Gulf deployment, periodics had always been conducted on dry land.

At sea, with the high demand placed on very few aircraft and the prospect of hostilities in the very near future, the technicians had to come up with a faster, more efficient process of handling the periodics. They succeeded admirably. While the first one took 20 days—delayed by a supply problem—subsequent inspections took less than two weeks. Major Pete Nordlund says there's one main reason why the technicians were able to do what they did—dedication.

In day-to-day operations, the aircraft technicians paid special attention to corrosion and vibration control. Lieutenant-Colonel Larry McWha says, "The Sea Kings were getting old and brittle and even with normal use, the constant strain on the airframe brought on by corrosion and inherent vibration made them prone to metal cracks." But the air techs' vigilant attention to cleanliness and the first rumblings of a vibration kept any problems to a minimum. Consequently, McWha says, "the Gulf birds, even when flown at high speeds, were the smoothest flying Sea Kings in the fleet."

The Sea Kings were used for more and more tasks as the deployment went on—and the available flying hours of each aircraft were being rapidly gobbled up even before the fighting started. In addition to the operational tasks of mine surveillance and merchant ship hailings, the Sea Kings were being used increasingly for ship to shore logistics runs. Tonnes of parcels and mail were coming in with every Hercules flight, and the Task Group was always in need of equipment spare parts in order to keep its ships and aircraft operational and ready for action. In addition, the Sea Kings were the main means of moving diplomatic, military and media visitors between ships and the shore, as well as for transporting squadron and Joint Headquarters staff to various national and multi-national conferences.

In addition to managing the aircraft availability and the ship patrol-rest cycles, there were unique problems associated with specific pieces of equipment. TERRA NOVA had recurring problems with her Phalanx Close-In Weapon System. The crew tried everything to fix it but they just couldn't keep it up and running. Parts were taken off PROTECTEUR's second Phalanx, the one on top of its hanger, and used to replace defective parts in TERRA NOVA's mount. But the system just wouldn't work properly, and that was beginning to affect morale.

Commodore Bruce Johnston of the Joint Staff back in Ottawa, visited the Task Group in December. When he was on board PROTECTEUR—a ship he had commanded just a couple of years previously—he went to the room below the Phalanx Close-In Weapon System where all the gun's electronics were. On the door of the room was a sign that said, "If it flies, it dies!" Obviously, the system was working well and the crew felt confident in its capabilities.[6] But when Johnston went to the same room in TERRA NOVA, there was a sign on the door which read, "NO, IT AIN'T FIXED YET!"

> On one of the occasions when the crew had fixed the Phalanx, they asked for a high-speed aircraft to test the system—a helicopter couldn't go fast enough to simulate an incoming missile. So I called up Colonel Romeo Lalonde in Qatar and said, "we need an aircraft out here. I see your next flight is at such-and-such a time, can your CF-18s come by, give us a high-speed pass to test the Phalanx, and then carry on?"
>
> There was a long pause, and then he asked, in a small, disbelieving voice, "Is it loaded?"
>
> It was loaded, because it takes a while to load and unload them, so I said, "Well, I can't tell a lie,—yes, it is loaded, but you have my word that the switch will not be on, it will not fire."

---

6. Actually, keeping PROTECTEUR's bridge-based Phalanx operational was no easy feat because of the lack of cooling water. By the time the already warm water in the Gulf had travelled through pipes to the top of the bridge it had warmed up considerably more.

His voice grew higher as he asked, "Are you asking me to trust you? You want me to send an airplane out there to trial out this thing that can shoot it down in two seconds? And you want me to trust you?!"

Anyway, I convinced him that it would be safe, and with the air force's usual co-operation and efficiency that we had grown to rely on, he ordered airborne the two CF-18s that he had on five minute standby. Twenty minutes later, the two CF-18s strafed[7] TERRA NOVA and the Phalanx worked—with no harm to the aircraft.

But the gun wouldn't stay fixed. Commander Stu Andrews says,

The system is exceptionally complex. There's so many layers of complexity that the actual faults can be so deep-seated that they are not at all apparent when you look at the symptoms or do your diagnosis. For months, I had these gurus coming out from all over the world—England, U.S., from other ships—anybody who knew anything, and they'd all just stand around and scratch their heads. They'd make it work for a while and then it would fall over again. One positive thing that came out of it was my technicians became, without question, the best technicians that we had in the navy for a number of years. Because they spent entire days with their heads in that thing.

Every week the ships had to send to Commodore Summers a report listing all the faults and all the work that had been done on the various ship's systems. Andrews says that process really underlined the problem: "ATHABASKAN's would go in and it would have two lines—'replaced two light bulbs', or something like that. Mine would be about 15 pages long."

Finally, just after Christmas, TERRA NOVA, which had been moved south out of harm's way for a week because of her Phalanx problem, went into Bahrain to have the system replaced. Maritime Command had to charter a British cargo aircraft, because the system was too big to fit in a Hercules transport. When it arrived at the airport, however, the authorities would not let it in because it was a weapons system. One of TERRA NOVA's quick-thinking crew told them, "don't worry about

---

7. Strafing involved having the aircraft fly at high speed about 50 feet above the water, straight at the ship. No bullets were fired.

it—it's a sonar system." They let it in. The work was done in a local shipyard and by the time the ship was due back on patrol at the beginning of January, the new system was installed and working.

Preparing for the Long-Haul

Managing the patrol-rest cycle of the three ships in the Gulf for a short period of time was one thing, but Maritime Command was faced with a major problem: there was no end in sight to the deployment, and the ships and crews could not go on forever. They would both have to be replaced at some point.

There was, however, no replacement for PROTECTEUR. The navy had only two other supply ships—HMCS PROVIDER and PRESERVER. PROVIDER was the oldest of the navy's three replenishment vessels. She had been built on a commercial design and had no operations room. Fitting this ship out for replenishment, enforcement, and command and control activities would be a major undertaking, if not actually impossible.

PRESERVER was not in any way ready to go to sea. In July of 1990, she had begun an intensive refit program at Halifax-Dartmouth Industries Ltd., which entailed her being lifted out of the water (dry-docked) and stripped down.

In October 1990, faced with an indefinite deployment and with no ships ready to replace the ones in the Gulf, the military officials in Ottawa and Halifax worked out a plan to replace the crews, at one month intervals, starting with PROTECTEUR in January. The crew of ATHABASAKAN would be changed over in February, and TERRA NOVA in March.

Summers, Miller and McClean agreed that the crews would need a break, but stated their preference that the changeover be accomplished by sending replacement ships, fully crewed, to the Gulf. Financially, however, that was a problem. The Department of National Defence had just spent over $100-million refitting the three ships it had sent to the Gulf.[8] It made much more economic sense to keep using the same ships, and just fly new crews over.

In light of the arguments being put forward by its Gulf commanders, Maritime Command briefly considered delaying the changeover. But there were several factors that ultimately decided the issue, not least of which

---

8. National Defence, *1993-94 Estimates—Part III: Expenditure Plan* (Canada Communications Group, Ottawa: 1993), pp. 14-15.

was that Vice-Admiral George had promised the families in Halifax that he would rotate the crews within six months and it was a promise he was reluctant to break. Moreover, because of the stressful conditions in the Gulf, many senior officers felt it was necessary to relieve the ships' companies before they burnt out. In addition, the navy had already scheduled the aircraft which would transport the new crews into the Gulf because there was a question about whether or not flights would be able to get into the area once hostilities started. After several reviews, the decision became final when Mr. Bill McKnight, Minister of National Defence, announced in the House of Commons, that the crews would be replaced.[9]

When first adopted in mid-October, the January 10, 1991 turnover date for PROTECTEUR was fine. It was only after the subsequent adoption of U.N. Security Council Resolution 678 on November 29, 1990, that the Canadian date was thrown into conflict. That Resolution allowed for the use of force to evict Iraq from Kuwait if Iraq had not withdrawn its troops by January 15, 1991. In all likelihood, the allied attack on Iraqi forces would start then or very shortly thereafter. The commanders in the Gulf relayed the message back to Halifax and Ottawa that the proposed changeover, in light of the January 15 U.N. deadline, was not a good idea. It was too late: the decision had been made.

The officers didn't give up and tried a different approach to convince their superiors to change their minds. They suggested they wait for two weeks before changing PROTECTEUR's crew. They reasoned that if the war had not started by then, it wouldn't for sometime. That was not just a guess. McClean, as captain of the only refuelling ship in the central Gulf, had been in a good position to study the situation. While refuelling the various allies, he would talk to the other ships' captains on the telephone. And all of them were of the same view: if hostilities did not start very shortly after the January 15 deadline, the multinational alliance could start to fall apart. It was a major feat of diplomacy that the allies had managed a consensus on the deadline in the first place; if that deadline passed and no action was taken within a very short period, some would start to get cold feet.

McClean played one last card. He asked Admiral George to let him and some of his key people stay so that there would be some experienced hands left in the ship. The Admiral said no. And his reason was very simple: "If I make you leave nobody else has an excuse. Nobody else can

---

9. House of Commons, *Debates,* October 23, 1990, p. 14582.

say they're more important than you. So we'll start with you and everyone else will have to go too." McClean couldn't argue with that—"Nobody could have convinced me they needed to stay more than me!"

There was nothing more that the Gulf commanders could do except make sure that the changeover took place with the least risk to the people involved.

It was important that the crew sent to PROTECTEUR have a good working knowledge of a replenishment vessel—the routine, the engines, the electronics. The best way to do that was to use PRESERVER's crew. The navy set about gathering them up from their new assignments.[10] But not all the crew members could be taken away from their new duties, so the navy had to take sailors from elsewhere. A further complication was that no one else, apart from those already in the Gulf, had been trained to operate a supply ship armed with a 3"/50 gun mount, two Phalanx Close-In Weapon Systems, and electronic warfare equipment.

En route to the Gulf, PROTECTEUR's crew had worked out the procedures for the newly armed ship. They produced battle orders and procedural manuals for all the new systems, and how they were integrated into the ship, as well as instructions for manoeuvring and fighting the ship. These were all sent back to Canada. McClean and his replacement, Captain Dennis Cronk, talked on the phone, as well as in person— Cronk and a number of his key people flew over to the Gulf a couple of times in the months leading up to the changeover so that they could see things first hand. This gave Cronk a cadre of his ship's company who were familiar with the ship. Cronk himself was not overly concerned about taking over an armed supply ship because his special training in the navy was as a weapons officer.

After all these preparations had been completed, a Sea Training Staff flew out to Bahrain with the new crew who left Halifax on January 1, 1991. The replacements relieved PROTECTEUR's crew on January 6, and after a few days of familiarization training, the original crew flew home to Halifax, leaving PRESERVER's crew to take over the ship.

The new crew had to be trained for operating in a war zone. In order to do that safely, the ship was sent out of harm's way, to the Gulf of Oman. This was an unsettling situation for the Task Group, because it meant its logistic support and its whole helicopter repair facility would be in the Gulf of Oman—a day's steaming away.

---

10. When a naval ship is sent to an extended refit only a skeleton ship's crew is kept to oversee the work. The other crew members are redistributed through the rest of the fleet.

In the weeks prior to the changeover of PROTECTEUR's crew, Maritime Air Group had been trickling in replacements for the ship's air department and the air crews. By the time PROTECTEUR left to do workups in the Gulf of Oman, most of the new helicopter crews and support staff were already trained in their new jobs. But while that part of the air operation was proceeding smoothly, moving the supply ship with its aircraft maintenance department away from ATHABASKAN with two helicopters on board could present support problems. To avert this, Commodore Summers aranged for the Sea Kings to use the airport at Sharjah in the United Arab Emirates as a stop-off point when transporting people or parts between the two substantially separated ships.

PROTECTEUR left Dubai on January 11 to start what was to be a 10-day training program. But first she spent one day in the southern Gulf with ATHABASKAN and TERRA NOVA fuelling, so that her crew could get used to the equipment. Then they went out to the Gulf of Oman to practise the boarding routines, the chemical warfare defences, and the ship's anti-air defences. The training program was a demanding one, using all 24 hours in the day, but the crew was enthusiastic and met all the challenges. On the fifth day—January 17—Captain Cronk said they were coming back in. Miller was confident of Cronk's abilities but he worried that it was just too quick.

> *I knew I could trust him. He was a senior captain with lots of expertise and experience but I was worried that he was maybe too keen to come back into the Gulf (fighting had started between the time he sailed out to the Gulf of Oman to do his workups and the time he came back through the Strait of Hormuz). I still remember him calling me and saying, "I'm ready Dusty, I'm ready."*

> *It was great that he was so enthusiastic but I wanted him to be very sure. I said, "As soon as you poke your nose through the Strait of Hormuz you're going to have three ships alongside of you, you're going to be fuelling night and day, you're going to be busy, and you're going to have to adjust to a non-training mentality, a war mentality. You really want to take the time to make sure you're fully prepared for that eventuality."*

The crew would have to be ready both physically and mentally to deal with being in a war zone. They needed the extra training time to get up to speed and work as a team—most of the members had come from PRESERVER and had been sitting ashore while that ship was in refit while other crew members came from different ships. Miller and Cronk spoke with the Sea Training Staff who said PROTECTEUR's crew was close, but in their opinion was not quite ready. They still hadn't done several of the exercises. The Sea Trainers said another couple of days would make all the difference. Cronk agreed to take an extra couple of days, but even with that, his ship managed to complete three weeks of training in eight days.

> When PROTECTEUR came back into the Gulf on the 20th of January, her ship's company was used to doing exercises rather than actual operations. They wanted to finish up a few exercises, so they did a man overboard exercise when they came into the logistics box. All the ships there thought this was for real, and all of sudden there were helicopters overhead, and everybody was coming to her assistance. Cronk knew immediately that there could be no more exercises. They were in a real war zone and he couldn't afford to cry wolf.

When the hostilities began, the Canadian ships were kept in the main logistics area in the southern Gulf. After the Logistics Force moved northward to be closer to the carriers they were resupplying, PROTECTEUR was assigned the outrider job of refuelling all the coalition's picket ships.

> This was partly because she was vulnerable to a missile attack— the outrider job kept her out of Exocet range—but mainly because Cronk was a senior naval captain with a destroyer background who could easily and capably take on an autonomous role.

Just One More Thing ...

While the crew of PROTECTEUR was changing over in early January, ATHABASKAN was undergoing a change of her own. Just before hostilities started Miller had been faced with a major decision. The navy offered to test an upgraded version of the Sea Sparrow missile system—the AIM-7M—for fitting in ATHABASKAN. The AIM-7E missiles currently on board were an earlier version and Maritime Command asked Miller if he wanted a new system which would give the ship a solid state missile head with 50 per cent more range and greater reliability.[11] It was hard to refuse such an offer with hostilities about to begin. But at the same time, hostilities were about to begin! Was it wise to give up a defensive weapon that the operators knew worked in the

---

11. The new missiles were the same ones used by the air force's CF-18s flying out of Qatar, so there would be a nearby supply if ATHABASKAN ran out in the course of the war.

hopes of gaining a better system—one that might not work? If the allied action was going to start on January 15, Miller wanted all five helicopters operating and all three ships out in the Gulf, together, working as a team. He didn't want one ship in port having a missile system installed. But he kept coming back to how much better the new missile would be. Despite all the arguments against taking the time to fit the system, there was no getting away from the fact that the ships and their crews would be safer with the new Sea Sparrow on board ATHABASKAN.

While Miller weighed the pros and cons of replacing the Sparrow missile, Maritime Command was testing the system in HMCS HURON at the U.S. Navy test range off the coast of Puerto Rico. By January 9, the trials were over and the navy knew that by changing some electronics in the launching mechanisms—the two arms that slide from the ship with the missiles hung underneath—an air force missile could be fitted in and successfully fired from a navy ship.

Maritime Command had told Miller that once the system was fitted in ATHABASKAN, it would have to be tested by firing a couple of missiles.

> To fire missiles in the Arabian Gulf, just before war, was not a good idea. And if we were going to do it, ATHABASKAN would have to go out to the Gulf of Oman, or somewhere well away from what was going on. Well, when they'd proven the system with HURON, they'd also proven this Golden Bird test missile that is hung off the rail and electronically proves the system, doing everything except firing off the rail. So it tells you that it will fire off the rail; that you have got an operating missile system without ever having to fire a missile. So I said, "Well if this all works, if you can get missiles into the United Arab Emirates"— which meant flying them in and trucking them down to the jetty, all with the approval of the local military—"then, okay."
>
> The timing was such that Captain Al Dunlop[12] in Halifax was calling me, saying, "I've got the missiles loaded in a Herc, we just heard that the trial has been successful in HURON. Do you want them? If you say yes, the Herc is going to take off—the pilot is on the other line."
>
> So I'm doing a countdown, thinking today is January 10, war is going to start in five days—how long is it going to take to fit

---

12. Captain Dunlop took over as Deputy Chief of Staff, Readiness, when Captain Jim King was posted to the Royal College of Defence Studies in London in January 1991.

the missiles? How much better is this one? I've looked at its specs, and if we are going to be in a war, were we not obligated to take it? We'd done everything for our ships' companies, to make sure that we had the best that we could get out there to survive. So I took a deep breath and said, "Yes."

And I could hear him say on the other line, "Okay, he wants the missiles—Take Off."

On January 10, the missiles and the team that had done the trials in HURON, flew into Dubai. On January 11, ATHABASKAN, after first meeting PROTECTEUR in the southern Gulf to help train the crew on replenishment at sea, sailed into port for the changeover. The technicians worked in two shifts, 24 hours a day, fitting and testing the new system.

Meanwhile, Miller and his staff, who were setting up the Combat Logistics Force, needed somewhere to work. Normally they would have transferred over to PROTECTEUR, which was the alternate command ship, but she was in the Gulf of Oman going through training exercises with her new crew. So Miller and five members of his staff—Lieutenant-Commanders Jim Hayes, Paul Maddison,[13] and Greg Hannah,[14] Chief Petty Officers Dave Ashley and Al Dunn—transferred to TERRA NOVA. The ship was never designed to accommodate a squadron staff and they had to use the sonar control room as their quarters—an exceedingly cramped arrangement. Hayes remembers sitting with the noisy air conditioner directly above his head, having to do his job while afflicted with blinding headaches from the cold air and noise.

In addition to the cramped quarters, TERRA NOVA did not have all the communications circuits. She did, however, have the main commander's satellite system—but only the one. So for two days, the staff were crammed into a small, makeshift ops room, hoping that nothing would delay the outfitting of ATHABASKAN.

I got really nervous after two days went by. It had nothing to do with the support I was getting from the ship—they were bending over backwards to give me everything that I could possibly want. But after a while, not having all of the stateboards, not having all of the facilities, and not having all of the

13. Lieutenant-Commander Paul Maddison joined the Squadron Staff in January when Lieutenant-Commander Greg Romanow became the Canadian liaison officer aboard USS MIDWAY—see Chapter 9, p. 161.
14. Lieutenant-Commander Greg Hannah had replaced Lieutenant-Commander Kevin Laing who had flown home to Canada at Christmas to take up a new posting—see Chapter 10, p. 183-184.

*communications that ATHABASKAN had, I felt I was not
going to be able to do the job, that I was always missing a piece
of the picture.*

As it happened, by the 13th, ATHABASKAN was ahead of schedule, and the system was fully installed by the 14th. Her old Sea Sparrow missiles were offloaded and the new ones stored in the ship. At 1030 the squadron staff had transferred back on board by helicopter and by noon, the ship was back with the Combat Logistics Force in the southern Gulf. A test run in which the new missile system tracked a couple of CF-18s went perfectly and ATHABASKAN was certified at 1700 (5:00 p.m.) as having the AIM-7M system fully operational.

The Best Laid Schemes ...

Once the allies began their attack against Iraq, it became nearly impossible to replace the crews on board TERRA NOVA and ATHABASKAN. But by February, Maritime Command, recognizing that those crews and staff officers would soon begin to burn out, began making other plans to continue the Canadian deployment.

The three ships in the Task Group had been especially equipped for their Gulf duties—no other ships in the navy were fitted with the necessary systems. In preparation for a long deployment, the navy began fitting out HMCS HURON and RESTIGOUCHE to replace ATHABASKAN and TERRA NOVA in mid-April. The Department said its new plan to rotate ships instead of crews, "ensures combat effectiveness will be maintained with minimal interruption in Canadian presence in the Gulf. Ships will not have to be withdrawn for two or three weeks [as was the case with PROTECTEUR] while new crews undergo workups on board an unfamiliar vessel."[15]

The new rotation plan also included a replacement for the squadron staff. Miller would be relieved by an officer from the west coast.

Captain Ted Heath had been the squadron commander on the west coast who had been at sea in charge of the Canadian ships during the April-May exercise in the Pacific. The navy had made arrangements for a logical flow of the new operations officers to come in, while Miller was still in charge, to learn the job, and gradually take over from the current staff. Heath was supposed to come in for the final week of the transition and take over from Miller. The command ship ATHABASKAN was to be replaced by a similarly outfitted HMCS HURON at a later date.

---

15. Department of National Defence, *News Release* January 31, 1991, AFN: 08/91.

Maritime Command, however, was nervous that if Miller was replaced, Canada would lose the job of running the Combat Logistics Force. The senior officers wondered if Canada had the job because the Canadian Task Group had performed so well enforcing the U.N. embargo—doing 25 per cent of the interdictions with only three per cent of the naval ships in the Gulf—or whether it was because Miller had a personal rapport with the U.S. Admirals. Certainly there was a foundation for such a concern. When talk of replacing Miller reached American ears, the suggestion came back that if he was replaced, maybe the command of the Logistics Force should be given to another nation.

In fact, a French captain had already suggested that as he was a more senior captain than Miller, he should be given command of the Force. He sent a message to the Americans suggesting that he take command of the Force when the Canadian changeover occurred. As a courtesy, Miller invited the French captain's operations officer to visit ATHABASKAN's operations centre and watch the squadron staff at work. The officer was duly impressed and reported back to his captain who then acknowledged that his ship, although more modern, was not equipped or crewed to handle the complexities of the supply operation. He had no squadron staff, only a ship's staff; he did not have the same communications equipment or frequencies; and he did not have the same data link terminal that provided the picture of the entire Gulf.

The French navy, in contrast to the Canadian navy, was using primarily French-made equipment and was not entirely compatible with other navies, in particular with that of the United States. In a situation such as the Gulf, where several navies were working together, the operation depended on communications compatibility.

In any event, the change of command became a non-issue. Not only had Summers spoken to Rear-Admiral March and been assured that the job would remain Canada's, but as it happened, the war ended and the Combat Logistics Force disbanded before Heath was scheduled to depart Victoria.

CHAPTER EIGHT

"Good Day, Captain.
This is Canadian Warship ..."

"We are not blockading. Blockading is an act of war."[1]

Defence Minister Bill McKnight
to reporters in Halifax, August 24, 1990

It may sound like semantics, but the difference between a blockade and the U.N.'s embargo enforcement operation in the Gulf was a very important one to the Canadian government. The objectives of a fleet blockade are military, with one navy preventing another from leaving its base and controlling its seas. That is considered an act of war. What the U.N. was doing was a step down from that—it was trying to cut off Iraq's trade, denying the country essential supplies, in the hopes of forcing a diplomatic solution to the growing crisis.

Enforcing the U.N. trade embargo required that the navies involved co-ordinate their efforts. Therefore, at their September meeting in Bahrain, the naval representatives decided to divide up the Arabian Gulf and Gulf of Oman into 16 patrol areas or "boxes". These were then assigned to the various navies based on their capabilities and preferences.[2]

Canada, with just three ships, took responsibility for two sectors, which necessitated the Task Group using PROTECTEUR in a destroyer's role. The sectors that Canada patrolled depended on which ships were on station. When ATHABASKAN and TERRA NOVA were on station, they took sectors Charlie 5 and Charlie 2 (see Map 2). When one destroyer

---

1. "Tears flow as ships leave Halifax for Persian Gulf" by Kevin Cox, in *Globe and Mail*, August 25, 1990, p. A1.
2. There were also sectors, designated as anti-air warfare sectors, which overlapped the boxes. The sole job of the ship assigned an anti-air warfare sector was to protect against a surprise air attack. Meanwhile other ships, working in their assigned patrol areas, would do the interdiction. The Americans, British and later, Australians, provided the anti-air warfare ships.

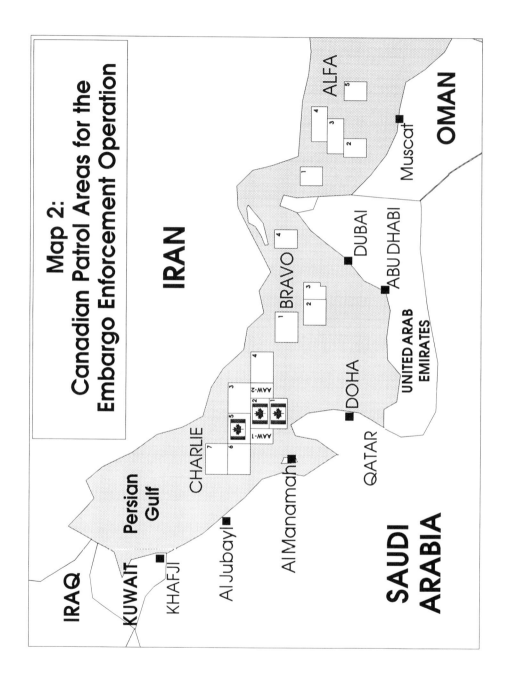

Map 2:
Canadian Patrol Areas for the
Embargo Enforcement Operation

and PROTECTEUR were on station, the destroyer would be in either Charlie 5 or 2, but the supply ship, which would be a prime target for an Iraqi air attack, was kept out of Exocet range, in Charlie 1. The three "C" sectors later came to be known as Canada 1, 2 and 5.

Other countries with three ships were more cautious, taking just one box so that they could be sure of being able to keep one ship on station at all times. Some countries could not manage a 24-hour-a-day, seven-days a week patrol, but were able to put a ship on station for a certain period of time before having to dock for supplies and maintenance, manage the changeover of ships and crews, or, as in the case of the French, continue with regular Indian Ocean patrols.

At the September meeting, the allies had selected a Maritime Interdiction Force (MIF) Co-ordinator, Rear-Admiral Fogarty, to keep track of all these national commitments. The reports from each of the ships involved in the enforcement operation were filed into Rear-Admiral Fogarty's staff, who kept track of which naval vessel was where and which merchant vessels were traversing the areas. The admiral's staff produced a monthly schedule that made sure there was another ship ready to replace one that was leaving a patrol area. This ensured that the coalition had at least one ship on patrol in each of the 10 boxes at all times and that no merchant vessel slipped through unchecked.

The multinational force "hailed" each vessel in the area by asking its name, registration number, cargo, point of origin, destination, date of departure, and date of arrival. While these questions were being answered, the enforcement vessel would be checking its registry and making sure that the information it was receiving jibed with the information in its records.

Lieutenant-Commander Kevin Laing says a typical hailing by the Canadian ships went as follows:

> Merchant ship proceeding on course 280 at 15 knots, this is Canadian Warship four miles on your port bow, flashing you with white light, Channel 16, over.

After communication was established, the Canadian ship continued,

> Good Afternoon Captain, this is Canadian Warship conducting operations in accordance with U.N. Resolutions 661 and 665. I am obliged to ask you some questions and would appreciate your co-operation, over.

The usual reply was "yes, go ahead" and the question and answer session would proceed. If the Canadian ship was satisfied, the vessel was permitted to proceed. But if the merchant ship was identified as being of further interest, it was boarded. The communication was then,

> Merchant vessel this is Canadian Warship. At this time Canada intends to exercise its right of visit and search under international law. Canada intends no harm to your vessel, its cargo, or crew. Please stand by to accept the Canadian inspection team.

ATHABASKAN, TERRA NOVA, and PROTECTEUR were the first non-U.S. Navy ships to operate on the front line. The other allies thought the Canadians were foolish to move so far forward considering the Iraqi air threat. But after seeing the "Crazy Canucks," with a supply ship and a 33-year-old frigate, handle life on the front line, the other allies began to move forward.

Because the Canadian ships were operating in an alien, hostile environment, undertaking an entirely new type of mission, they had no standard operating procedures. In their place, Summers, as Task Group Commander at the time of accepting responsibility for the central Gulf patrol areas, laid down a battle doctrine, or list of instructions, for conducting the mission.[3] This battle doctrine rested on a few key assumptions including that when a Canadian ship was in the C5 patrol area—the most northern of the three Canadian boxes—there had to be allied anti-air warfare ships stationed in the adjacent sectors. Summers also wanted the two Canadian ships on patrol to be operating in neighbouring boxes in order to support each other and provide reliable communications connections. Most of the boardings were expected to take place in the Gulf of Oman and the Canadian Task Group was to be kept fully up-to-date on the movements of the various naval and merchant ships via the Link 11 data link[4] information system. The battle doctrine also assumed there would be ample warning time of any Iraqi attack.

The doctrine incorporated the procedures and tactics which were developed, trialled, and used in the execution of the embargo enforcement mission. It was broken down into six areas: standing operational tasks,

---

3. Information on the battle doctrine was taken from a paper by Lieutenant-Commander Kevin Laing.
4. See Chapter 6, pp.118-120 for information on this tactical data link.

merchant ship interdiction, weapons control, rules of engagement, patrol areas, and the detailed operational status of each ship in the Task Group.

The procedures for conducting interdictions included very detailed instructions for communications with the merchant ships in all circumstances of co-operation and compliance. There were also four boarding plans set out for use in various situations from one where the threat was minimal, to one where the ship was not co-operating at all and the possibility of having to seize the vessel was high.

With these procedures firmly in mind, ATHABASKAN and TERRA NOVA sailed out of Bahrain on October 1, to take up their positions with the Americans in the busiest sector of the Arabian Gulf. Upon arrival, the Canadian ships immediately began a reconnaissance of their patrol areas. They sailed around them, getting an idea of what the shipping patterns were, whether they were used as fishing areas by dhows, whether ships could anchor there, what type of ocean bottom was underneath them, and what kind of air traffic used the air lanes overhead. But within six hours of arriving on station, ATHABASKAN's boarding capabilities were put to the test. A charter vessel, TIPPU SULTAN, which was heading to Iraq to evacuate Indian nationals from that country, had not been inspected in the Southern Gulf. The Canadians were asked if they could attempt a boarding in the rough sea conditions which had already forced another ally to abort its planned inspection. After much staff discussion of the risks, Miller decided the decision should be Commander Pickford's, as captain of ATHABASKAN. Pickford agreed to try. A Sea King helicopter located the vessel, which was to the north of the Canadian sectors, and informed the ship it was to be boarded by a Canadian team. By this time it was dark and windy and there were six-foot swells on the sea, but the Canadian Task Group was up to the challenge of launching a boarding under such adverse conditions. An eight-man inspection team, led by ATHABASKAN's Executive Officer Lieutenant-Commander Roger Girouard, used a Rigid Inflatable Boat (RIB) to travel over to the merchant vessel. Once there, they had to leap from the RIB onto the side of TIPPU SULTAN and climb up a ladder which had been lowered, with both ships rising and falling with the six-foot waves. After completing the boarding, the team searched the ship but found nothing which contravened the U.N. embargo. The ship, whose Captain was co-operating fully, was given the go-ahead to continue its journey, and the inspection team lept back into the RIB for their journey back to ATHABASKAN.

Some of the squadron staff wondered if the allies were testing the Canadians. Lieutenant-Commander Jim Hayes thought "it was very odd because there was an American ship and a British ship there and ourselves, and we were asked to do it." If it was a test, the Canadians passed with flying colours. Commander John Pickford says that the feeling of success "permeated throughout the entire ship and really set the tone" for the remainder of the deployment. The Americans were particularly happy that the Canadians had proved their ability to handle the enforcement function, because it freed up the U.S. ships to concentrate on air defence. They provided two ships to the sectors near the Canadian Task Group to do some interdiction, but it was the Canadian ships in the middle that handled the majority of the shipping transiting the Gulf.

The difference between what the Canadian navy trains for in peacetime and what occured in the Gulf was tremendous, just in terms of numbers. The navy's radar operators normally expect to deal with about six radar contacts—ships and aircraft—at a time. These are handled by a computer, but updating the movements of the ships and aircraft has to be added manually. For example, if a ship which is being tracked on a course of 090 (or true east[5]) at 20 knots suddenly completes a starboard turn (turns right), the operator has to catch the turn. (The computer symbol can be programmed to keep going 090 forever, but it'll end up on land.) Consequently, keeping track of six contacts can be a little hectic. Sailing out of Halifax harbour, a navy ship may see two or three merchant ships, plus several buoys that would be stationary on the radar. In the middle of the Gulf, within a 30-50 kilometres radius, there would be 30 ships (both merchant and escort) and approximately the same number of aircraft for a total of about 60 contacts that had to be plotted and co-ordinated on the ship's display. So a ship's operations staff that had been trained for six contacts was being faced with 10 times that number. Fortunately, the intensive training over the 10 days prior to leaving Halifax was successful in that the operations staff were not totally surprised at the situation in which they found themselves. And after the first few days of handling so many radar contacts, the operators began to recognize very quickly if something on the screen changed or was a little out of the ordinary. They became very good at watching the shipping and commercial flight routes and reacting when a vessel or aircraft was not

---

5. The gyroscope is divided into the 360 degrees of a compass. 000 is true north, 090 is true east, 180 is true south, and 270 is true west.

on the correct path.[6] Which, considering that the number of contacts displayed on a radar screen resembled, according to Lieutenant-Colonel McWha, "flies on an outhouse," was quite an accomplishment. All contacts were reported to Rear-Admiral Fogarty's staff on an hourly basis.

The Canadian presence in the central Gulf counted upon the U.S. providing air defence. On the whole, this was not a problem because the Americans kept an anti-air warfare ship on patrol just north of the Canadian deployment.

I was very aware of that ship's movements. If this particular ship went away, I would call the U.S. Admiral and quickly order our ships to patrol the southern parts of their sectors. It didn't happen often, but it happened a couple of times. And the disappearance usually didn't last long—just long enough for us to worry. There was one time though when it lasted about six to ten hours, making us very nervous.

Despite the occasional lapse, co-operation among the allies was very good. For the most part, the Canadians worked with the British and Americans in hailing vessels passing through the "Canada sectors". Often, one naval ship would conduct a boarding while another would standby in case of trouble.

Not all the ships which passed through Canada's sectors were challenged. Allied vessels and ships that had already been challenged elsewhere, were among those that were allowed to proceed without being boarded. Also, if there were indications that a boarding of an Iraqi ship would be opposed, it would be allowed to proceed out to the Gulf of Oman where it could be boarded in safer waters and taken to a holding anchorage.

The multinational force preferred to deal with opposed boardings in the Gulf of Oman, far enough away from Iraq that the ship's captain would not be able to summon help. In one case, a captain, brandishing a gun, opposed being boarded, forcing the Americans to resort to inserting an armed boarding party by helicopter. The ship was put to anchor and the cargo seized; the captain was told he could then proceed on his way. Instead he went into port and reloaded with a new cargo, and again attempted to sail into the Arabian Gulf. He was stopped a second time.

---

6. Not many civilian airliners strayed from the established flight routes. Most were uncomfortably aware that there were 90 missile-firing ships in the Gulf that could shoot an aircraft out of the sky.

The Multinational Interdiction Force Co-ordinator, Rear-Admiral Fogarty, and his staff, were responsible for making the initial determination of which ships warranted boarding. Miller, however, did not always agree with the American's evaluation and occasionally decided on his own initiative to go ahead and board a vessel. Not losing his sense of humour, however, Miller made light of the situation in a report to Commodore Summers.

> *In early December, after we had had a couple of differences of opinion with the Americans over which ships should be inspected, I had lunch on board the American battleship WISCONSIN with her officers and a senior member of Admiral Fogarty's staff. Later I sent a message to Commodore Summers which read, "I boarded and conducted tour" of a "Vessel of Interest," meaning the WISCONSIN, and found the "Vessel's Master was most co-operative. Inspection correct. Vessel cleared to proceed .... Great lunch served."*

The interdiction effort was extremely successful from the seagoing side. Nothing was going into Iraq by sea, other than the occasional small, pirate vessel which travelled into Iraq along the northern coast.

The Canadian ships, adopting the motto, "You sail, we hail," intercepted an average of 15-20 vessels every day. By the end of the war, the Task Group had completed 1,877 interceptions and 22 boardings. The Canadians established the records for enforcement: in one day ATHABASKAN challenged over 30 ships, and TERRA NOVA boarded eight vessels. TERRA NOVA came by her record by being the right ship in the right place at the right time. The Dutch had dredging equipment in Iraq and had promised the U.N. that when their contract ended in December they would take their equipment out of the country. To do so, they collected up a number of tugs, took them to Iraq, loaded their equipment on board, and then began the trip south out of the Gulf. TERRA NOVA intercepted and boarded the first one in the train, and then spotted the next one coming over the horizon. She immediately moved northwards and boarded that ship. Only to finish in time to see the next one appear. And then another, and another. By the time the small Canadian frigate had finished, she had moved considerably northward out of her sector, and had boarded eight vessels. Her crew was exhausted but exhilarated—it had been an extraordinary event in a normally boring routine.

Using a highly unmanoeuvrable tanker for enforcing U.N. sanctions was a novel move, not just to the navy, but to the merchant ships. Captain Doug McClean remembers one day in particular. PROTECTEUR had come up slightly behind and to the side of a merchant vessel that had not yet been checked. Using the normal message over the commercial distress frequency to get the ship's attention, PROTECTEUR announced, "Good day Captain. This is Canadian Warship and we're here enforcing United Nations Resolution 661. We'd like to ask you a few questions." There was no response. PROTECTEUR moved in closer and tried again. "Good day Captain. This is Canadian Warship ..." Still no response. McClean, with growing apprehension, tried once more and added a warning that the merchant vessel had better comply at once. All McClean heard back was a mystified ship's captain, plaintively explaining, "I want to comply but I don't see any warship. All I see is an odd looking ship off my starboard bow—is that anything to do with this?" McClean, taking great umbrage at that, replied sharply, "Yeah, it's the one with the guns on it!"

By using a supply ship to interdict commercial vessels, and having five Sea King helicopters available to help with the enforcement mission, the Canadian Task Group out-performed all others. With only three ships in the Gulf, Canada conducted 25 per cent of the total challenges.

That the Canadian ships were able to challenge so many ships was due in large part to the Sea King helicopters. The Canadian aircraft were the only allied helicopters in the Gulf equipped with forward-looking infrared sensors (FLIRs). This gave them a night-time capability which the other helicopters didn't have. It was thanks to the efforts of Major Chris Little of Equipment Requirements at Maritime Air Group Headquarters that the Canadian choppers had the sensors. When the staff officers had first sat down to decide which equipment to include in the Sea Kings, Lieutenant-Colonel Larry McWha did not suggest fitting the infra-red sensors because "I did not think it was going to be humanly possible to get enough of them and get them installed and integrated into the aircraft." Major Little thought differently, and he made it happen. McWha was glad he did.

When the Sea Kings left on a mission, they were supplied with a list of ships that were not to be hailed—for example, supply ships for the alliance or merchant ships that had already been cleared by allies operating in the southern Gulf or Gulf of Oman—and a list of ships whose movements should be noted, but not necessarily hailed. Everything else the helicopter could go ahead and hail. Using radar or night vision goggles, the aircraft would pick up a contact and close in on it. Depending on the haze, the Sea Kings could use their stabilized binoculars up to 10 miles away to determine the ship's general shape and direction. By heading towards the ship's stern, the helicopter could expect to close the distance undetected, using the forward-looking infrared sensor to make sure there were no weapons or crew members with small arms. After reading the ship's name and port of registry, the helicopter could then pass the information to the Canadian ship operating in that sector and she could then hail the merchant vessel on the radio. Or, the Sea King could go ahead and hail the ship itself.

In addition to the equipment, the Canadian Sea Kings had another major advantage over the other helicopters in the Gulf: the Canadian pilots were experienced in low-level flying. Because the aircraft are normally used for anti-submarine warfare, the pilots are trained to operate at altitudes of between 40 and 150 feet in order to use the dipping sonar which is lowered from the aircraft into the sea. Lieutenant-Colonel McWha says "people who don't fly in that mission, don't fly that low. They're not used to it." The Canadians were comfortable flying that low—even at night with their lights out.

TERRA NOVA did not have a helicopter on board but had the use of the aircraft in the other ships in the Task Group. Commander Stu Andrews says, "I wouldn't accept the word of anybody over the radio." If a Sea King was not available to confirm the information, "I would have to go driving in at the stern, at night, at high speed and get really close and try to light up their stern to confirm their name. It made for some hairy rides."

In addition to seeking out and hailing ships, the Sea Kings stood ready to be used for inserting armed boarding parties aboard unco-operative vessels. This new manoeuvre had been demonstrated to the Canadians by the British guided-missile destroyer HMS GLOUCESTER while the Task Group was moving through the Red Sea. Using PROTECTEUR as the target vessel, five armed personnel with flak jackets and helmets slid down a rope from a hovering Lynx helicopter onto the ship's fo'c's'le[7] and seized control of the ship. The helicopter then brought in a second armed group of marines. The demonstration showed it was possible to

---

7. The Canadian navy has developed a vertical replenishment method for ships which do not have a flight deck which uses the fo'c's'le as the receiving area. It is the one area of the upper deck which is not encumbered with antennae and weapons systems, making it the safest area for a hovering helicopter.

get five men safely onto a ship's deck in about 30 seconds, a great improvement over having men climb up the sides of an unfriendly vessel from a Rigid Inflatable Boat.

When the Task Group reached Bahrain, with the British demonstration in mind and information on rope type tension, the Canadians used a towing hawser[8] to set up a training program in ATHABASKAN's helicopter hanger. The Task Group had no trouble finding volunteers to undertake the training for an armed boarding party— most of the crew members saw this as an exciting change of pace. The volunteers were first trained in the hanger, then from a helicopter hovering very low over the flight deck, and finally from about 30 feet up. Everything went very well, until the first practice run using a destroyer, TERRA NOVA.

> *We flew them over and they went down on the fo'c's'le, no problem at all. And then this one, very keen, fellow walked over the breakwater in front of the gun on the bow to get to the ship's bridge—the steel ladder goes straight up one side and down the other side—and he got his leg caught at the top when it slipped between the rung and the shield, and he went over and his leg stayed where it was. He broke his leg but he was more in distress over messing up an exercise that had not been formally authorized. He kept saying, "Geez, I'm sorry sir. But it had nothing to do with the program, it was just my stupidity. I'd hate to have it cancelled because of me."*

> *I had authorized the insertion program as an operational requirement, then we worked up the training and we did it ... then we told Maritime Command what we were doing.*

> *There was some opposition. For example, Maritime Air Group's immediate reaction was "why would anyone want to jump out of a perfectly servicable aircraft without a parachute?" But we took a video of the thing and flew it back to Halifax so they could see what we were doing. They were still somewhat hesitant, but they gave final approval for the exercise and told us to carry on.*

---

8. A rope that is used for towing another ship. Towing hawsers used to be made out of steel which created enormous handling problems for the crew members who had to drag this rusty and grimy steel rope from the bow of the ship where it was stored to the stern where it would be attached to an ailing vessel. Today's towing hawsers are made out of more flexible nylon.

The Canadian routine for inserting an armed boarding party—called VISIT, for Vertical Insertion Search and Inspection Team—included using two helicopters so that one could use its machine guns to cover the other one as the team slid down the rope. The Canadians became extremely proficient in this manoeuvre—10 men from two helicopters were inserted on board a ship within 1 minute and 55 seconds. As it happened, however, the Task Group never used this method for boarding a ship, mainly because the squadron staff decided not to forcibly board a ship in the central Gulf where the ships were operating. The area was too close to Iraq and if the Iraqis had been as well organized as the allies thought they should have been (but actually weren't), the Canadian helicopters and insertion team would have been in great danger of attack.

Around Christmas time, when things were getting very tense, the squadron staff added to the Task Group's concept of operations. In the event of an attack by the Iraqis on allied forces, the ships were told to take defensive moves "Chaff Tango," "Chaff Oscar" or "Barber Pole." "Tango" meant if there was a large oil tanker nearby, the Canadian ship should go behind it and use it for cover. "Oscar" referred to the same manoeuvre using oil rigs for cover. And "Barber Pole" was the code name of a "safe spot."[9] If the Iraqis struck before the ships were ready, and missiles were flying, Miller would issue "Barber Pole" and the three Canadian ships—which could conceivably be in three different locations in the Gulf—would all converge on the same spot. That plan for a safe spot lasted until approximately the beginning of the war.

> *There was a period of transition. Because we knew that the 15th of January was the deadline, then marching up to that deadline was a period of great tension. If the Iraqis had thought like western military people, they would have walked back a week— I would have—and conducted a pre-emptive strike. As an Iraqi, if I figured my intelligence was good enough and the allies were going to use force, I would have hit them hard on land and in the ocean. After all, the Iraqis had 660 aircraft that could have made a real mess out of the carriers and certainly if they could have gone at us at a time where we might have been resting or sleeping or picked a holiday or whatever, they would have capitalized on one of the ten principles of war.*

---

9. Lieutenant-Commander Jim Hayes selected the name "Barber Pole" because it is the name of the east coast operational squadron. The name comes from the Sambro Light out of Halifax, which is red and white.

Hussein didn't. But there was no way for the Canadians to know that he would not take advantage of that one window of opportunity. So as time marched on, and January 15th loomed closer, the ships increased the level of their weapons training, performing drills and taking part in both national and allied exercises while continuing to patrol their assigned sectors.

During this very dangerous period before the actual fighting began, one of the Sea King pilots got an unexpected—and unwelcome—chance to try out some of the air group's defensive manoeueuvres.

Each Sea King had been fitted with a radar warning receiver, which makes a buzzing sound if a missile targets the aircraft and gives the pilot the bearing of where the missile is coming from. The pilot—who would be understandably nervous if the warning sounded—was trained to follow a sequence of moves to save himself and his aircraft: he was to change altitude, fire his deception devices, and do a hard manoeuvre to change his lateral position.

One night, a Sea King from ATHABASKAN was on a training flight in the north central Gulf, when its warning radar went off, showing a missile approach from the north.[10]

> *Immediately, the pilot fired his flares, went 90 degrees to the right, and dropped 150 feet. The problem was he was flying at about 150 feet! The sea came up very quickly!*

Luckily, Lieutenant-Colonel Larry McWha was in the aircraft. He had been momentarily distracted by the pilot's firing of the flares and when he looked back he saw the altitude descending down through 30 feet at a speed of 750 feet a minute. He knew they were going to crash. In a blink of an eye he grabbed the controls, levelled the aircraft, and then began the climb back up again—after touching a tail wheel in the water.

McWha was understandably less sanguine about the experience than Miller, who saw a bright side to this otherwise unnerving episode.

> *We learned a big lesson out of this: always dwell a pause of two marching paces before reacting.[11] Then emergency reactions will lead to survival instead of disaster.*

---

10. Actually, the radar warning receiver had been activated by an allied radar operating in an unexpected mode.
11. Military-speak for: think first, act second.

Throughout the lead-up to the allied action against Iraq, and during the 6-week period of fighting, the Canadian Task Group put a heavy emphasis on the value of the embargo enforcement mission. While the Americans were more concerned with fighting and winning a victory over Iraq, the Canadians recognized the symbolic nature of the multinational embargo enforcement operation: the world would not stand idly by and allow Baghdad's aggression to go unchecked. At the same time, however, the Canadian Task Group was ready to take an active role in supporting the allied navies' offensive against Iraq. Thus was born the role of Combat Logistics Force Co-ordinator.

CHAPTER NINE

"You're going to be busy"

When Miller took over as Commander of the Canadian Task Group in October, he had no idea that three months later he would be in charge of co-ordinating the movements of not three, but 60 ships. In fact, if he had been asked if he wanted the job of Combat Logistics Force Co-ordinator he probably would have said no. After all, he was being kept busy running the Canadian part of the embargo enforcement operation and he fully expected to continue that work after hostilities began. The Commodore, however, had other ideas.

At the beginning of January, Commodore Summers met with Rear-Admiral March to discuss Canada's naval role once fighting began. At that meeting, the officers agreed to a tentative role for Canada of guarding the supply ships. That role was expanded at the monthly multinational conference held in Dubai aboard the Australian supply ship HMAS SUCCESS on January 9—Canada's Captain Miller would be the co-ordinator of a newly formed multinational Combat Logistics Force.

Summers phoned Miller with the news, telling him, "We wanted to keep the Canadian ships together, so I offered your services to run the logistics." Miller, taken by surprise, was shocked—"You what?!" Summers was prepared for Miller's reaction. "What else are you going to do?" he asked curtly. "If we split the three ships up, what are you going to do? You and your operations staff wouldn't be needed, you'd just be watching the war"—and then he added the kicker—"you may as well go home." He paused for only a moment before conceding, "So you're going to be busy!"

Summers hadn't made the decision lightly. He had seen an early plan from Vice-Admiral Stanley Arthur's planning staff that showed the three Canadian ships being split up among the various combat units. Neither

Summers nor Miller was happy with that prospect. They wanted the Canadian ships to continue to operate together, as a clearly identifiable Canadian contribution. Summers says,

> We were probably the most senior in terms of time in the Gulf. That superb naval staff that we'd put together, was, in my estimation, the best in the Gulf, and it would be a shame to marginalize that capability by splitting up our force. So I looked at that whole thing and decided this was not in Canada's or the navy's best interests, nor mine, in my responsibility of trying to maintain control and national command over these forces.

He looked at what would be the best role for Canada—one that would make the best use of the squadron staff and would be a meaningful contribution to the coalition's efforts. He didn't have to look far.

The Americans had a problem with their initial planning for the naval operations in the Gulf: how to keep their ships refuelled and resupplied in the event of a protracted conflict. By early January, when war seemed inevitable, they still had not developed a solution to their logistical resupply problem. Summers believed he had the answer.

He approached Rear-Admiral March in USS MIDWAY with the idea that Canada could be of the most benefit to the coalition by organizing the logistics for the international naval force. March agreed that Canada should take on the role.

Despite Miller's initial reaction, the Canadian navy was uniquely prepared to handle such a mission. In addition to having worked closely with a number of different navies on a regular basis, and to having the necessary equipment for inter-naval communications, Canada had a major advantage in its people.

> *The Canadian ships in the Gulf were made up of men and women from all across Canada, from all backgrounds. We had in the ship's company, Italian, French and Arabic speakers, to name a few, and when working with ships from other nations we regularly sent messages to them in their own languages. Can you imagine, if you are serving in an Italian ship and you get a message from the Canadians in Italian that you would like them to do something, or would they mind doing something? You can just see the usefulness of having that kind of capability.*

The role of the Combat Logistics Force was to keep the front-line combatants supplied with fuel (oil, jet fuel, hydraulic fluid, lubricants), ammunition (bullets, cannon shells, missiles, rockets and bombs), and spare parts (tires, clamps, nuts and bolts, circuits and wiring, tubes and computer chips). The requirements were huge. For example, every 48 hours each of the four carriers required 1.5 million gallons of JP5 aviation fuel, and 200-300 lifts[1] of ammunition. In addition, there were 100 other ships of varying sizes that had to be supplied.

The Pachyderm Palace

The Canadians began this huge operation by picking a 20 by 20 nautical mile area in the southern Arabian Gulf—nicknamed the "Pachyderm Palace"[2]—in which the allied combat support vessels, landing support ships, ammunition ships, general cargo ships, destroyer tenders and tankers could anchor after either entering the Gulf or returning from taking on cargo at a supply port. This area was divided into two mile squares numbered 1 to 10 from south to north, and called by the names of Canada's 10 provinces running east to west (see Diagram 1).

> *We had regularly up to about 25 destroyers and about 35-odd other ships, oilers, command, hospital ships, you name it. Everyone knew, though, that it was a Canadian operation. We had huge amphibious ships coming in, saying they wanted to go to anchor at Saskatchewan 2, because their supply ship was in Manitoba 3.*

The northern part of the Pachyderm Palace was the Mobile Area, in which at least one tanker and those ships that did not want to anchor maintained a clockwise direction of movement.

Escorts from the various countries were assigned patrolling sectors defined by the grid, in order to provide maximum protection to valuable logistic ships. In addition, there was a 20-mile deep protection zone—the northern part was referred to as the Yukon and Northwest Territories—patrolled by destroyers and area air defence vessels surrounding the logistics area. Supply ships were escorted north from the Pachyderm Palace to the carrier battle groups.

Initially the only escorts in the Combat Logistics Force (CLF) were the two Canadian destroyers, ATHABASKAN and TERRA NOVA.

---

1. A "lift" refers to the contents of a cargo net which is slung under a helicopter for delivery to a unit. The cargo net can hold several pallets.
2. The Americans referred to it as the "Ponderosa" or "Virginia City."

Combat Logistic Force Holding Area

"The Pachyderm Palace" (Canadian) "The Ponderosa" (U.S.)

Yukon and
NorthWest Territories

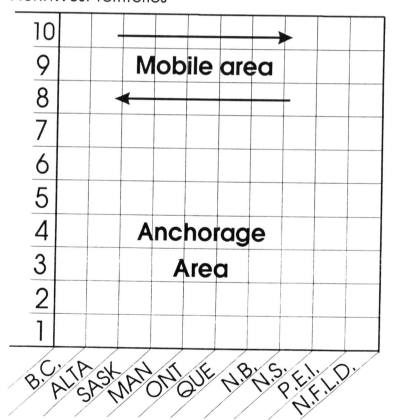

Note: 2 nautical mile by 2 nautical mile squares

Many of the destroyers and frigates of the other navies were committed to the carrier battle groups. Slowly, however, other countries made their warships available for escort work, so that at one time or another during the hostilities, escort and supply ships from Argentina, Australia, Belgium, Canada, Denmark, France, Italy, the Netherlands, Norway, Spain, U.K., and U.S served with the CLF.

Each of the navies involved in the Logistics Force operated under national command—and that meant each of them had different restrictions in terms of where they could and could not go in the Gulf. Because of these national restrictions, Miller did not exercise full tactical control of the ships in the CLF, but instead had the responsibility for tactical co-ordination. In an ironic twist, however, the U.S. command ship, USS BLUERIDGE, which carried Vice-Admiral Arthur, the American Admiral in command of the entire multinational naval operation, was part of the CLF, and subject to Miller's tactical co-ordination. Likewise, USS LASALLE, the command ship used by Rear-Admiral Fogarty in his role as Strike Force commander, and the two hospital ships, were designated part of the logistics force.

The U.S. designated Miller a Warfare Commander with the codename UNREP SIERRA (Underway Replenishment, Surface Forces). He was responsible for escorting the supply ships into the Gulf through the Strait of Hormuz, protecting them while at anchorage in the logistics area, and then escorting them north or to port. When Miller's command ship, ATHABASKAN had to leave the area to perform escort duties, Miller assigned another ship's captain—either TERRA NOVA or another country's vessel—the task of guarding the area, and also had him act as a relay for his instructions.

Each area of the Pachyderm Palace had its own threat, and ships were placed in the various sectors depending on their capabilities to counter particular threats. For example, the sectors to the northwest of the Pachyderm Palace had a significant air threat because they were nearer Iraq, whereas a sector on the south side had a minimal air threat but a possible surface threat, because it was closer to the coast and possible terrorist action. Miller, therefore, wanted to have the CLF's best anti-air warfare ships on the northern side and the best surface capable ships on the south. The least armed ships, such as the Danish and Norwegian, could be kept on the eastern side because there was very little threat there at all.

Setting It Up

There were only a few steps involved in running the logistics supply train, and on paper, it looked pretty simple. But there were teething problems, beginning with the setting up of a Canadian liaison with the American forces.

One of the key components of the logistics operation, was having a Canadian officer on board USS MIDWAY. When Summers negotiated Canadian command of the Combat Logistics Force, he suggested to Rear-Admiral March that there should be two Canadian officers—one from the surface side and one from the air side of things—aboard the American carrier. March agreed. Summers then told Miller they needed a knowledgeable officer, who had been involved in the scheduling to be in the carrier, as the Canadian liaison officer—nicknamed the "Canadian Connection." Summers wanted Lieutenant-Commander Greg Romanow. But Romanow was doing the scheduling for the Task Group and Miller did not want to let him go. Miller was blunt with his commanding officer: "If you take him, I don't have a scheduler. You're telling me I'm going to be responsible for doing all this, but you're taking my scheduler away."

The two officers exchanged strong words over the issue, with Summers saying he was taking Romanow, and Miller resisting the move. The two men became more and more agitated until Summers finally said, "Well, obviously we're not getting anywhere. We can't talk to each other anymore on this. Maybe we'd better call each other back in an hour or so after we've calmed down." Both men hung up.

Miller was in the captain's cabin in PROTECTEUR and the captain, Doug McClean, was taken aback by the ferocity of the phone conversation. He talked to Miller about possible solutions to the problem. Although Miller did not want to lose Romanow, he actually agreed with Summers that he was the best man to do the liaison job onboard the American carrier.

At that time, in addition to Romanow who was the scheduling officer, Miller had two Squadron Watch Officers—Lieutenant-Commander Jim Hayes and Lieutenant-Commander Greg Hannah. Miller was happy to have Hayes do the scheduling job, because he had done that on a number of occasions when Romanow was off duty. But that still left the problem of a Watch Officer who was fully conversant with the battle orders, weapons control, and the adaptation of the schedule to operations. Fortuitously, while Miller was trying to figure this out with McClean, the Sea Training commander arrived with his crew to do the work-ups for PRESERVER's crew which had flown in to relieve those on board PROTECTEUR. Commander Mike Pulchny came into the cabin at the tail end of the conversation, and said, "I've brought an extra officer, in case I needed to do work-ups in ships in different areas and I needed a liaison with you." The extra officer was Lieutenant-Commander Paul Maddison—someone that Miller knew and trusted. So Maddison joined Miller's staff as the Squadron Weapons Officer,[3] Hayes took over as Squadron Combat Officer, and Hannah became the Squadron Operations Officer. (Maddison and Hannah thus became the two Squadron Watch Officers, each on duty in the operations room of ATHABASKAN 12 hours a day.)[4]

Miller phoned Summers and told him about the solution that had miraculously appeared. Everything had been worked out and Summers was going to have Romanow (who was at a function in Dubai and knew nothing of how his name and job were being bandied about).

> *As soon as Romanow walked on board, I said, "Pack your bags, you're going to USS MIDWAY." He said, "I'm what?! I'm going where? Does my wife know?" I said, "Of course your wife doesn't know!"*

Romanow transferred over to MIDWAY on January 5 and became part of the staff of the Battle Force Anti-Surface Warfare Commander, Captain J.W. Parker. As such, Romanow kept track of the American operations and their ships and tankers, as well as the other allied tankers.

Romanow studied the surface ship taskings that the battle force commander had. Romanow also looked at, in general terms, what was required for logistics. For example, how full of fuel did the commander want his ships at any one time. In gross terms, he might say he wanted them at 80 per cent fuel, every three days. Romanow then relayed that information to Hayes in ATHABASKAN—the two of them working in tandem for the next two months. Hayes kept track of what ship was at what fuelling state, how much fuel they were burning, and when they had to be refuelled. The same thing was done with ammunition. In the case of food for the carriers, a lot of that resupply was done by large aircraft from shore.[5]

---

3. Luck was on Miller's side, not only in finding another officer at such short notice, but also in finding this particular one: Maddison who had just finished a year on the staff of a task group commander, the Commander of the Standing Naval Force Atlantic.

4. Maddison stayed with ATHABASKAN until mid-February when he was relieved by Lieutenant-Commander Mark deSmedt. Maddison returned to Canada to prepare HMCS HURON to take over from ATHABASKAN in the Gulf.

5. The sustainment requirement for food alone was tremendous: one carrier has 5,000 people on board.

Until we got some kind of indication that the carriers needed fuelling on this particular day, or that it was a go, what I got was general instructions from the U.S. admiral in USS MIDWAY who was co-ordinating all the carrier operations. He didn't want to worry about all the logistics so he said, "you figure it out, as to which ships need what fuel, when, and I'll tell you what tanker is coming, when, from the U.S. side of things, and you organize the allied tankers".

Summers also assigned a member of his staff, Major Jocelyn Cloutier, to work the air side in MIDWAY. Summers reasoned that by sending the best people, they would not be marginalized by the Americans.[6] Summers felt confident that if there was anything taking place that could affect his responsibilities as operational commander of the Canadian forces, Romanow and Cloutier would both be in a position to give him a 'heads up' and to argue the Canadian perspective.

Running the Operation

It all appeared pretty straight forward. But with every large operation, it's the details that stand ready to trip everyone up. For example, Canada and Europe use the metric measurement system but the Americans are still using the imperial system. There were also different threads on the fuel and oil hose fittings. Fortunately, the Canadian navy is experienced at coping with this type of problem: PROTECTEUR had the fittings to ensure she could fuel any of the allies. The one exception was the British. They had with them a fitting which would allow their destroyers to be fuelled by an American ship; however, they only had five of them and there were more than five tankers in the Gulf—at its peak the CLF had about a dozen tankers assigned to it. Consequently, this big, brass, heavy fitting had to be flown to whichever allied tanker was most likely to end up refuelling British ships.

That sounds like a simple operation, but it wasn't. The tanker would be informed by a helicopter that a part was being delivered and then would proceed to deliver it. The ship's officers would see this great big, heavy—it weighed a ton—brass part arrive on their deck and think it was a mistake, the part didn't belong to them. Asking the helicopter crew what it was for, didn't help, because they didn't know. They'd just been told to deliver it.

---

6. Summers had picked his people well. After Captain Parker was put in charge of combat search and rescue missions in the northern Gulf, Romanow took over the logistics chair and was given his own operations room and a staff of 25 people.

So then the messages back and forth would start: "There's been a mistake. We've just received ...."

"No, there's no mistake. The part is for refuelling British ships."
"But we're not about to refuel any Royal Navy ships."
"It's in case you do."
"But it doesn't fit on any of our equipment."
"No, but it fits on their's. When they arrive for refuelling, you have to send this part over to them."
"Well, why don't they just carry it with them?"
"Because they've got 18 ships in the Gulf and only five of these fittings."

And so it went. Everytime one of these fittings had to be delivered somewhere, the phone lines buzzed.

The national restrictions on each navy also had to be factored into the taskings. Some navies could only go as far as 27.30 degrees north latitude, so they could not be used to escort supply ships to the carriers in the northern portion of the Gulf. Other navies had an easterly boundary of 54.0 degrees east longitude so they couldn't go further west than the eastern edge of the logistics area. The Danes in their corvette OLFERT FISCHER, for example, could not go further into the Gulf than the eastern edge of the Pachyderm Palace but they wanted to do something useful. Miller, therefore, asked them and the Norwegians, who contributed their coast guard cutter ANDENNES to support the Danes, to be the permanent guards of the eastern sections of the Pachyderm Palace. On occasion he also used them, and TERRA NOVA, which was equipped with the sophisticated Canadian Naval Electronic Warfare System (CANEWS), to escort ships through the Strait of Hormuz.

The Western European Union also provided ships—the U.K., Italy, France, Belgium, and the Netherlands each contributed ships at one time or another—under the command of an Italian who reported to a French admiral in the Indian Ocean. They wanted to work as a bloc; just as Canada wanted to be seen to be contributing as a Canadian entity, this group wanted to be seen to be contributing as a Western European Union military entity. Initially they wanted just one sector, on the eastern side of the Pachyderm Palace. Miller knew that using four ships to patrol one relatively safe sector would be a waste of assets. The French ship in particular was bristling with anti-air warfare capability. So the WEU agreed to take on two sectors and occasionally Miller used one or two of the WEU ships to do specific taskings such as escorting a tanker to refuel the carriers or a supply ship into port.

There were differences in the military ethos as well that presented a unique problem. Hayes, who was doing the scheduling, at one point had to send messages to various navies to encourage them to stay on duty. After a lengthy period at sea, with no break, many of the ships began heading into port, leaving Hayes with only two Canadian ships and one French ship. ATHABASKAN had been at sea for over 30 days straight, and the Americans, as per their usual way of operating, "had been at sea forever." Hayes sent a message to the departing ships saying, "I would really appreciate it if you would lend some support." Many of the ships came back.

Then there was the problem of a Royal Navy task force which came into the southern Gulf, and decided that the southeast box of the Pachyderm Palace was the best place to be stationed. Miller sent a diplomatic message to their tactical officer to tell him that the Combat Logistics Force was operating in that area, and while he would be delighted to have the British take responsibility for a box or two, he would prefer that the three Royal Fleet Auxiliaries be stationed in the CLF mobile area and the three Royal Navy destroyers take on a bigger area, as part of the co-ordinated multinational effort. He received a very nice message back, apologizing for moving in on an underway logistics co-ordination effort, and offering to dovetail operations with the CLF. The British, who at that point were not part of multinational Combat Logistics Force, decided that once their minehunters arrived, they would move west of the Pachyderm Palace out of the way. However, they would provide an escort and a tanker to the CLF, and, for familiarity purposes, they would cycle their new ships through Miller's logistics organization.

Miller and his staff kept track of all the ships in the CLF on several large stateboards in the staff office on the starboard side of ATHABASKAN.[7] These white plastic boards contained information on each supply and escort ship, what it carried, what its tonnage was, where it was allowed to go based on the national restrictions, where it was, where it was going, when it last fuelled, who it could fuel, and what it's next job was. These boards were kept up to date, by hand, on a continual basis. The operational staff did not use a computer for a couple of reasons. One, all the computers on board were being used to run the weapons

---

7. Because the Tribal class destroyers were built as command ships they have a dedicated facility for a squadron staff.

and sensor systems. Taking one of the displays in the operations room and using it to run the scheduling program, would have meant taking it away from a weapons system or a surface search co-ordinator. The word processors on board were also in constant use, producing such things as weapons orders and battle orders and documenting operations.

The operations staff did look into getting a computer to run one of the available programs for this kind of operation—for example, the registry of shipping—but they decided it was easier to have a book which they could physically go through and a board which was prominently displayed and easily referred to. And that was the second reason for not using a computer for the logistics scheduling. The books and stateboards were constantly being referred to by the various staff members; if the information was on a computer, it would have meant having two, three or four officers hunched over a little computer screen.

The one computerized system that Miller's CLF team did have was the Joint Operational Tactical System. It was located in the staff office, and it provided the location of all the ships in the Gulf, including a readout on all the merchant ships—where they had come from, where they were going.

Moving the Goods

Miller's staff issued instructions on a rolling three day basis.

We had a plan of which ships we'd have to escort, which merchant ships, ammunition ships, logistics ships, and we put them in a three-day message that would say, "ATHABASKAN, your job for the next six hours is to escort this tanker from this position to that position, remain in that area while it fuels these ships, and then bring it back to the logistics force box, and we'll have another task for you, and probably for the tanker. And you're to start tomorrow morning at 10:00."

It's one thing to put that out in a three-day rolling program, and another to make sure that it happens. It was my staff's job to actually call up ATHABASKAN, or whatever, and say, "did you get the message?" Everyone then scrambles, and normally you get a "what message?" because messages take a while to get through. Even though they're immediate you have a queueing system.

So, all for the better if they say "yes, we got the message and yes, we'll be in that spot, and we'll do it." Then come 10:00 next morning, my staff officers are saying, "right, TERRA NOVA should be in that spot, with that ship, and they should be going that direction. Is that happening on the radar scope?" If the answer is yes, and they actually appear to be moving the right direction, everybody's happier than a clam. If it's "What the heck is TERRA NOVA doing down there? Why is she going the wrong way? Why isn't that tanker coming in here?" then they're on the phone, saying "what are you doing, where are you going, why aren't you where you are supposed to be?"

That didn't happen very often, but it did happen. It's like an air traffic control area where you have to put people in a holding pattern because all of a sudden a storm comes in and then everybody had to adjust what they were doing. So occasionally there would be a minor problem or the ships would have had to challenge or board a vessel which was their primary job. They'd call my watch officer and say, "this is what we're doing, and we're going to be a little bit late, but should be no problem." It happened. It was a matter of being on top of it, and I think that's where my staff were exceptional. They were on top of every little movement that had been ordered and rarely—in fact, there were only two occasions out of a couple of hundred taskings— did it go wrong.

Several times during the war, Miller used TERRA NOVA for escort duties through the Strait of Hormuz. He chose the Canadian frigate because it was well-equipped to deal with any threat posed by small craft from Iran (which was still an unknown quantity), and as proved by the Mediterranean tests, its radar absorption material and small size made it virtually undetectable. Also, being Canadian, it was easier for Miller to send TERRA NOVA off on an assignment on the spur of the moment, than it would have been for him to demand a quick response from another navy's ship.

The two-day round trip involved TERRA NOVA travelling through the Strait to the Gulf of Oman and picking up the vessel or vessels requiring an escort into the war zone. One time the frigate was sent to escort through the Strait an 80,000 tonne American aircraft carrier bristling with weapons and aircraft, which left Commander Stu Andrews wondering, "Who's escorting who?"

Andrews says the interesting part of his escort journeys occurred at night, when there was heavy traffic of small vessels going back and forth between Oman and Iran. These were most likely smugglers plying their trade, but as Andrews says, "at night you have no idea what they are. All it is, is a bunch of very small, fast moving contacts coming right at you. And they come right at you, zipping just under your stern or just in front of you. We would come up to full readiness on those occasions, because we didn't know what these guys were about to do, or what weapons they had."

Providing an escort to a hospital ship presented a new set of problems. Escorting any ship entailed being prepared to protect the vessel from an air attack. This was not a major problem in the case of a large tanker, which could absorb a hit without sustaining major damage. However, hospital ships were different: they could not afford to take any hit. Preventing that involved putting TERRA NOVA at risk. She would have to use her chaff system to seduce the missile away from the target ship or failing that, her Phalanx close-in weapon system to destroy the incoming missile. Because these systems are for self-defence, they have a very short range. The challenge was to manoeuvre TERRA NOVA so that she would be between the threat and the hospital ship, while keeping the frigate's Phalanx gun in the correct firing position. Because the TERRA NOVA's Phalanx was aft, Commander Andrews had to keep the ship's stern to the threat. But by turning the stern of the ship outwards to the threat, TERRA NOVA was then heading into the ship it was trying to protect, instead of going the same way beside it. To satisfy those two contrary requirements involved some violent manoeuvring. TERRA NOVA performed this mission once before hostilities began for MERCY during exercise Imminent Thunder—which despite being an exercise was really during the period of greatest risk because of the possibility of a surprise pre-emptive air attack—and once during the fighting.

There were up to 12 allied tankers in the Combat Logistics Force at any one time, and they all wanted some of the action. None of them wanted to sail around doing nothing so Miller's staff assigned each its own patrol area. There was always a duty tanker in the northern Mobile Area that steamed clockwise on a racetrack circuit, so that any ship coming in would be fuelled almost immediately. All it had to do was show up. So the tanker would be on a 24-hour notice to provide fuel within 30 minutes. After only a couple of days of that job, the crew would be pretty tired and the tanker would be reassigned to a less demanding mission. For example, it would have to go from the Pachyderm Palace to the carrier operating area to fuel a ship, but because it took 10 hours to get there and back, the crew would get a rest en route. The tankers were rotated through the northern patrol area approximately every three days so that the work was shared equally.

Miller's staff didn't just require an abundance of scheduling skills to make this system work; diplomacy was also in high demand. This was especially the case when an Argentinian ship needed refuelling and the nearest tanker to her was a Royal Navy ship. It took some cajoling on the part of the Canadians, but the British finally agreed to refuel their former enemies—although they kept two Royal Navy escorts close by while the operation was underway.

Only once did a tanker complain that it did not feel it had had enough business during the day. Miller played with the schedule and the next day they were given four ships to refuel—by midnight, they were saying, "Okay, okay, thank you. We won't complain again!"

The Air Plan

The Canadians also did the air co-ordination for the 45 helicopters of eight different types operated by the navies of the Combat Logistics Force. This responsibility fell onto the shoulders of Major Peter Nordlund, Squadron Air Operations Officer. Nordlund had been doing the flying program for the five Canadian Sea Kings. That in itself had been a challenge because each helicopter could only fly so many hours before it had to be serviced; Nordlund had to make sure that only one aircraft at a time was in for servicing. During the war, however, his responsibilities increased substantially as he juggled the taskings of up to 45 helicopters.

He contacted all eight of the navies operating helicopters and found out when each of them wanted their choppers to fly, for how long, what the capabilities of the helicopters were, and what the individual navy's air requirements were. He then prepared a large stateboard on which he logged each of the types of helicopters, what their weapons load could be, what their tasking was, when they were going airborne and when they were coming back to their ship, what ship was their parent ship, and what sector was it in. From this Nordlund put together a daily flying program which was discussed and finalized at the evening's briefing. The stateboards in the staff office contained the schedule for the current 24 hours, and the tentative plan for the next 48 hours. On an average day, he juggled the daily activities of 12-20 aircraft; but there were times when he handled as many as 45 and as few as two.

Like the ships they flew from, the allied helicopters had varying capabilities. Some aircraft had equipment that was especially suited to mine surveillance, others were better equipped for over-the-horizon ship surveillance. In addition to the different capabilities, all the navies had their own national regulations governing the use of their helicopters. The Argentines, for example, were not authorized to fly beyond visual sight of their destroyer. For that reason, Nordlund assigned them a patrol area of about five miles radius around their own ship. Each type of aircraft had its own cycle of how many hours it could fly before it had to go in for a certain number of hours of maintenance. For example, the Canadian Sea Kings could fly for 12 hours straight with only stops for fuel and crew changes. Another type of aircraft could fly for six hours, have two hours of maintenance, and then fly for another four hours. Nordlund had to identify those cycles in his planning. As ships came in, and a day or two later left the logistics force area, Nordlund had to adjust his scheduling to the newly available assets. Usually the helicopter which became available did not have the same capabilities or operational parameters as the one that had just left. So the juggling continued, around the clock.

During the interdiction period, the Sea Kings were flying about 12 hours a day, mostly at night because their infrared sensors could detect ships and read their names on their hulls in the darkness, as well as being able to detect mines in calm seas. The cooler night air was also easier on the aircraft and their crew members. Once the fighting started, when Nordlund was able to draw on allied resources, he tried to keep at least one helicopter airborne at all times.

In addition to hailing ships, the helicopters were needed for surface surveillance to protect against any small terrorist craft—a major worry to the Combat Logistics Force. When the CLF was in the southern Gulf, there were numerous dhows around because the Logistics Force was placed on the edge of their traditional fishing grounds. The allies could not know if the small craft coming towards them were just going about their daily business or if they were about to launch an attack. After all, during the Iran-Iraq war in the 1980s, the people in the dhows often carried handheld missile systems. To be on the safe side, the helicopters with the Combat Logistics Force devised a way of keeping the fishing vessels away from the fleet. One of the crew members would put on a gas mask and hold up a picture of a skull and cross bones to get the message across that the small craft were entering a dangerous area. Only occasionally did the helicopters have to use a more direct method.

> *The first time we had to use force was on January 30, 1991,*
> *when a dhow was proceeding towards one of the huge Logistics*
> *Force carriers. It would not turn away despite our warnings*
> *and ATHABASKAN had to fire across its bow. Two days later,*
> *the gunner in a Sea King helicopter fired shots across another*
> *vessel's bow. It immediately turned and sailed away. That was*
> *the first shot fired from a Sea King in the war—and the gunner*
> *was a woman.*[8]

Master Corporal Karin Lehmann was the gunner. She and the rest of her Sea King crew were on patrol when they spotted a dhow whose captain refused to turn his craft around despite signals from the helicopter. In describing the incident later, she wrote,

> When it became evident that he had no intention of turning around, Captain Brulotte [Michel Brulotte, the Sea King pilot] contacted our task group's control centre to advise them of the situation. He then hovered the Sea King near the dhow and we made further attempts to warn him off. Finally I fired several bursts of tracer over his bow and it had the desired effect. The dhow immediately turned 180 degrees and beat a hasty retreat.[9]

The helicopters were also used to look for floating mines. Although the Combat Logistics Force was kept in an area that was far away from the mined areas, there were over 1200 mines in the Gulf at the time—many of them left over from the Iran-Iraq war—and a lot of them had come loose from their tethers.[10] An additional task of oil slick surveillance was added to the Sea King's repertoire later in the war when ATHABASKAN was asked to escort, first the American Aegis cruiser

---

8. Media reports during the war erroneously attributed "the first shot fired in anger since the Korean War" to two CF-18 pilots who fired their 20mm cannons and a Sparrow missile at a small Iraqi patrol boat. (See *Ottawa Citizen*, Jan. 31, 1991, p. A3; and *Globe and Mail*, Jan. 31, 1991, p. A7). We believe the sequence was ATHABASKAN first, followed by the CF-18s and then the Sea King.

9. *Airforce*, Vol. 15, No. 3 (Oct-Nov-Dec 1991), p. 6.

10. The naval force did not know at the time how many new mines were put into the Gulf by Iraq. After the ceasefire, the Iraqis provided the coalition with a plan of what mines were where. The Geneva Convention stipulates that countries who sow mines in wartime must keep track of where mines are laid so that they can be removed after hostilities. Also, if tethered mines break from their moorings, they must be equipped with a device that disarms them when they reach the surface. In the Arabian Gulf the weather broke some of the tethers on the mines so that they became free floating. And later investigation found that many of the free floaters were still armed. There was a suspicion that the Iraqis had laid them incorrectly, either through incompetence or on purpose. See, "Moored mines contravened convention" in *International Defense Review*, No. 7/1991, p. 737.

PRINCETON, and then the hospital ship COMFORT, in waters off the coast of Kuwait. The helicopters scouted a clear route for the ships which otherwise ran the risk of having their water intakes suck up crude oil into their machinery.

The CLF's Three Phases

As a result of the changing tactical situation, there were three distinct phases to the co-ordination of the logistics effort. In the first phase, the Combat Logistics Force operated in the southern Gulf while the carrier battle groups operated in the south central Gulf. In the second phase, the CLF was still co-ordinated out of the southern Gulf, but the carriers moved north. In the third phase, with the almost complete reduction of air and surface threats, the CLF moved north as well.

First Phase

During the first phase (see Map 3), the supply ships responded to whatever ships needed them, whenever they needed them. After the first few days, however, the resupply operation settled into a fairly regular schedule. Some ships needed supplies less than others. The carriers, for example, had their own supplies delivered to them every three or four days, so the Combat Logistics Force did not have to worry about them. But each of the destroyers in the battle group needed refuelling every three or four days. That presented a scheduling problem. Since the CLF did not want to have to refuel 20 destroyers all on the same day, and since the refuelling operation takes a destroyer out of the action for anywhere from one to eight hours,[11] Miller's staff created a staggered schedule, whereby five destroyers a day would be refuelled.

In order to keep a sealift operation going throughout the crisis, allied ships en route to the Gulf, needed access to some kind of system that would give them information on the conditions in the Gulf. So from the beginning to approximately the middle of Phase One, Rear-Admiral Fogarty asked Miller to position destroyers in the Gulf of Oman, just before and just after the Strait of Hormuz, and one near the Pachyderm Palace. Any ship entering the Arabian Gulf would be able to call the destroyers and ask, 'What's the situation in the Gulf?' The destroyer would then give them an update on such things as where the latest mine

---

11. The time it takes to refuel depends on various factors such as the sea state, but the most important variable is the type of system used to send the fuel from one ship to another. A pressurized system such as that used by the Canadian navy is very fast, whereas a gravity-fed system which is used by some navies' older ships is extremely slow, literally depending on gravity to trickle fuel from the tanker to the combat vessel.

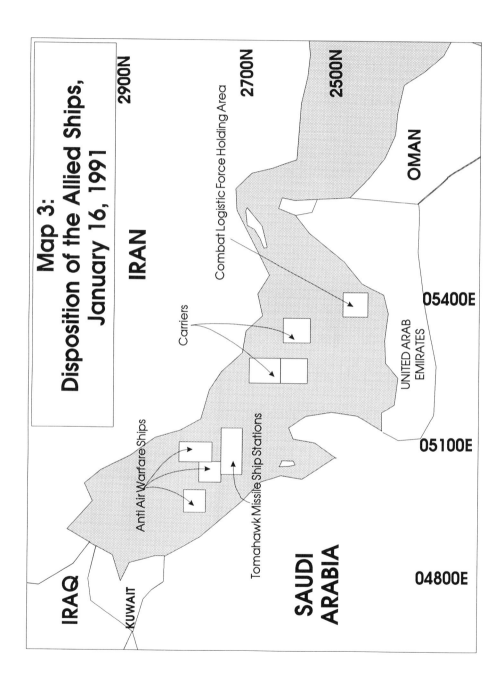

Map 3:
Disposition of the Allied Ships,
January 16, 1991

had been found, what the sea state was, and what special precautions needed to be taken. The destroyer would also take the opportunity to check the destination of any merchant ship. Those going further than Bahrain had to be escorted. Every ship entering the Gulf, including support ships, would check in with the destroyers on picket duty.

> In early February, I sent out the Norwegian and Danish ships to escort one ammunition ship coming in from the Gulf of Oman. They got to the one ship and he called me and said, "We've picked up this one ship, but you should know there's 32 more that have fallen in behind!" I knew the amphibious force was going to be coming up at some stage of the game, and they had their own escorts, and could make their own way. But here they were, these HUGE amphibious carriers, 32 of them, with all their support and troops, and they have fallen in behind the Norwegian, who's saying "I hope you don't want me to look after ALL these vessels!"
>
> I reassured him, "No, no. They're looking after themselves." So they all came in, but the escorts were nervous the whole time.

The amphibious force wanted the CLF's protection but didn't want to interfere with the logistics group's operations. Commander John Pickford of ATHABASKAN recalls that one of his officers displayed a unique brand of diplomacy in handling these ships. In ATHABASKAN's operations room, Lieutenant Rick Glover, "saw these little radar tracks" heading straight towards the Logistics Force box,

> ... and he wasn't having much luck in telling them to go north. I think he got tired of talking to his opposite number so he got on some other line and talked to a three- or four-ring commander and in no uncertain terms told him he'd better get his damned ships out of the CLF area. Then on the radar screen you could see all these radar blips suddenly turn northward!

The amphibious force ended up on the eastern portion of the CLF's operating area where it could stay out of the way.

Captain Coumatos, the Commander of the amphibious squadron, went over to ATHABASKAN, where he met with Miller and discussed the plan for the next few days. Coumatos' squadron was to conduct a special mission off Kuwait and Iraq in preparation for the amphibious assault that was, at that time, expected to happen. In the course of the conversation, Coumatos asked if Miller and his crews were watching CNN, only to be astonished to find out that the Canadians were unable to tune it in. The American then offered "a little gizmo" that the Canadians could fit onto a piece of their electronic warfare equipment—a piece of passive sensing equipment which listens for frequencies in the air and would tell the ships if they were being targetted by an Exocet missile. He explained that there was no threat in the frequency range where the "gizmo" would be attached, so the Task Group would not be hurting its defences in any way. "I've got some spare gizmos, I'll send them over, hook them up to your antenna, and you'll have CNN. We're finding it very handy."

> *So we hooked it up. Initially I thought it was a mistake, because now we've got sailors on watch for five hours at a stretch and then five hours off; and on their five hours off, they'd go down and be glued to CNN. By the time they came back on their seven-hour shift, they'd be starting to get a little tired. Well, they recognized this pretty early on—after the second day, everyone was dragging round, mumbling, "I can't watch CNN anymore, I just can't do it!" So they actually policed themselves in the timing of whether they watched it or not.*

Second Phase

As the air and surface threat diminished, the Americans decided to move their carriers about 80 kilometres further north in the Gulf. The logistics force, however, remained in the southern Gulf, and thus faced a 190 kilometre trek to the carriers' new operating area (see Map 4). When the carriers had been in the central Gulf, it had taken the tankers and escorts only eight to ten hours in total, to get to the carriers, refuel them, and return to the Palace. Now, with the carriers closer to the Iraqi coast, more or less in the northern part of the Gulf, the ships of the CLF were facing a 10-12 hour transit one way. This would place a tremendous strain on the CLF's assets. Then the Squadron Staff came up with the idea of a supply train—several supply ships and their escorts—leaving every six to eight hours, so that they had one going up and one coming back. In this modern-day version of convoys, resupply ships left the logistics area at specific times.

> *A rough rule of thumb we used was that escorts would be 20 hours away from the logistics area. Since I was most familiar with my own ships, I used Canadian assets at either end of the*

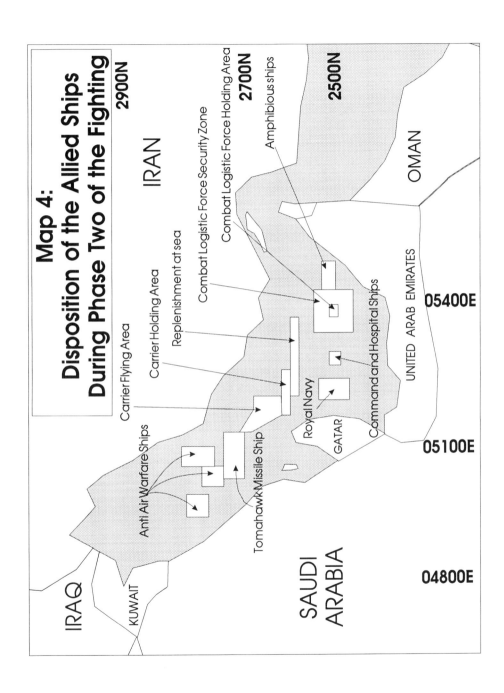

Map 4:
Disposition of the Allied Ships
During Phase Two of the Fighting

2900N

IRAN

Carrier Flying Area

Carrier Holding Area

Replenishment at sea

Combat Logistic Force Security Zone

Combat Logistic Force Holding Area

2700N

Amphibious ships

2500N

OMAN

Anti Air Warfare Ships

Tomahawk Missile Ship

Royal Navy

QATAR

Command and Hospital Ships

UNITED ARAB EMIRATES

05400E

05100E

IRAQ

KUWAIT

SAUDI
ARABIA

04800E

supply line to allow me close control and ensure the supply ships followed specific routes and directions.

This worked well. The train schedule provided a good solution to the additional transit distance the logistics ships had to make to get to the front line strike ships and carriers. Escorts and supply ships were assigned to a particular group going north at 1900 local time, while another group at the carrier line would leave at 2000 local. Those supply ships missing the train would have to wait for the next scheduled departure. Using this method, which was easy to co-ordinate, fewer escorts were required.

Even so, the extra transit distance stretched Miller's escort assets to the limit during this phase of the operation. The problem was exacerbated by the fact that the new northern operating area of the carrier battle groups was beyond the national limits of several of the navies providing escorts to the Combat Logistics Force. Also, as time wore on, more ships needed time in port for maintenance and repair.

Phase Three

Some relief came in mid-February, when the allies decided to move the CLF's home base northward, into the southern part of the carrier operation (see Map 5). PROTECTEUR was then assigned the "outrider" role, in which she picked up in Bahrain all the stores for the escorts working in the central and southern Gulf, the Strait of Hormuz and the northern Gulf of Oman. She then steamed from Bahrain out to the Gulf of Oman, resupplying escorts along the way, before heading back to Bahrain for more supplies. With this additional responsiblity, Miller and his staff were co-ordinating a logistic effort that was 800 kilometres long, an operation they referred to as "The Desert Turnpike" (see Map 6).

With the move north, Rear-Admiral March added to Miller's tasks by telling him, "you're in the middle of us, so you look after all of the escort positioning—who the escorts are going to be to protect the carrier group while you're here. You may as well do that, because then you've got the logistics and you know who's going to be where."

What Rear-Admiral March was asking, made sense. He did not want to have to worry about surface ships when his staff had their hands full co-ordinating the air strikes, with planes flying off four carriers. The tasking order for the air strike co-ordination was about two-inches thick for just one day, and the Admiral's staff had to read it extremely carefully to make sure that a plane took off at the right time. Having four carriers

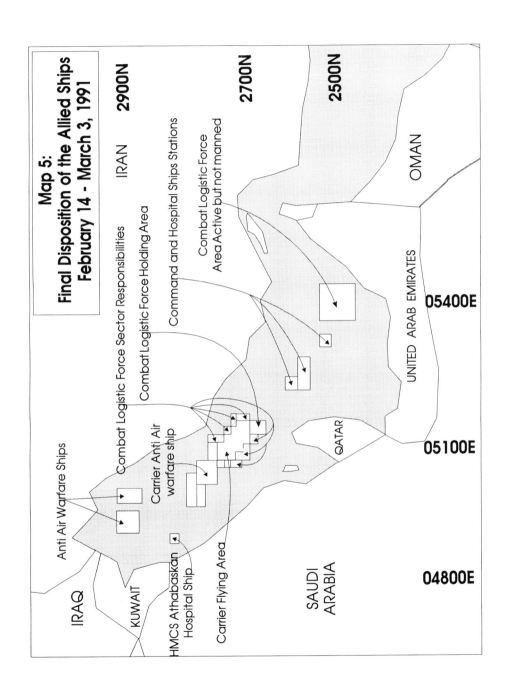

Map 5:
Final Disposition of the Allied Ships
February 14 - March 3, 1991

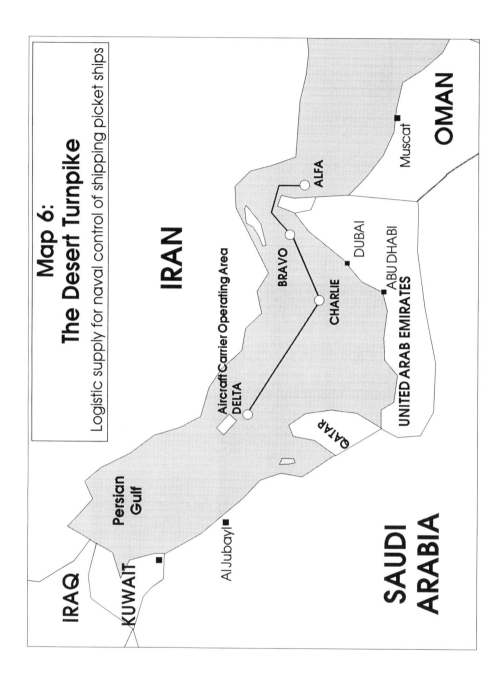

Map 6:
The Desert Turnpike

Logistic supply for naval control of shipping picket ships

operating in the same area took a tremendous co-ordination effort, so March's staff did not want to have to be concerned about the surface side of things.

So Miller's CLF operations expanded to include the patrol of eight sectors around the carriers' southern deployment area. The guard ships in those areas were thus providing de facto protection of the CLF home base, now located next to the carriers. Resupply operations were run by having supply ships steam north through the protected sectors along one edge of the carrier deployment area, and south through the protected sectors along the other edge. With the escorts for both the CLF and the carriers now under his control, Miller became responsible for the co-ordination of approximately 60 ships.

Ironically, at the same time as Miller took on responsibility for a larger number of ships, Nordlund found the number of helicopters available to him drastically reduced. Nordlund explains that, "because the CLF box was that much closer to the actual fighting forces in the northern part of the Gulf, there was not as great a requirement for the escort of the tankers back and forth to the warships. Therefore, these ships, with their helicopters, were now being sent right up north themselves."

Because the Combat Logistics Force was now operating closer to Iraq and Kuwait, the mine threat increased substantially during this phase of the war. Nordlund, therefore, used the available helicopters—which for the most part, were just the five Canadian Sea Kings—almost solely for mine surveillance. Because the best sensor for detecting mines is the "Mark 1 eyeball", he changed their schedule so that the aircraft were operational during daylight hours.

It was because ATHABASKAN carried two helicopters that Miller felt comfortable responding to U.S. Rear-Admiral March's request for a ship to escort a tug to USS PRINCETON which had hit a mine off the coast of Kuwait.[12] The helicopters provided surveillance capability the ship needed to pick its way through the Iraqi minefields. In fact, the specifics of Rear-Admiral March's request—that the escort ship have a helicopter and a good anti-mine capability, and "I'd prefer it to have a Canadian flag flying from the stern"—dictated Miller's decision to send ATHABASKAN.

12. See Chapter 5, pp. 86-87.

ATHABASKAN had had her degaussing system adjusted while in Augusta, Sicily, and she had been fitted with mine avoidance sonars which picked up contact mines at enough of a distance that the ship could manoeuvre out of harm's way. The ship had also practised her damage control techniques[13] extensively in the event of being hit by an influence mine. All this was also true of TERRA NOVA, but what tipped the balance to ATHABASKAN was its helicopter capacity—the Sea Kings had proven invaluable in helping to spot mines and pick out a clear path for the ship.

No sooner had ATHABASKAN returned from escorting PRINCETON and her tug to Bahrain, when, on February 24, she was asked, to go north again to escort the American hospital ship COMFORT from the central Gulf, first to Al Jubayl in Saudi Arabia, and then to the Kuwaiti coast north of Ras Al Khafji. The ground war started at 0400 local time on February 24, and the plan called for the hospital ship to be in position off Kuwait just hours after the fighting started.

The tasking had its memorable moments. Commander John Pickford says, "we were patrolling the vicinity of COMFORT's anchorage. At 2:00 o'clock the Operations Room Officer called to give a normal report of a SCUD launch, when suddenly we had its Link track [the expected trajectory as determined by an airborne warning system] and it was closing in on us. We went to action stations." The adrenalin was really flowing. "I can tell you, when you're lying in your rack at 2:00 in the morning and you go to action stations, with the alarm ringing, you cannot bend over and tie up your shoelaces. It's impossible." Fortunately, the missile was downed by a Patriot missile and the alert cancelled.

While ATHABASKAN was providing protection to COMFORT off the coast of Kuwait, Miller used TERRA NOVA to relay his instructions to the logistics force. He continued the functions of the CLF until March 2, when the ground war ended. Miller officially ceased his UNREP SIERRA duties on March 3 when all logistics requirements reverted to the responsibility of each individual nation.

---

13. To minimize the effect of being hit by a mine all doors and hatches to every deck are closed, all compartment doors are kept shut, and the ventilation system is reduced. With these precautions, if a ship is hit by a mine, only the area of impact would be affected, and the ship would still stay afloat.

Chapter Ten

"You guys need me here!"

Keeping 1,000 sailors happy while under constant threat of attack is impossible. Keeping those same 1,000 sailors from getting fatigued, bored, and depressed is almost achievable. Almost.

The seriousness of the situation in the Gulf, and the knowledge that everyone there was needed, produced a sense of camaraderie and a professionalism that cannot be created in a peacetime exercise. During a normal prolonged peacetime exercise, the navy expects to have to send about 10 per cent of its personnel home for compassionate or training reasons. But during the eight-month deployment in the Arabian Gulf, only a handful of sailors went back to Canada—less than one-half of one per cent of the Task Group—and each was sent for a compelling medical or compassionate reason. Miller credits the low repatriation rate to the two Padres on his staff; they remained in close contact with the ships' companies, and constantly monitored the ships' morale.

> *Also, every crew member was so psyched and so critical to the success of the mission that they had been sent on, and they knew it, right to the ordinary seaman who joined yesterday—everyone was as important as the Captain of the ship, when it came to the survival of that ship, in a tense situation. And they knew that. It was amusing because the Docs, the medical officers that we had in each of the ships, said that they felt like Maytag repairmen because they'd never had such a healthy ship's company. I think that is attributed to the same thing. No one dared to get sick, because we all depended on each other.*

Miller and a Padre interviewed each of the five people that did go back. In one instance, the reason for repatriation was complications arising from the birth of a child, with the possibility that the either the wife or the baby could die. In Halifax, Captain David Morse, Commander of the Fifth Canadian Destroyer Squadron, personally looked into the situation, talking to the family and the doctors. His conclusion was that the sailor should come home. But Miller's interview with his crewman did not go as planned.

> *I said, 'you realize there are things going on at home, and the situation is extremely serious and you really have to go back.' And he told me, "No, she's going to be okay. We've talked, and it's all right. You guys need me here!"*
>
> *I agreed that yes, we did need him, "but your family is forever, and everybody has agreed that your presence is going to help the situation at home, and you really should go. I can't order you to go, but you know what the situation is, and it's serious."*
>
> *He knew that he had to go, but he was really reluctant. He asked me, "What are you going to do? Who's going to take my job here?" I assured him we'd manage and that his supervisor had a couple of other crew members who were prepared to take over. I told him, "I'm comfortable that we can cover off your job if you do go. So it's your decision."[1]*

That reaction—one of heavy responsibility for the rest of the crew members and the success of the navy's mission—was not limited to the one sailor. The other four felt the same way—as did every other member of the ships' crews. They had all been through the same training, right from the beginning in August, and they had grown together as a team; no one wanted to let the others down.

> *When I had a chance to brief the ships' companies on whatever subject, I made it quite clear that we had become a team, and that every member of that team was as important as anybody else. They may have a different job, but they were just as important. That was very important to the engineers who were slugging it out in the boiler room, and the army fellow who was standing there all day, holding the air defence system, and the ordinary seaman who joined just a few weeks before the ships*

---

1. The sailor did go home, but, a month later, once his wife and child were out of danger and more family members had come to the rescue, he flew back to the Arabian Gulf and rejoined ATHABASKAN.

*sailed. That was the key, I think, to the success of each of the
ships—that they recognized we couldn't do without any one
person that was there.*

Everyone wanted to do a good job, to prove that they could be
depended upon, that when the stakes were high, they could come through.
On his last day on board ship before being rotated back to Halifax in
early January, Sea King technician Master Corporal Patrick McCafferty,
after 132 days away from home, wrote in his diary, "We have gone
through good times, bad times and endured a lot of hardships but some
of us do not want to leave." He summed up the feelings of dedication
and accomplishment felt by those in the Task Group:

> During our tour the technicians would routinely work 20,
> 30 or 40 hour shifts to keep the aircraft flying. Rest,
> relaxation and sleep were luxuries we all went without for
> extended periods of time but the dedication to our jobs never
> waivered. I'm not saying that at all times everyone was in a
> good mood or in good spirits but the overall performance
> was truly above what was required or expected. We have
> become a family in a sort of way and are very proud of
> what we have done and the reason for doing it.

Just before Christmas, Lieutenant-Commander Kevin Laing, the
officer who put together the task group's weapons control instructions,
and who sailed from Halifax with Miller, was offered the plum position
of Executive Officer of one of the new patrol frigates—HMCS
VANCOUVER. In order to take the job, he had first to complete a six-
week course on the new ships; unfortunately the course began January
7. Miller wanted Laing to take the job and assured him that because of
the upcoming crew rotations of each of the three ships, they would not
be on continuous patrol for the next three months, so that the Squadron
Staff could make do with one less Watch Officer than the three they
currently needed.

Although the Task Group had left Halifax with only two Squadron
Watch officers, the Staff had been buttressed with the addition of a third
in October. At that point in the deployment, Laing and Lieutenant-
Commander Jim Hayes, who had been taking turns standing watches so
that they never got more than seven hours break at one time, were
beginning to feel the strain. Miller, therefore, had added a third Watch
Officer—Lieutenant-Commander Greg A. Hannah—so that a rotation
schedule could be set up to give each of the three officers some rest.

Hannah, whom Miller had known at the Maritime Warfare Centre, had been working on shore as the operations and communications officer in the logistics detachment. With his background and his recent experience with the Task Group, Hannah was well prepared to replace Laing as Watch Officer. Laing left the Task Group on December 27.

> *I think that was the most difficult thing for anybody—to actually leave while we were in the middle of a mission. The same thing with Captain Doug McClean in PROTECTEUR. I certainly had tears in my eyes, and so did he, when we said good-bye, as he boarded the aircraft and flew off.*

McClean says leaving the Gulf in January "was far and away the worst thing I've ever had to do in my naval career. We had worked so hard and the ship's company was so well trained and motivated, that leaving the Gulf was a heartbreaker. And it was extremely difficult to sell to the ship's company." Calling the leaving "devastating," McClean remembers "there were a lot of tears being shed by 400 people on the day we left the ship—and there were some pretty tough old chiefs there—because we felt like we'd not been allowed to finish the job."

It was especially hard on Miller to lose McClean. They had sailed together previously as navigations officer and operations officer, respectively, in HMCS MARGAREE in the late 1960s. During that time they had developed a good working relationship which easily transferred to the Arabian Gulf operation.

> *Doug McClean and I worked very compatibly—it was almost psychic. When I wanted things to happen a certain way, I'd call him up and he'd say, "you know what we should really do ...." and he'd tell me exactly what I was about to tell him.*

But the small size of the Canadian navy meant that Miller had also served with McClean's replacement, Captain Dennis Cronk. Miller had been Cronk's Executive Officer on board HMCS GATINEAU on the west coast in 1980. So losing McClean was a blow, but he was being replaced with someone else whom Miller knew and trusted—essential conditions for day-to-day dealings in the high tension atmosphere of the Gulf.

Master Seaman Peter Nowlan, Miller's signalman, went home very reluctantly when the crew of PROTECTEUR was relieved by the crew of PRESERVER. Although Nowlan was attached to the squadron staff, he was also part of PROTECTEUR's crew, and as such, had to return to Canada. Nowlan wanted to stay, and Miller wanted him to, but the naval staff had made the decision that they could not be selective; there were too many who wanted to stay, right up to Captain McClean. Also, Nowlan was a member of the squadron staff posted aboard PROTECTEUR, but with war imminent, she was no longer going to be used as an alternate command ship. Therefore, there was no need to keep a staff cadre in her.

> Nowlan actually did make it back to the Gulf—just in time to rejoin ATHABASKAN while it was sitting off the coast of Kuwait in a minefield, escorting a U.S. hospital ship. I remember his shocked reaction. "What are you guys doing here? When I left you were in the Central Gulf! If I'd told my wife this is where I was going to end up, she'd never have let me go!"

The work in the gulf was not glamorous, and after awhile, even with the tension of war, it became tedious. But the officers and crew knew they could never slacken in their diligence. Lieutenant-Commander Jim Hayes, after he became Senior Combat Officer in early January, did not have anyone to relieve him. When he went off duty to get some rest, the messages that he was responsible for reading piled up, awaiting his return. The messages amounted to the thickness of a Toronto phone book by the end of a day, and they had to be read meticulously. It wasn't always obvious what another ship was saying and how it would affect the scheduling that day. Twice his exhaustion overcame him and he allowed himself a couple of extra hours sleep; it took him so long to catch up again that he decided sleeping in wasn't worth the aggravation.

Lieutenant-Commander Paul Maddison had the long midnight to 0700 watch during the six weeks of fighting. For the most part, the work was routine and boring. But he had a morning ritual which provided a vivid reminder of the war going on just to his north, in Kuwait and Iraq: at 0500 hours he would go up to the flight deck and look south to see a line of flashing lights in the sky, moving north. It had taken him a couple of days to realize what those lights were—the American B-52 bombers out of Diego Garcia flying north for their daily bombing run on Iraq. Seeing the aircraft would always make Maddison think about the Iraqi troops on the ground, and wonder how many of them would die that day.

Their work in support of the front-line ships meant the three Canadian ships were needed at sea at all times. Port visits were a thing of the past once the fighting started, except for emergency repairs. By the time the war ended and ATHABASKAN sailed into Dubai, she had been at sea for 49 days without a break. Commander John Pickford says he could have stayed longer if the war had gone on longer— "We were just into it. It was the way of life." He was spending 18-20 hours a day on duty, refreshing himself with an afternoon nap, so that he would be ready for whatever surprises the night might throw at his ship.

From January 2 to March 2, TERRA NOVA was at sea constantly except for a 24-hour port visit to Dubai for mechanical repairs. Commander Stu Andrews remembers the monotony. "Most of your days out there were deadly boring. You'd move around and do a few hailings, but there was nothing else you could do. You could never stand down your guard to entertain yourselves; you could never stand down your guard even to do extensive training."

Still, despite the tension and the tedium, the navy's operation in the Gulf, both before hostilities and after the fighting started, ran relatively smoothly.

Although the three ships in the Gulf were old and often denigrated by the media as being inadequate for the job,[2] those on board were confident that the weapons systems fitted in the aging hulls coupled with the careful deployment decisions made by the squadron staff, would be sufficient to keep them from any undue risk. That assumption, of course, rested on the premise that all weapons systems on board were up and working. That, however, was not always the case.

> For a long time, TERRA NOVA had trouble with her Phalanx weapons system. It was averaging about an 80 per cent on line system, whereas all the others were close to 100 per cent. You'd flick them on, and there was absolutely nothing wrong with them. In eight months I think one of them may have gone down for an hour. Just incredible. So TERRA NOVA's was abnormal. Every time it went down, if TERRA NOVA was in a sector where the threat was higher, she would have to be taken out and put further south until the system was fixed. There's a bit of pride involved there. It started to affect morale.

Finally, Commander Stu Andrews decided he had lost confidence in the system. Consequently, Summers and Miller had no choice but to move TERRA NOVA south off the coast of Qatar. Andrews says, "I don't know if they invented the box [patrol area] for me or what, but they put it in, and it was like at the end of the world. It was just nowhere. It was really discouraging. In my night order book, for the week that we

---

2. See next chapter, "The Second Front—the Media."

were down there, we invented a new name for this thing everyday, like 'the box at the end of the world'."

This was not an acceptable operational situation; a replacement Phalanx had to be fitted. Extensive arrangements were made to fly a new mount to Bahrain, and the new system was fitted in the ship over Christmas.[3] Once it was proven operational, TERRA NOVA resumed her normal patrols in the central Gulf until the fighting started, when she became an escort ship as part of the Combat Logistics Force.

It's the Thought that Counts

As with soldiers and sailors everywhere, keeping morale high over a lengthy deployment depends on regular contact with the people back home. Delivery of the mail was therefore given a high priority.

You could feel the electricity in the air when the mail was due, and I made sure that we had a helicopter ready to go immediately to pick up the sacks. In fact, I was too quick to send the helicopter in to meet the aircraft the first time we had mail arriving.

The problem is there's bags of mail and they all have to be sorted along with the other supplies that came in on the flight. The supply techs had to figure out what went to which ship, and where each ship was, and then get it ready to go.

To have a helicopter sitting on the tarmac, burning fuel while they're unloading the cargo was putting a lot of pressure on them. So I got a call from the commander of the Logistics Detachment. He said, "You know, really doing it fast, it takes us about three hours to get this stuff sorted out. So how about scheduling your aircraft four hours after the arrival?" So that's what we did. And when that helicopter arrived on board, there was no shortage of volunteers to unload it, sort the mail and distribute it. Within ten minutes the letters, care packages, and parcels would be all through the ship, and people would be whistling and cheerful. Then there would be a hush over the whole ship while they all read their mail.

The sailors on watch in the ops room, however, would be tensed up because they wanted to read their mail, but they couldn't. So they devised a routine where they would relieve each other in the jobs that they were doing. They'd take a proper turnover,

---

3. See Chapter 7, pp. 130-132.

they'd keep their eyes down, looking at what was going on, and then someone would relieve them, within the watch on a 10-15 minute basis. So, if you were the standby, you'd read your mail as fast as you could read it, and then whip in to relieve the next fellow. You had to do it that way. Mail meant everything.

The Sea Kings were the key to a succesful mail delivery system. The air crew and technicians who maintained those hardworking machines became quite attached to them. In fact, that attachment was fostered by an idea launched by Lieutenant-Colonel McWha. He suggested that the technicians give each of the five aircraft a nickname prompted by the machine's personality. The first one to be named was aircraft 417. Because of its reliability and the way it always seemed to be hovering around during major operations, it was called "Big Bird" after the famous Sesame Street character who also seems to be constantly hanging around. Master-Corporal Pat "Rat" McCafferty, the resident artist, painted a picture of the character on the side of the Sea King. He designed other appropriate pictures for the other aircraft as they were named. "Hormuz Harry" had a goofy-looking camel, "Chicken Hawk" had an ugly, mean-looking little bird, "Lucky Louie" had a big, grinning, sharp-clawed, well-fanged, fat cat, and "The Persian Pig" was adorned with a silly, clumsy-looking pig.[4]

Special dates were remembered. Even Halloween.

Howard Dill of Windsor, Nova Scotia, who grows the world's biggest pumpkins, and who had just watched the local TV station broadcast a message from a sailor who suggested a pumpkin or two might remind them of home, called the Admiral and said, "Admiral I've got a 350 pound pumpkin here and I want to send it to those guys out in the Gulf." So they crated up this huge pumpkin along with a lot of little pumpkins, trucked them out to a Hercules aircraft, and sent them to Bahrain. I was in PROTECTEUR with Captain Doug McClean at the time the crate arrived. We watched it craned on board and opened by the crew.

The ship's cooks carved a beautiful design on the pumpkin—even carving 'Halloween' into the mouth—and while we were admiring it, the ship's air officer came up to me and said, "You know, sir, what we should do is fly that pumpkin around the Arabian Gulf for Halloween!"

---

4.   Thanks to Lieutenant-Colonel Larry McWha for his descriptions of these characters.

I looked at him and said, "If you think I'm going to authorize a pumpkin flight in the middle of the Arabian Gulf with 90 missile-firing ships out there, you've got to be crazy!"

He looked a little dejected, so I asked him, "Do you have a training flight to do tonight?" that night being Halloween night.

He shook his head, "No, sir, I don't have one scheduled tonight."

Doug McClean kicked him and said, "Of course you've got a training flight!"

The officer, not picking up the hint, continued to protest. "No, I don't." .... Then the penny dropped. "Well, I guess we could always do some crew training."

I said, "Well, if you've got training to do, I'll authorize a training flight for tonight and if you happen to have a 350-pound pumpkin in the rear end of that aircraft with the cargo door open, all lit up, and it flies around, that's okay."

So that's what we did. The pumpkin was put in the back and lit up with chemlights. And I sent more messages about that pumpkin to the ships to make sure it didn't get shot down than I did for just about any other flight we made.

So the Great Pumpkin flew around the ships in the central Gulf on Halloween night, and I got messages from our allies that went mostly like this: "You Canadians are crazy. You were crazy in the First World War, you were crazy in the Second World War, you're still crazy, and don't ever change."

There were other "crazy" moments.

When the media joined us in the Suez Canal, they did interviews with the ships' companies for the express purpose of showing them on local television so that the sailors could send a message back to their families to tell them they were doing okay. One sailor got in front of the camera and said he was okay, he was a little bored, and that he missed things back home like Greco pizza. He hadn't had a pizza as good as Greco for some time. The next thing you know, Greco Pizza was sending out the components of 1400 pizzas—dough, toppings, and cheese— complete with boxes decorated with a picture of a yellow ribbon. So we were able to have Greco pizza night in the middle of the

> *Gulf. You could call down from the bridge for a pizza "all dressed" and the joke was, because it had taken more than 30 minutes to get there—it had taken more like 30 days from Halifax—it was free!*

Other companies supplied beer, magazines, "freezies," board games, and Christmas trees. A steady stream of VIPs from Ottawa and Halifax attended intelligence briefings and met the ships' crews through December. These included Minister of National Defence, Bill McKnight, Associate Defence Minister Mary Collins, Deputy Minister Robert Fowler, Chief of the Defence Staff John de Chastelain, Vice Chief of the Defence Staff Vice-Admiral Chuck Thomas, Commander of Maritime Command Vice-Admiral Robert George, Commander of Maritime Air Group Brigadier-General Barry Bowen, and Liberal Defence Critic Bill Rompkey.

Christmas in the Gulf

On December 12, a group of local Halifax personalities visited the Task Group. General John Cabot Trail entertained the ships' crews, and Marcel Dionne set up the "The First Annual Desert Sand Hockey Tournament" in Bahrain. The crew of ATHABASKAN played against the crew of PROTECTEUR, who had Dionne as a ringer. PROTECTEUR won the game in an overtime shootout. Michael "Wacky" Wheatley, an electronics entrepreneur in Halifax, gave each member of the Task Group a Sony "Walkman," engraved with the sailor's name, for Christmas. On the evening of December 15, ATHABASKAN's flight deck was used to stage a Christmas variety show put on by a Canadian entertainment troop from Toronto whose members included singers Laura Hutton and Suzanne Gratton, ventriloquist-comedian John Patterson, and musician Rod Philips.

Christmas was a difficult time to be so far away from home, but the ships' officers and crews did their best to ease the homesickness, including having a helicopter from ATHABASKAN fly "Santa Claus" around the ships on Christmas morning.

Lieutenant-Commander Greg Romanow managed to arrange for a unique Christmas greeting from the squadron staff. Miller and his officers dressed in Arabic clothing and posed for a photo in front of a Sea King helicopter onboard ATHABASKAN. Romanow sent the photo to a friend from HMCS IROQUOIS in Halifax who arranged for the printing of the photo on the front of a Christmas card. Inside, the message read,

"Season's Greetings from the Arabian Gulf. Wishing you Peace and Prosperity in the Coming Year." The squadron staff were each given a box to send to their friends and families. Things were shaping up not too badly for a Christmas away from home.

But then there was the "ugly incident" of the two Christmas Trees! Commander Pickford, Captain of ATHABASKAN, tells the story.

> There are two artificial Christmas trees used by the wardroom and the Captain's cabin. Miller and I sent the steward down to the storeroom to get our tree. This sailor was actually Miller's steward because the Commodore had taken my steward when he went ashore to the Joint Headquarters. So Miller's steward didn't know which box; he just grabbed a tree and brought it up. Dusty and I spent one really nice night before Christmas, when it was quiet on patrol, decorating the tree with items sent from schools and others back home. A couple of nights later, we went up to a briefing, and when we came back down our tree was gone. IT WAS GONE!! And this little tabletop tree was there instead. So I got hold of the XO [Executive Officer] and said, "I want that tree back."
>
> He said, "Well sir, there's been a problem. The tall tree is supposed to be in the wardroom where we have 40 people, and the little tabletop tree is for the Captain in his cabin."
>
> Well, I didn't know, I hadn't been there before. And we luuuuved that tree. I mean, who cares about the Iraqis; this was important! So I made them bring the tree back up. And they all brought it up, grumbling, and overemphasizing their unhappiness.
>
> Later, we went down to the wardroom for Christmas dinner, but it was kind of hard to say, "Oh, XO, nice Christmas tree" because they had the little table top one with two decorations on it!"

On Christmas Day, Ordinary Seaman Greg King, the youngest crew member in ATHABASKAN—barely 18—became "Captain For the Day."[5] He had lunch with two friends in the Captain's cabin and had several petty officers scrub out the ordinary seamen's living quarters! He

---

5. This is a navy tradition.

also was given a five minute call home to the surprise and delight of his family. Christmas Day dinner was an official meal for the ship's crew in which the officers, including Miller, served in the galley.

Despite these attempts to make the day more festive, however, for most of those aboard ATHABASKAN and PROTECTEUR—two of only about half a dozen allied ships on patrol that day—Christmas, always the hardest time to be away from those you love, was a fairly dismal affair.

To give the crews a break over the holidays and before the allied attack on Iraq began, Miller arranged for the Americans to take over the Canadian patrol sectors so that the Task Group could head into port for some rest and celebration. On New Year's Eve, PROTECTEUR and ATHABASKAN went into port at Dubai (TERRA NOVA was in Bahrain having her Phalanx gun replaced) and the squadron staff took Miller ashore—the only time that the entire staff left the ships—for a Desert Barbeque. The group left the port in Toyota 4x4 land rovers "with kamikaze pilots for drivers," according to Dave Ashley, and headed into the desert. The vehicles bounced up and down sand dunes until they got to one massive one. Ashley's driver said it was "70 at the bush"—the land rover had to be doing 70 km per hour when it reached a particular bush in order to make it up the dune. It took three tries to get to the top.

When the group made it to their oasis destination their hosts dug a hole in the sand into which they placed rocks. On racks laid across the top of the hole, they barbequed chicken and lamb. Ashley and Jimmy Hawkins found a way up a large white dune with sand like pure salt, and they sat at the top with a cardboard carton of wine, howling at the moon. Miller, not realizing that the two Petty Officers had made their way to the top by winding their way up along the side of the dune, tried to join them by running straight up the front. He couldn't do it. For every three steps he took forward, he slid back four. The two Chiefs howled even louder.

Miller had other problems that night—he was almost kicked by a camel. During their hair-raising ride across the dunes, the staff had come across a herd of wild camels. Figuring they could get some great pictures for the folks back home, everyone piled out of their vehicles and began snapping away. People were standing close to the camels while others took their pictures. Miller and his steward, Leading Seaman Gerry Doucet, were getting close to one camel and the photographer kept saying, "a little closer, a little closer." Miller was edging closer when he suddenly noticed Doucet running away. Surprised, Miller looked to see what the sailor was running from—a camera-shy camel who was lashing out with his hind foot at the bothersome Canadians. Miller ran.

Good times finish too soon. The New Year's celebrations in Dubai were only a brief respite in the tensions of patrol—for the next two months, the destroyers stayed at sea.

The terrors of war were driven home to the ships' companies at 2330 on January 16. Just hours before the allied attack on Iraq began, sailors were told to line up outside the sick bays to get a week's supply of nerve agent pre-treatment tablets—pyridostigmine bromide—and atropine injectors. Officers took their place along with the crews, waiting for these necessary medical defenses to the horrific weapons of modern warfare. ATHABASKAN's Commander Pickford remembers, "it was a really eerie sight because we had the red night lighting. The sailors standing there were a sombre group, but they were a very confident group."

The Home Front

Back home, the navy helped set up support systems for the families of the sailors in the Gulf. These were needed for everything from coping with the loneliness and the fear, to helping with everyday concerns such as car breakdowns. The focus of the support groups was the Family Support Centre, a multi-service facility established on most major military bases to respond to family needs. In Halifax, the Centre's activities included Spousal Networks made up of volunteer spouses from each ship, an Operation Friction Newsletter which provided information about programs available for the spouses, and an Emergency Child Care Network in which parents offered their services on an emergency short term basis.

The families at home were under a tremendous strain. While most were used to their loved ones going away to sea, what had always helped them get through those lonely times was the date circled on the calendar indicating when the ships were to return home. For this deployment, most of the families had no such date. The deployment was an indefinite one, and the people left behind could only cope one day at a time. Add to that the risk of injury or death from being in a war zone, and the pressures were tremendous.

Specific problems were met head on. When Paul Koring's article appeared in the *Globe and Mail* detailing the low morale of the ships' crews,[6]

---

6. See the next chapter, "The Second Front—The Media".

Rear-Admiral Dick Waller, Chief of Staff at Maritime Command, held a meeting of all the families and discussed their concerns. The navy believed that the best way to keep its sailors happy and their minds on their jobs was to keep their families informed. When the ships first deployed, Captain Jim King, Deputy Chief of Staff, Readiness, invited the families to a meeting at the community centre in Shannon Park, the married quarters in Halifax, and he talked to them about where the ships were deployed and what they were going to be doing. He also dealt with other concerns such as mail and training course interruption. The questions and answers were recorded and sent out to Canadian Forces Base Esquimalt on the west coast.

One answer that probably wasn't sent west was King's response to a woman who was concerned about her husband's career. She explained to King, "My husband was supposed to go on a course and the course has already started, so clearly he's not going to go on this one and no one has told him what's going to happen. What's the policy?" King was feeling pretty confident about his briefing by this time, so he didn't miss a beat before replying, "Well, there's no doubt in my mind, that when those guys get back, the first thing's that's going to be on their mind is what are they going to do next in the navy?" He remembers looking out at this stunned audience, "and all of these women were looking at me, and I could see them saying, 'you idiot'. I immediately corrected myself, with, 'Sorry ladies. The second thing on their mind.'"

The navy also arranged for a special 800 number which played tapes made by the ships' crews. Every day, the three ships would put together information on what they were doing, and what special occasions were celebrated. There were also personal greetings to family members back home who were celebrating anniversaries, birthdays, or the birth of a child. These written messages were sent back to Halifax where someone read them onto a tape which was then hooked up to the 800 number.[7] There were several phonelines to each of the English and French versions of the tape, and they averaged 300-500 calls a day. A typical day's message tape—for example, October 24, 1990—ran:

> From TERRA NOVA—the Persian Excursion continues.
> Today is the two month anniversary of our departure from
> Halifax, bound for the Gulf, though it seems like only

---

7. It took a few tries to find the right person to read the messages on the tape. Because it was supposed to be a personal look at the navy's day-to-day life in the Gulf, the reader had to be someone who could read the messages with feeling and not like a military order. The families who phoned the 800 number to hear the tapes made no bones about letting the navy know when the message reader was too stilted.

yesterday. Our last day in Manamah was spent shopping and relaxing under hot, sunny skies. Last minute phone calls, letter writing, kept the crew busy as preparations for patrol number three near completion. Happy Birthday Jamie, how does it feel to be a teenager. Old I bet, love Dad.

PROTECTEUR sends—it's now two months since our emotional send-off from Halifax. It's remarkable how a large group of strangers have been accepted and have adapted to navy life with little psychological damage. It should be interesting to see how the army folks cope with life in the field on their return to Canada. Leading Seaman Fex extends Happy Birthday greetings to his wife Shelly. Petty Officer First Class Jan Blinks is celebrating her birthday and sends best regards to her friends in Halifax. Captain Don Feltmate wishes his wife Theresa a Happy Birthday—"You're not getting older, you're getting better."

Dateline ATHABASKAN—News of plans for a crew change in the New Year has the ship busy with talk and plans. There is now light at the end of the tunnel. Details are yet to come but no doubt the phones will be busy on our next port visit. Meanwhile, the off watch hours are taken up with woodworking and deep sea fishing, until the lures were lost. Secret preparations are also underway for Halloween. Lieutenant-Commander Dave Hudock and Lieutenant Bruce Belliveau wish Cathy and Doug Noullett a very happy fourth anniversary and are wondering if the stork has arrived yet.

Finally, Captain Miller, the Task Group Commander, "wishes his star daughter, Amy, a very Happy Fifteenth Birthday. I.O.U. special dinner on return. All my love, Dad."

The navy gave each crew member a 15 minute free phone call from a designated ship's phone for every three weeks away. In addition, the crew members were allowed two five-minute phone calls per week, where operational circumstances permitted. This provided the men and women in the Gulf with a chance to speak with two separate family members, such as a spouse and a parent.

Various businesses back home were also lending moral support to the Gulf effort. Greco Pizza and Farmers Co-Operative Dairy in Halifax both printed yellow ribbons on their food containers. Schools[8] and

8. The list of the names of the schools which sent letters to the sailors in the Gulf is 15 pages long.

individuals across Canada took it upon themselves to boost morale and show appreciation of the sailors' work by writing letters. Miller had about 10 pen pals from all different parts of the country, including a navy veteran from World War II, Jack Pullen. Hearing from a man who had lived through the fears and frustrations of war 45 years before was especially comforting.

The letters were very important to everyone: the mail was a way of keeping in touch with ordinary life back in Canada and of giving crew members a break from the tension of daily life in the Gulf. And everyone, from the ships' captains to the ordinary seaman, took the time to answer the letters they received.[9] In each ship there was a bucket outside Sick Bay containing all the unanswered letters addressed to "A Canadian Sailor in The Gulf" from schools, Scout troops, Lions Clubs, and numerous other organizations. Whenever a sailor finished his watch, he would walk past Sick Bay and pick a letter out of the bucket. In that way, just about every letter sent to the Task Group in the Gulf—and there were thousands—was answered, up until the last few weeks of the deployment when fighting was underway.

It Helps to Have a Sense of Humour

Despite everyone's best efforts, however, there were occasions when something would happen to dampen spirits. Fortunately, a sense of humour—never in short supply—could help save a situation.

After USS PRINCETON hit a mine off the coast of Kuwait and ATHABASKAN escorted the badly damaged ship out of the minefield, the Canadians sent 17 cases of Labatt's beer to help boost the morale of the stricken American ship. Other navies sent their sympathies and words of support to the Captain of PRINCETON who gratefully acknowledged them in a public message to the allies with the words, "Thank you for all the condolences ... but next time send beer like ATHABASKAN!"

Lieutenant-Commander Jim Hayes remembers that at one point during the war, some well-meaning but insensitive official sent a message to ATHABASKAN explaining that due to a shortage of body bags, each bag would have to hold more than one body. Hayes was in the communications room when the message came in. "The communicator, a young Able Seaman from Newfoundland, was just furious. I asked him

---

9. Answering the letters from the Canadian public also gave the crews a chance to do some P.R. work for the navy, which does not have a high profile in Canada except on the east and west coasts.

what was wrong and he spluttered back, 'This damned message. If I'm going to use a body bag, no other damn bastard's going to use the same one!'"

The subject of body bags was on the mind of an Australian officer that Commander Stu Andrews was speaking to in Bahrain. An Australian ship had departed from port, just before TERRA NOVA was about to sail. Andrews was on the jetty talking to an Australian officer from the American flag ship, who said the Australian supply system had sent 300 body bags to this ship with a crew of 300. The crew members were apparently going around asking each other "who puts the last guy in? Or is there a zipper on the inside so that he can do himself up?" Although Andrews and the officer had a good laugh over the black humour of the situation, Andrews realized that it wasn't really a joke that he could share with his crew once he got back on board. He saved it until everyone was safely back in Canada.

That same black humour was evident in a parody on what was happening in the Gulf put together by an ATHABASKAN crew member and published in the ship's routine orders shortly after the war began on January 16:

> There you have it in a nutshell—defiant. After watching a radio on T.V. on CNN of a recording of a speech by Saddam and interpreted by some fellow in Jordan and analyzed from the White House to just about every other house around the world, the predominate word of the day is ... defiant.
>
> So Mad Ass (as General John Cabot Trail reminds us is Saddam spelled backwards; it's not exact but he is a Caper so it's close enough) has decided to continue to smash the face of the Iraqi people into the fist of the coalition's combined might, or so it would seem.
>
> I'm not sure I understand what's going on anymore, not that I did in the first place. There's Iraq (Iron Mike Tyson), Kuwait (Pee Wee Herman), Saudi Arabia (not quite sure), oil, land rights, Palestine, Israel, West Bank, historic sites, temples, missiles, and a whole cast of crazy people. Let's bring this closer to home and see if we can't figure this one out. Imagine if you can ....
>
> It all started in the early days of August, the unthinkable happened, Nova Scotia invaded the little potato rich Prince Edward Island, who was planning on building a bridge link

with the mainland. Ontario was quick to condemn the action (Ontario depends heavily on P.E.I. for its spuds), and quickly gained support for its condemnation from British Columbia, Alberta, Saskatchewan, Manitoba, and New Brunswick. Newfoundland and Quebec had their own unique problems and did not want to get involved. The Territories just didn't give a shit about some southern squabble.

The Ontario-led coalition (which we will refer to as Canada), was swift in its action and quickly had all federal aid to Nova Scotia cut in a hope of forcing her out of P.E.I. by economic means. Nova Scotia was defiant, determined the will of her people could overcome the sanctions (plus she was sneaking a bit of stuff in from Maine, U.S.A.).

Canada became more impatient saying "Get out of P.E.I. you dirty rotton blue nosers or else we will kick you out." Nova Scotia's answer was "Go bark up a tree you non-fishing inlanders."

Canada became intolerant of the situation and after five months of giving the federal aid cuts a chance, they started an offensive bombing war against Nova Scotia.

Now when someone starts dropping massive quantities of bombs on your head, you got to stand back and say to yourself, "Hey, these guys are serious." That's what Nova Scotia did. She tried to draw the attention of the world away from the fact that she had invaded P.E.I. and tried to gain an ally in the process. Nova Scotia said she would withdraw from P.E.I. if Canada let Quebec separate from Canada and become the distinct society she wanted to be. Canada said, "No deal, you fish-eating maritimers." Quebec said "Ne m'amene pas dans ta guerre." Nova Scotia was unsuccessful on both counts. Nova Scotia then said "You better stop bombing the proud people of Nova Scotia or else we are going to start firing our large, slow, and highly inaccurate missiles at Newfoundland." (Nova Scotia blamed the Newfoundlanders for killing Meech Lake. Another feeble attempt to link Quebec's distinct society clause with the war.)

"Canada continued to bomb Nova Scotia, and true to her word, Nova Scotia started firing her Haddock, Cod, and

Flounder missiles at Newfoundland. The first missiles landed in the capital of St. John's, destroying an outhouse and killing Uncle Joe's favourite cow. Newfoundland, not being one to take a kick in the teeth laying down, said "Byes yer in fer it now." Only after intense negotiating by Canada, did Newfoundland agree not to attack with her massive trawler fleet, but she reserved the right to fish in Nova Scotia waters at a later date, and if she continued to be attacked could not promise that she would not retaliate.

"After a month and many tons of ordnance being dropped on Nova Scotia, she decided to save some of her assets from destruction and started sending the newer ships in her trawler fleet to Maine, U.S.A. (remember George's Bank?, go figure). Maine promised to impound these vessels until after the whole mess is sorted out. Canada accepted Maine's statement, but still remained cautious (you can't trust those Americans any farther than you can throw them).

"So as it stands now, Nova Scotia is still in P.E.I. and determined to stay there. Canada is still pounding Nova Scotia from the air and occasionally sneaking commando teams in by the well established and secret "Sri Lanka" route. All this sounds silly? It's amazing how something so serious can sound so silly, ain't it? Where will it all end? You can bet your last looney that Nova Scotia will leave P.E.I., but the big question is when it's all said and done, and the final tally is in, will all this have been worth it? Nobody has a crystal ball, I guess we'll just have to leave that one for the history books. This world we live in can be pretty screwed up at times, don't you think?"

Keeping up the morale of 1000 people under threat of attack, thousands of miles away from home, doing an unglamorous but essential job, was no easy task. It took discipline, hard work, and leadership.

The navy, and in fact the whole Armed Forces, had trained their people well. They knew their jobs, they knew how to work hard and play hard. The ones in the Gulf were only a small fraction of the incredible team which was a part of a war for the first time since Korea 40 years ago. Everyone, from our contingents in Bahrain, Qatar and Saudi Arabia, to our

Admirals in Halifax, Esquimalt, Ottawa and Norfolk, to the loadmasters in Air Transport Group, were working 20 hour days in a focused effort to suport the front line folks.

The City of St. John's acknowledged this effort when it hoisted a huge banner for their returning sons and daughters, which read "Thanks for bringing them all back home alive."

We didn't lose a single person—a remarkable feat when one considers friendly fire alone could have spoiled the day. It was ingenuity and plain old Canadian pioneering spirit which contributed to this miraculous result—nothwithstanding an enemy totally overwhelmed by a high tech allied fist.

Chapter Eleven

The Second Front—The Media

One of the sailors returned to my squadron staff after having spent a month back in Canada as a result of having been caught up in the rotation of PROTECTEUR's crew in January. He flew to Bahrain aboard the regularly scheduled Hercules aircraft flight from Halifax. (The Air Transport Group crews who flew those planes became one of the many groups of unsung heroes to the successful Canadian military operations in the Gulf War.)

He was picked up by one of the Sea King helicopters sent from the ship to retrieve all those spare parts, mail and people critical to our survival. This occurred on February 25, 1991, as HMCS ATHABASKAN, having transited through two sea minefields and circumnavigated Hussein's oil slick, sat off the coast of Kuwait providing escort protection to the U.S. Hospital Ship COMFORT. The air was filled with acrid black smoke coming from the destroyed oil tanks along the Kuwaiti coast. The sailor's first reaction was, "Where in the world are you?" His second reaction was, "Nobody in Canada knows you're where you are. If I'd known where you were I might have thought twice about coming back. There's nothing in the newspapers that say's you're off Kuwait—everyone back home thinks you're safe and happy in the southern Gulf outside all the action. Holy Smokes!!"

That the Canadian public was generally unaware of the vital role the navy was playing in the Gulf was in large part due to the nature of naval warfare. Ships fight wars at sea, away from the inquisitive eyes and ears of a reporter. Although there was space provided in the ships for visiting members of the press, it was limited—PROTECTEUR had four bunks specifically for the media; the other two ships occasionally were able to free up a bunk or two—and getting to the ships was difficult. Whereas before the fighting started, ships were making regular port visits, after January 16, the ships remained at sea except for emergencies, and a reporter had to wait for space to be available on one of the helicopters' supply flights to get either on or off a ship.

Thus, the Canadian media, kept out of the war zone press pools organized by the allies, tended to concentrate on the activities of the very visible CF-18s in Qatar. At one point there were 30 reporters at the CF-18 base covering 36 pilots.[1] The navy never had that kind of overcoverage problem.

On the whole, the navy maintained a good relationship with the press people who covered the Canadian ships in the Gulf. Before the Task Group left Halifax, Public Affairs Officer Lieutenant Jeff Agnew[2] put together a communications plan to keep the families and the general public informed of the navy's activities. The plan, which emphasized "candor and openness," attempted to balance two objectives: keeping the pressure off the ships' companies so that they could get on with their job, while providing as much information as possible to the media. Agnew's five-part plan provided for media access during the ships' preparations, their departure and en route phase, the deployment in the Arabian Gulf, the deployment of relief crews, and the return to Halifax.

Agnew's office was kept hopping throughout the eight-month mission. (In one busy day in August, he and his staff answered 242 queries from the press.) Prior to departure, they arranged for interviews with sailors from specific towns in Canada, for briefings by various officers, and for the attendance by over 200 journalists at the departure ceremonies. After the ships left, the Public Affairs Office helped maintain national support for the mission by keeping journalists apprised of the Task Group's activities and by arranging for quick delivery of the various packages from communities and businesses (including the 350 pound pumpkin).

The initial coverage of the navy's deployment generally was either supportive or skeptical. Watching the activity down on the docks everyday, many reporters concentrated on the dedication of the civilian and military workers involved in the refitting of the ships. The local media from different communities conducted interviews with "hometown boys" and their families, and the general tone was one of appreciation and support.

---

1. Christoper Young, "The Role of the Media in International Conflict," *Working Paper 38*, A report on a two-day seminar held in Ottawa 12-13 September 1992 (Canadian Institute for Inernational Peace and Security: December 1991), p. 7.
2. Agnew was promoted to Lieutenant-Commander as of September 1, 1990.

Others, however, stepping back from the excitement and the stories of individual achievement, focused not on the dockyard activity of readying three ships for war, but on the age of the ships and their perceived inadequacies. Columnists and reporters reminded their audience of the delays in the Canadian Patrol Frigate and Tribal class destroyer update programs which had resulted in the navy having to send a 31-year-old frigate (TERRA NOVA) to a war zone.[3] Politicians were criticized for their past neglect of the navy and their willingness to put Canadian sailors at risk in "outdated, outmoded ships that are sitting ducks for modern weaponry."[4]

At the same time as the ships were being readied for the Gulf deployment, the national media was preoccupied with the "Oka crisis" in which native Canadians in Kahnewake and Kanesatake had blockaded roads and challenged authorities in pursuit of their land claims. The army had been called in to help the provincial authorities, and reporters from the larger newspaper chains were covering the conflict in detail. Consequently, there were fewer resources available for the naval activities in Halifax. National editors were more inclined to view the army's actions in Quebec and the navy's preparations for the Arabian Gulf as evidence of a defence policy in disarray. The story was not that the army and navy were doing the best with what they had; rather, it was that the government was responding in an ad hoc way to individual crises, without benefit of a comprehensive post-Cold War defence policy.

Paul Mooney, a Canadian Press reporter who has covered the military for many years, made sure that his stories did not cast aspersions on the dedication and quality of the people in the navy, but laid the blame for any inadequacies squarely on the shoulders of the politicians. Mooney joined the Task Group at Gibraltar and stayed with the ships for several weeks. One of his early stories took a critical look at the Task Group's deficiencies, including the unorthodox use of a supply ship for patrols, an antiquated anti-air system, and an overtaxed air transport system.[5] But throughout the article, Mooney left no doubt who he blamed for the problems. He quoted one officer as saying, "It's the baling-wire and bubblegum scenario. The government sends us and we do the best we can with what we have." An analyst is quoted as saying, "they had to go

---

3. Jeffrey Simpson, "The ships Canada might have had, but for delays and cost overruns," in *The Globe and Mail*, August 21, 1990, p. A16.
4. Catherine Ford in *The Calgary Herald,* August 25, 1990. Also see, Marjorie Nichols in *The Ottawa Citizen*, August 25, 1990, p. 3.
5. "Navy fit for Museum" by Paul Mooney, in *The Ottawa Citizen,* October 17, 1990, p. A3.

with what they had." And in case the reader missed the point, Mooney bluntly stated, "this operation has brought into sharp focus the continual neglect of the Forces by successive Canadian governments."

At the same time as Mooney joined the ships in Gibraltar, Lieutenant-Commander Ian Thompson came aboard as the Senior Staff Officer, Public Affairs, for the Task Group Commander, Commodore Ken Summers. When Summers moved ashore as the Joint Commander, Thompson moved with him to Bahrain where he continued to act as the point man for reporters wanting interviews or to travel with the ships during their embargo enforcement patrols.

Miller met individually with every reporter assigned to the Task Group, at the beginning of his or her assignment. During that meeting, Miller explained the military situation and he outlined the navy's rules. There was really only one: material being sent via the ships' communications systems would be reviewed for operational security concerns. Thompson says the reporters "could write about anything they wished to and in the manner they wished ... there was no censorship because we don't have a law of censorship in this country. But we asked them to sign an agreement that if they wanted to use our transmission facilities, then they must clear for operational security." This included such information as what times the ships were on station, their specific geographic position, what date ships were leaving their patrol areas, and their times of arrival in port. In other words, the media would not be allowed to provide Iraq with any kind of information that could help it in the war and would put the lives of Canadians at risk. "For me," says Mooney "it was pure common sense that you did not mention the time of arrival at a port, for example" because of a possible terrorist attack. "I never put that in my copy. ... As someone who has covered a lot of military affairs, you don't do anything that's going to put your own people at risk."

One officer on the squadron staff—Lieutenant-Commander Greg Romanow before his transfer to USS MIDWAY in early January—was assigned the responsibility of reading all the media reports before they were sent. Any security problems were relayed to Miller, who then sat down with the reporter and asked him or her to find another way of saying the same thing. That meant getting rid of the specifics and using general terms to describe the event. For example, instead of saying "HMS Battleaxe intercepted an Indian freighter at 27.1 degrees north latitude 51.00 degrees east longitude," it would have to be reworded to say "a

British ship, working in the central Arabian Gulf, intercepted an Indian freighter." If, however, the reporter could prove that the information had already appeared elsewhere, the story was left alone.

Paul Koring of the *Globe and Mail* says he was asked to delete the name of a British ship from his story about an interception of an Indian freighter full of refugees. He refused—"I made no changes at their request"—and he says he was still allowed to use the satellite link. Koring says "the deal I made at the beginning was, 'look, if you object to it, I'm not sending it. I'm not having you censor it. If you raise an objection which you think is factual or involves national security, I'll consider it. But if I don't want to change it you don't have to let me send it.'" Overall, however, Koring found the navy to be "very accommodating."

If they were not using the navy's communications system to send their stories, then the reporters were left to their own consciences as to what they could report—and if their consciences weren't geared up for wartime reporting, there was always a public affairs officer ready to jump start them. One evening, up on the bridge, Rob Gordon of CBC Halifax, overheard a conversation regarding a secret exercise. Gordon says when the officers realized they had a journalist in their midst, they were shocked. He left the Task Group the next day, as scheduled, and discussed the story with his editor. While the decision on what to do with the information was still up in the air, a military public affairs official called Gordon and strongly suggested that he not report the story. He didn't, noting that there were various production reasons for that but also that the navy's concern played a role in the decision. He says, "You had to take it into account, because if you didn't play ball with them, you weren't going to get out to a ship the next day, or suddenly it would be very difficult to interview somebody. They had all the cards."

Gordon's situation was somewhat unusual, in that most of the information which the navy would not want published was time-sensitive. Therefore, if the reporter waited until leaving the ship so that he or she could avoid the navy's restrictions, enough time would have elapsed that the event would already have occurred and the information about it would no longer be secret.

Dealing with what the press wrote was one thing, dealing with how they went about collecting their stories was another.

After the American amphibious force entered the Gulf in February and lined up next to the Pachyderm Palace while waiting for their call to action, the Combat Logistics Force added protection of the marines to its list of duties. That involved warning away small craft and airplanes that could carry people armed with anti-ship missiles. Also, the allies did not want anyone taking pictures of the American force.

Major Pete Nordlund says there were several small civilian aircraft carrying two or three reporters that had to be warned away from the Logistics Force. The aircraft and their passengers "had no due regard to air safety—they would not tell anybody they were coming, and they wouldn't talk to anybody." The reporters might not have been so brazen if they had realized that the ships' crews, sensors and weapons systems were responding to the small aircraft as if they were those of the enemy.

For those reporters who took to the sea instead of the sky in search of stories, there was a wealth of material. Most of the journalists who visited the Canadian ships stayed aboard for anywhere between 5 days and three weeks. During that time, they had access to briefings on the general situation, as well as to observation of tactical operations, the equipment—some of it in use with the Canadian navy for the first time—and to interviews with the crew members, including the 34 women who were in a combat vessel in a war zone for the first time in Canadian history. Reporters were given the freedom to roam around as they pleased and talk to whomever they wanted,[6] as long as they didn't interfere with the ship's operations. Such extraordinary access and limited competition for stories, served as a sharp contrast to the media who were covering the ground action. They were being tightly controlled, with their main means of obtaining information limited to media "pools" and official briefings.

Of the reporters who sailed with the Canadian Task Group, only one filed a story that was perceived to be so patently unfair that it caused an uproar—both in the Gulf and at home. It happened just after the Task Group arrived in the Gulf.

> *I guess it was about 1:00 in the morning when Greg Romanow said, "I think you'd better read this article. There aren't any security implications, but there is definitely a morale implication." I read it, and agreed with Greg. I couldn't imagine the sailors saying some of the things that were quoted in the article.*

What had Miller and Romanow so concerned was an article by Paul Koring of the *Globe and Mail* which dealt with the ships' morale. Koring had just spent five days aboard ATHABASKAN, observing the operations and talking with the crew members. The story he wanted to file, began,

---

6. A military escort was required to accompany a reporter into the operations room.

"I didn't join the navy to get into a war," the steward said. That lament is echoed often among Canadian sailors, especially younger ones on the lower decks ....

It went downhill from there. Koring focused on the crew's fears, frustrations, boredom, and desire to go home. He quoted crew members who were worried about the change in deployment area ("Now we are in the [missile-range] circles and I think they have been lying to us all along") and who resented the supply ship PROTECTEUR being in port noting that her crew members "are going to get an extra $4-a-day pay while we take the risks and float around here." He reported that one sailor was so scared he was sent back to Canada and another was sent home for being drunk and assaulting a superior officer. He added, however, that "a number of requests for compassionate leave that usually would warrant repatriation have been denied."[7]

Miller remembers asking Koring to make some changes before filing his story.

I had Paul Koring come in, and we talked about it, and I said, "That's not true." He conceded that he had picked up on some rumours and had emphasized some negative aspects of his observations.

I said, "Well, that's not fair. The story's not a security problem, but it's a morale problem. You're going to affect the morale of the families back home and you're going to affect our morale, and it's not true, and you know it's not true. I can't tell you to take it out and change it, but if I were you, I'd take it out and change it."[8]

So at 1:00 a.m., knowing that this was going to be published, I sat down and went through his article point-by-point. I dragged in those people that he interviewed, and each of them denied saying what Koring had quoted them as saying. The Doc, especially, was going beserk because he was quoted as saying "There have been some very suspicious accidents just as we came to Bahrain."[9] So I wrote down a 3-4 page message to the Maritime Commander, Vice-Admiral George, and I called his Chief of

---

7. *The Globe and Mail,* October 5, 1990, p. A1.
8. Koring says he was never asked to change his article.
9. The implication being that some crew members were trying to get sent home for medical reasons. This was untrue. One crew member did have to be sent home because he had had abdominal surgery before he left and he developed problems en route.

*Staff, Rear-Admiral Waller. I told him the article was coming
out and it would say that morale is bad. I assured him that was
not the case.*

*The article made crew members a little warier of the press. No
one was naive enough to think that all the articles written about
us were going to be positive and glowing, but we did expect
them to be objective. And this was not an objective article.*[10]

Where Koring had gone wrong, was in not understanding the naval
psyche: sailors bitch and moan just as part of their existence. As Master
Seaman J.B. Eldershaw wrote, in a letter to the Editor of the *Globe and Mail*,

I am currently serving on board HMCS ATHABASKAN
in the Persian Gulf. I am writing in response to an article by
Paul Koring, Fear of War Shadows Canadian Sailors (Oct. 5).

The article leaves one with a false view of what's actually
happening. It is my opinion that Mr. Koring only reported
on a very small number of individuals.

Everyone involved with this deployment should be a little
scared and of course we all would like to know when we
will be home. I'm sure the majority believe in our task and
are doing their very best.

.... Let me make this very clear; our morale is very high. In
fact, I have never seen it higher and I've served aboard
ATHABASKAN for the past four years.

Sitting around and waiting is always boring and this gives us
a lot of time to think of things to complain about. The
expression that a sailor is not happy unless he is complaining
was coined for a very good reason. ...[11]

When Rob Gordon visited the Task Group in mid-November he found
the same complaints among the crew members that Koring had
witnessed—they were not getting enough shore time, they should be given

---

10. Koring did not file his story until the end of his stay on board ATHABASKAN, so that he was
safely on land by the time his article appeared in print. Later, Koring wanted to attend an onboard
cocktail party, to which he was specifically not invited. Summers refused Koring admission to
the party, "for your own safety." The ship's crew was so angry at what Koring had written about
them, he probably would have risked a physical assault had he boarded the Canadian ship. See,
"Globe reporter barred from Qatari gathering" by Paul Koring, in *The Globe and Mail*, October
31, 1990, p. A12.
11. *The Globe and Mail*, October 15, 1990, p. A18.

war pay, and they should have been told they would be working in the Central Gulf. But Gordon has covered the navy for more than a decade and he knows that sailors complain. As he put it, "sailors complain a lot, especially about officers and conditions. I heard lots of complaints, some of them more strident perhaps than you would get if they were on exercise off Bermuda, but nothing really outrageous."

The ships' companies were told to be very careful about speaking to the press in future and according to Gordon, "they were very, very nervous about what I was going to report on, who I talked to." In particular, ATHABASKAN's officers and crew were wary of the reporter who came aboard immediately after Koring's departure. That was Martin Seemungal of the CBC. He was in trouble with the Bahraini authorities and was being thrown out of the country. The navy took him, via Sea King helicopter, out to the Task Group.

> *We wondered about him right away because when he was trying to get into Bahrain, he got a little obstreperous with the authorities. This was hot on the heels of Paul Koring, and we thought, 'oh boy, here we go again.' The guy's not going to be sympathetic to our cause; if he's dealing with foreign authorities that way, how's he going to deal with us?*

> *We arranged for him to come directly to the ship, so that he would be on Canadian territory and his papers would be valid. When it was time for him to leave, we dropped him off in another country to avoid any further problems with Bahrain.*

> *As it turned out, he was very good; he was objective and told his viewers what was happening. And he did everything himself— camerawork, interviews, reports, and production.*

Rob Gordon says Seemungal's problem arose during a visit with a representative of the Bahraini Ministry of Information which controlled media access to the country. Gordon had been warned beforehand to expect to spend up to two days with this official, talking to him about Bahrain, and what a delight it was to visit. Gordon did so, and after making the appropriate comments and responses to the official's questions, was given permission to proceed with his work. Seemungal, however, was not so patient. He put up with the tea-drinking propaganda sessions for only about an hour, at which point he protested the process in very strong terms. The Bahrainis told him to leave the country immediately. Luckily for Seemungal, ATHABASKAN was ready to take him aboard.

The navy, in fact, went to tremendous lengths to help some reporters. Ian MacLeod from the *Ottawa Citizen* was aboard ATHABASKAN over Christmas. His editors had impressed upon him that no matter what, he was to file a story about Christmas aboard the ship for publication in the December 26 issue of the newspaper. "I had trouble filing that story," MacLeod remembers.

> My computer and their computer and phone lines, for some reason were not compatible. So they tried to get a satellite link so that I could file my story by voice instead of modem. But they couldn't get the satellite link locked in, the ship was moving too much. I was getting pretty desperate. So [Lieutenant-Commander] Greg Romanow ordered the bridge to basically steer a straight course, even if that meant they would go outside their patrol zone, so we could maintain the satellite link long enough for me to call in the story. So they broke their patrol pattern, and as I understand it, the captain of the ship, Commander John Pickford, came down and rather calmly, but a little anxiously, asked what the hell was going on? The Americans had even phoned over and said, "Hey Canada, what's going on? You're out of your patrol area." Anyway, I got the story dictated in short order, and they resumed their normal patrol pattern.

From September through December, the Task Group hosted at least 60 reporters and technicians. Thompson says he was "generally very happy with the kind of coverage we were getting. It was very balanced and detailed enough. The bottom line was that the navy was doing a good job and that was what was being reported." In fact, the reporting was so positive, that in those first few months, some of the reporters "were getting hassles from their [editors] because they weren't putting out any negative stories."

Unfortunately, interest in the ships' activities peaked too early. During the first few months, print, television and radio reporters all took their turns sailing with the Task Group, detailing life on board, the functioning of the new equipment, and the operational mission. But there was a problem with extended coverage. Agnew says, "Once a member of the media got aboard a ship and determined that you were going out, drilling holes in the ocean, and no one was shooting at you, and they'd seen a couple of replenishments at sea, nobody wanted to go back again." Having seen it once, they could then easily keep abreast of the naval situation by checking with a Public Affairs officer, leaving them free to cover the action on the ground and in the air. After all, a reporter on board ship was a reporter away from more exciting land and air activity for several days to a week or more.

After the fighting started in January, coverage of the Canadian Task Group's activities in the Arabian Gulf dropped off substantially. Consequently, many people still do not know just what the Canadian ships did during the hostilities. The major command assigned to Canada's Miller—that of Combat Logistics Co-ordinator—was not perceived to be important: after all, the ships were not on the front lines, they were not attacking Iraq, and no Canadians were killed. That added up to "no story here."

That was the case with Canada's national newspaper, according to reporter Paul Koring. He says,

> "We, the *Globe and Mail*, chose not to cover the Canadians deliberately. I was a strong advocate of that, and my advocacy of it was based on two things. One, we only had four or five people to deploy, and I thought the Canadians were relatively irrelevant from a military standpoint. And two, I suspected that, given the press regime they had set up in the wake of early stories, including mine, that they would be draconian and unhelpful."

Southam columnist Christopher Young pointed out in his summary of a two-day seminar on the role of the media in war, Canada's armed forces do not perform the glamorous roles that the media rush to cover:

> Canada has a small army performing good, useful work in defusing dangerous situations. Our soldiers are helping *to prevent* simmering sources of conflict from boiling over into front-page headlines—the kind that send anchormen in shirts with epaulettes scurrying to distant corners of the globe."[12]

Young was talking about the army but his observation applies equally to the navy. Standing off a coast making sure that sanctions were observed and supplies were delivered, as Canada's navy did during the Arabian Gulf War, did not compare to the excitement of a U.S. battleship firing

---

12. Young, p. 27. Emphasis added.

Tomahawk missiles and a carrier launching attack aircraft at an enemy's military installations. No, it just wasn't as exciting. But it was just as important, and those on the front lines knew it.

On March 7, after the war had ended, Rear-Admiral Dan P. March, Commander of the Joint Battle Force, sent the following message to Miller:

> "Dusty, the job you performed as the trail boss of The Ponderosa, as we affectionately called the Logistic Force station, was nothing short of magnificent. Your Force took on a job not considered very glamorous but one as important as any in the Battle Force. The protection and escort of these valuable assets was a job that had to be done and done right. Without the assurance that supplies would be delivered where and when they were needed our mission would have been impossible to complete. Your Force rode shotgun over the herd with a tenacity and zeal that were a pleasure to observe. You can take great pride in the vital role you played in the overall operation, and the entire Battle Force and I are grateful you performed it so well. I'd sail the trail with you anytime. Fair winds and following seas, Dan."

CHAPTER TWELVE

"The day the war ended—we think!"

When the ceasefire was called on February 28, ATHABASKAN had been at sea for 45 days with no break. War's end, however, brought no immediate relief. The ship was in a minefield off the coast of Kuwait escorting the hospital ship COMFORT to an anchorage near Raz Al Khafji. With the smoke from the burning oil wells engulfing the ship, a lightning storm raging, black rain pouring down, and the immediate danger of being blasted by a mine, the crew felt they were in hell. The irony of it was they had just been released from the purgatory of war. It's no wonder that on February 28, Miller's diary entry ambiguously states "The day the war ended—we think!"

It took the ship about 18 hours to get out of the treacherous minefield to an area where the crew could relax a little. The hatches were opened and fresh air blew through the ship, giving the crew members their first breath of outside air in several days. The ship remained in some danger, however, until it could get south of Qatar because of the large number of floating mines, so for ATHABASKAN's two Sea Kings, there was no let-up in operations until the ship sailed into port at Dubai on March 3.

TERRA NOVA and PROTECTEUR had also headed for Dubai when war's end was announced. It was the first time all three ships had been together for months.

> It's a tradition in the navy that if you've gone through an arduous time, that "splice the mainbrace" can be ordered. The name stems from the time of sail, and refers to a cutting in two—you get double the advantage and therefore you get a double tot. But only the Queen, the Chief of the Defence Staff and the Governor General can order a "splice the mainbrace."

Commanders like myself instead have the authority to provide a tot called "Up Spirits"—order a free tot of rum to each person in every ship's company. So I did this in Dubai, to signify the end of the war.

The tradition of issuing a daily rum tot no longer exists but we still issue a tot at the end of special or significant duty. It was a great day and experience to see all 1,000 armed forces personnel on board the ships gathered on the upper decks in the hot blazing sun in great humour, chuckling and celebrating the end of a job well done. At 1100, each sailor was served 2-1/2 ounces of overproof rum, which he or she drank neat or mixed with water or coke in front of the officer serving the drink. (The tot is drank this way so the liquor cannot be saved up for drinking at a later date.) The ships carry the rum on board in case an officer orders a tot, but when I ordered it for the three ships, there was an initial scramble to make sure there was enough for everyone on board. A supply officer would be in deep trouble if he didn't have enough rum to serve the ship's company at least one tot.

Four days later, after the ships' crews had enjoyed a well-earned port visit, the Minister of National Defence, Mr. Bill McKnight, and the Chief of the Defence Staff, General John de Chastelain, arrived on board ATHABASKAN and announced that the three ships would be departing Dubai on March 12, with a scheduled arrival in Halifax on April 6 or 7. The news was greeted with cheers and excitement, and the sailors kept the phone lines busy calling home with the news.

Two weeks previously, on February 24, HURON had left Halifax en route to the Gulf to relieve ATHABASKAN to continue enforcing the sanctions against Iraq. She was to arrive in Bahrain in late April after a journey which included a stopover in the Mediterranean to conduct readiness trials and training off Gibraltar. She stayed on station until the end of June, returning home to Esquimalt, B.C. in early August.[1]

On March 9 the command of the Task Group passed from Miller to Captain Cronk, the commanding officer of PROTECTEUR, who would be in charge of the three ships for their homeward journey. The next day, the Squadron Staff, who had been at sea for 60 days straight, flew home. Moving the Staff out before the ships return home after an extended deployment or exercise is normal practice in the navy, because playing

---

1. Department of National Defence, *News Release*, June 7/91, AFN: 26/91.

host to a Task Group Commander and his staff puts a tremendous strain on a ship's company. Everyone has to be on their best behaviour, giving their top performance, and they don't get a chance to relax. So after a major exercise or operation, the Squadron Staff usually flies back to base ahead of the ship.

Some officers in Halifax and Ottawa had thought it might be best for Miller to stay with the Task Group, but Summers and Miller successfully fought that suggestion. Actually, they fought for a while and then just ignored the messages from Canada. Summers personally drove Miller to the airport for the flight home on board a Canadian Forces Boeing 707. Summers stayed behind for another month to close the headquarters in Bahrain.

ATHABASKAN, TERRA NOVA and PROTECTEUR undertook the month-long transit at a relatively relaxed pace with no planned exercise routines, although there was a limited amount of training. The ships reached Gibraltar on March 27, while HURON was still in port there, and ATHABASKAN transferred to her various pieces of equipment and unused ammunition. The government sent Canadian customs officials to Gibraltar so that the ships' companies could go through that process prior to arriving in Halifax. After the ships' companies cleared customs, the Task Group continued its journey, arriving in Halifax on April 7 to the sound of bands and cheers. It was sweet music to the homesick sailors' ears. Waving flags, balloons, and yellow ribbons, families, friends, and supporters waited on the dock to greet their returning heroes. In amongst the hoopla was a battery of civic and military VIPs—including Governor General Ray Hnatyshyn and Prime Minister Brian Mulroney—ready to welcome the naval Task Group home and thank the sailors for a job well done. It was a triumphant moment not seen since the end of World War II.

⌘   ⌘   ⌘

The navy went to extra lengths to make sure the crews knew they were appreciated. Everyone received an average of 30 days leave,[2] which they could take immediately (and about 95 per cent of them did) or within the next year. To arrange for that, the navy trained three caretaker ships' companies.

A ship in harbour, because it is filled with ammunition, fuel, and electrical equipment, needs a crew for security. So the navy has a duty

---

2. The navy used a formula to determine the exact length of an individual's leave entitlement, with the result that some received up to seven weeks. The average, however, was 30 days.

watch system in which about 20 crew members per day stay on board, checking all the security systems and fire alert systems on a regular basis. With a regular crew of over 200, it usually works out that a crew member is assigned to duty watch once out of every 10 days in port. But because the navy was giving every member of the Gulf Task Group a month off, this type of duty rotation didn't apply; the navy had to provide separate caretaker crews. These replacement crews met the ships in Bahrain and Gibraltar to learn the idiosyncratic workings of each vessel while en route home, so that they would be ready to take over for the crews when they hit port. Once in Halifax, the ships were locked up with limited access during the day and none at night, and a small duty watch comprised of the caretaker crews looked after each ship for a month.

> You can't possibly say 'thank you' enough to the Admiral and the staff that set that all up. When you look back at it, I'm sure they thought we were ungrateful, because all of a sudden we were gone. But each and everyone of us appreciated it.
>
> Rear-Admiral Waller told me "you're out of here for 30 days and I promise I'm not going to call you." And he didn't. I felt so guilty!

The Personal Toll

Despite the bands, the official welcomes, and the return to family, for many there was an anti-climatic feeling to the return. After the tension of the Gulf, the long work days, and the regimented routine of running the Task Group, the Squadron Staff, having flown directly from a war zone to the familiar sights of Halifax, had trouble adjusting to peacetime activities.

It wasn't until they got home that they realized what the stress had done to them. For a long time, Miller felt detached from the everyday goings-on, as if he was watching events happen, instead of being a part of them. For eight months, Canada and his home had been unreal to him, while the stress and tragedy of war had become real. Now, back in Halifax with his family, packing to leave for a new assignment in Ottawa, Miller had to work at making the "unreal world" real again.

Others suffered more physical manifestations of the war's toll. Lieutenant-Commander Greg Romanow lost his hair and his fingernails disintegrated. For the first 10 days after he arrived home, he slept for 17-19 hours at a time. Interrupted sleep patterns was a common complaint. It took Lieutenant-Commander Kevin Laing a long time to reset his biological clock to a normal routine after the months of five-and-seven-hour watches in the Gulf. He still doesn't sleep well.

Neither does Chief Petty Officer Dave Ashley. For about a month after he got back Ashley found that he would be instantly awakened by any sound at all. He would leap out of bed only to have his wife tell him, "it's okay, come back to bed—it's just the furnace," or a train going by, or a plane flying over. Especially the planes.

There was also a certain amount of culture shock attached to the stress reaction. Lieutenant-Commander Jim Hayes says "It's incredible you can be in a place like that and then literally hours later, you're someplace else, and you can watch a movie, or whatever." Hayes took his family to Disney World. While driving alone in the car at one point, he suddenly had heart palpitations and he thought he was going to have a heart attack. As it turned out, he was fine—he just wasn't used to relaxing. It was a skill he would have to relearn.

The transition for those who returned by ship to Halifax was much less severe. The more relaxed trip back home gave them time to adjust to a slower pace.

Speakers' Tour

When the crew of PROTECTEUR returned home in January, Lieutenant-Commander Jeff Agnew of the navy's Public Affairs Office in Halifax, began receiving requests from various schools, Legions, and other organizations for people to come and talk about Operation Friction. With Rear-Admiral Waller's approval, Agnew asked for a handful of volunteers from PROTECTEUR's officers and crew to join a speakers' program. About a dozen stepped forward, including Captain Doug McClean and his Executive Officer, Commander Frank Scherber. Agnew gave them a day's training in speaking techniques and video presentations, so that they would be prepared for any presentations they would be asked to give on the navy's work in the Gulf. When an organization requested a speaker, Agnew then asked one of PROTECTEUR's volunteers to take the assignment.

When the three ships returned home in April, Agnew expanded the program. Before their arrival in Halifax, he sent a message asking for 10 volunteers from each ship, including air force personnel. After a one-day "speakers" course, the 30 volunteers began accepting invitations from across Canada to talk about what they had done in the Gulf.

Most of the squadron staff and the ships' captains participated in the speaker's program. It had been an exciting time in their lives and they wanted to talk about it to anyone who would listen. For some, such as

Commodore Summers, taking to the lecture circuit was "cathartic," a way of putting the work in perspective and easing the transition back to a more normal military life.

For the navy, it was a chance to blow its own horn, let people know about its success, and remind everyone that it was, despite the end of the Cold War, still an essential component of this country's security policy. Agnew says "It was a golden opportunity to tell Canadians about their navy. We were getting requests by the barrelful." In addition to the speakers' circuit, there were three other parts to the navy's public awareness program.

First, PROTECTEUR with her original crew, was sent to Newfoundland. Agnew had suggested to his bosses that singling out a province in this way was appropriate because more than one-third of PROTECTEUR's crew were Newfoundlanders, and "because of all the provinces in the country, I would guestimate that by far and away, the most outstanding support from anywhere was received from Newfoundland." This close-knit island community likes to stay in touch with its military sons and daughters, so that when they are away on assignment—whether in the Arabian Gulf or in Bosnia—media outlets request interviews with them, individual islanders faithfully write letters, and communities send gifts from home. Agnew says, "allowing those Newfoundlanders to take their ship home to Newfoundland, show it off, and be heroes for a day, was probably as valuable internally to our own self-esteem and self-worth and purpose, as it was to the public's."

Second, TERRA NOVA was sent to the Great Lakes for her summer's deployment. Although she was due to go into refit, the navy delayed that program and left the Gulf equipment in her (although her missiles were swapped for dummy versions). That way, her crew could show and explain to people what they did in the Arabian Gulf. Agnew says "she was incredibly popular in the Great Lakes area. It gave Canadians a chance to see—inland in some of the largest media markets in southern Quebec and southern Ontario—what their navy did for them."

ATHABASKAN did not have time for such a tour: she was due into the shipyard for a long-awaited refit and modernization. But in July, before she sailed up the St. Lawrence to MIL Davie's yard in Lauzon, Quebec, she hosted an open house in Halifax.

The third part of the public awareness program, consisted of sending a Gulf-equipped Sea King helicopter across Canada to the various airshows. On board the aircraft were representatives from the army, navy and air force who had served with the naval Task Group in the Gulf. They went equipped with displays and a video, as well as the Sea King equipment and one of the Javelin air defence missiles used to protect the ships. They were able to explain to Canadians, firsthand, what they did while they were in the Gulf.

Awards

Every soldier and sailor who served in the Arabian Gulf received the Gulf and Kuwait Service Medal. For those who served during the period of actual fighting between the coalition and Iraq, a Maple Leaf has been added to the medal. The award was made on June 22, 1991, National Armed Forces Day, at ceremonies in Ottawa and other centres across Canada.

There were other awards for outstanding service. Both Summers and Miller received one of the military's highest awards—the Meritorious Service Cross. Lieutenant-General David Huddleston at Headquarters and Air Command's Colonel Romeo Lalonde also received that medal, as did three foreign officers: Lieutenant-General Charles Horner, Commander of the Joint Air Forces, Vice-Admiral Henry H. Mauz, Jr., Commander of the Joint Naval Forces, and British Commander Lieutenant-General Sir Peter de la Billiere. One special civilian, Mr. Bill Bowden, Chargé d'Affaires in the Canadian Embassy in Kuwait, who kept the embassy open under siege by the Iraqis, and who was taken "guestage" to Baghdad for two months, also received the Meritorious Service Cross—the first civilian to be so honoured with the award.

Commodore Ken Summers was also recognized by the United States and awarded the Bronze Star at an official ceremony put on by the Americans.

The Meritorious Service Medal went to two sailors: Chief Petty Officer Second Class Mary Wilson, Chief Supply Technician in PROTECTEUR, and Chief Petty Officer Second Class Dave Ashley, the Squadron's Communications Chief.

For the whole of the Canadian Forces' effort in the Arabian Gulf, 25 people were "Mentioned in Dispatches", including Commander Stu Andrews, Commanding Officer of TERRA NOVA. This very rare honour is awarded only in wartime.

A Commander's Commendation was awarded by Summers to all members of the Squadron Staff as well as to approximately 20 people in each of the three ships who deserved special recognition for their individual acts of heroism or responsibility. Vice-Admiral George presented the Maritime Commander's Commendation to Captains (N)

Dennis Cronk and Doug McClean; Commanders D. Dubowski, David Jacobson, and John Pickford; Lieutenant-Commanders Bob Alce, R.J. Booth, Graham Chamberlain, A.R.C. Cole, Cooper, John Gardham, P.W. Gregory, Jim Hayes, Leak, W.B. MacDonald, D.G. MacDougall, Greg Romanow, and W.J. Van Dinther; Major Pete Nordlund; Lieutenants (N) D.J.B. Charlton, R.T. Fowler, Dan Langlais and I.S. Yeates; Captains John Madower, (Padre) D.C. Melanson; Chief Petty Officer 1st Class F. Childs; Chief Petty Officer 2nd Class G.A. Cormier; Chief Petty Officer M.A. Ryan; Master Warrant Officer Beauchamp; Petty Officer 2nd Class K.A. Heimrich; Petty Officer 1st Class J.J.R. Bussieres; Leading Seaman Ryan; Military Family Support Centre; Intelligence Section MARCOM Headquarters; Deputy Chief of Staff Readiness Section MARCOM Headquarters; and Laurie Vasey (Family Support Centre).

Approximately 30 Chief of Defence Staff Commendations—a pin consisting of three maple leaves—were awarded, of which half went to members of the Canadian Naval Task Group. These included Lieutenant-Colonel Larry McWha, Lieutenant (N) Bruce Belliveau, ATHABAKSAN's Combat Officer, and Chief Petty Officer Second Class Serge Joncas.

Units were also singled out for military honours. The highest honour for a unit, the Canadian Forces Commendation—a flag which is flown by the unit for a year and then put away—was awarded to the three ships by the Chief of the Defence Staff on Decemer 31, 1990 in recognition of their embargo enforcement operations.

The Commendation also went to the Ship Repair Unit (Atlantic) and the Naval Engineering Unit, for the work they did getting the ships ready for the Gulf deployment. There was, however, a sour note to this honour. There was supposed to be a public ceremony at the shipyard attended by the various naval and union officials as well as the employees. Unfortunately, labour problems at the shipyard caused the Federal Government Dockyard Trades and Labour Council (East) to boycott the ceremony. Consequently, the Canadian Forces Commendation was awarded in a quiet presentation in Captain Roger Chiasson's conference room. Vice-Admiral John Anderson, then Commander of Maritime Command, sent a letter to all employees thanking them for the work done in the ships and expressing his dismay that they missed the presentation. Chiasson still feels that the unions did their members a disservice by forcing them to miss a well-deserved honour.

The Canadian Forces Commendation was also awarded to 423 Helicopter Anti-Submarine Squadron for the work it did to prepare and maintain the five Sea Kings which sailed with the Task Group. Those aircraft accumulated a total of 2,500 flight hours over the course of the eight-month mission. But the air detachments had looked after their machines so well that they achieved a mission availability and completion rate of over 97 per cent—possibly the highest achieved by any of the allied air units in the Gulf.

On November 11, 1993, the Governor-General announced that HMCS ATHABASKAN, PROTECTEUR, TERRA NOVA, and 423 Anti-Submarine Helicopter Squadron had all been awarded Battle Honours. This honour, which is displayed on an official commemorative board, follows the name of the unit. Thus, ATHABASKAN, which is the third ship in the Canadian navy to be so named, has as her Battle Honours, the Arctic 1943-44, the English Channel 1944, Korea 1950-53, and now, the Arabian Gulf 1991.

⌘   ⌘   ⌘

After the ships returned home, some of the local businesses sponsored an evening gala for the crew members and their families, in the armoury at the Citadel. The sponsors provided all the food, the refeshments and the entertainment. At that event, which occurred about two weeks after the ships docked, Miller was presented with a beautiful print of a tree with a yellow ribbon around it, next to an old Nova Scotia house. Miller, in turn, presented the print to the Family Support Centre in Halifax for display, so that all the families could appreciate it.

That evening at the armoury provided Chief Ashley with a very special memory that he says was worth more than any medal or any meeting with a high-ranking official. Ashley attended the festivities with his wife, his two sons and his daughter-in-law. Dusty and Ann Miller were there, and when she saw Ashley, she went over to him, put her arms around him, and said, "Thank you. Thank you so very much." "That," says Ashley, "made it all worth it."

For Miller, what made everything worth it, was a letter. It came from the children of Kuwait, and it was addressed to the Commander of the Canadian Naval Task Group. It simply said, "Thank you for getting our country back."

CHAPTER THIRTEEN

Lessons

The Gulf War was one of many firsts for the Canadian Navy.

- It was the first time Canadian ships, designed for anti-submarine warfare, sailed with the sophisticated Phalanx Close-In Weapon System for air defence.

- It was the first time the Harpoon missile system was fitted in a Canadian ship and certified for use by Canadian operators.

- It was the first time that many of the electronic sensors, including the Canadian Electronic Warfare System, were ever tested under operational conditions.

- It was the first time a Canadian supply ship, HMCS PROTECTEUR, was used operationally as a "destroyer" and as an alternate command ship.

- It was the first time that the navy had employed Canadian Forces women in a combat zone.

- It was the first time that the navy used the army to provide air defence on board ship.

- It was the first time Canadians had been put in charge of a multi-national logistics force.

- It was the first time since the Korean War that a Canadian ship, HMCS ATHABASKAN, sailed through a mined area in a combat zone.

- It was the first time that the navy relied on satellite communications to provide real time contact with commanders back home and at sea.

- And, finally, it was the first time that Canada used a tri-service joint system of command, putting into the operational theatre a representative of the Chief of the Defence Staff to command the national effort.

Not only did the navy rise to meet these challenges, but it succeeded beyond all expectations. The result will be long lasting. Sending three ships and their helicopters to participate in the allied action against Iraq provided an opportunity to use skills and equipment that for nearly 40 years, the navy had only exercised under peacetime conditions. From this initiation into the operational side of modern warfare sprang a number of key lessons which should serve as the basis for shaping Canada's navy in the years to come.

When you're needed, you go with what you have.

When the order came to deploy to the Gulf, the navy was awaiting delivery of its new City class patrol frigates and modernized Tribal class destroyers. These ships, equipped with anti-submarine warfare systems, area air defence systems, and point defence systems, as well as helicopters for over-the-horizon reconnaissance and tracking, will give the navy a true general purpose capability. In 1990, however, the navy had to make do.

> We once again learned that for any wartime venture you go with what you have, or more aptly, with what you can lay your hands on at the time. While we sailed in ships over 30 years old, we did manage to divert the latest in anti-missile defence systems to the ships in a dockyard fitting spree not seen since the Second World War. We found ourselves in the fortunate state of having equipment versions more modern than any aboard the U.S. ships despite the ages of our hulls.

Luck was on the navy's side in at least one area: in 1990 there were no submarines in the Arabian Gulf. Consequently, the Canadian ships and aircraft did not need most of their anti-submarine warfare equipment. By removing some of those systems, Maritime Command and Maritime Air Group had more room to fit air defence and mine detection systems. It is unlikely that the navy will be so lucky in future. More than 40 countries, in all regions of the world, now possess submarines. Even the Arabian Gulf is not immune from this proliferation. In the few years since the Gulf War, Iran has taken steps to acquire at least three submarines. Thus, in future multinational operations, Canadian ships will likely need their anti-submarine warfare capability.

The navy will also need to keep its other defensive equipment up-to-date because old threats never entirely disappear. Iraq's nuclear and chemical weapons capability may have been destroyed after the war, but Baghdad is already attempting to rebuild. Other countries are also interested in acquiring these weapons of mass destruction. For those that can't afford a nuclear research program, there are always the cheap and plentiful chemical weapons—often referred to as the poor man's nuclear bomb.

Such a threat means the Canadian Forces must maintain a nuclear-biological-chemical (NBC) defensive capability. In the navy that means having ships that are able to close up and maintain a contaminant-free environment for extended periods of time. And for both the navy and Maritime Air Group, it means supplying NBC defence suits and masks to the officers and crews, as well as providing realistic training opportunities.

The Arabian Gulf operations proved once again that sea control remains a key naval role, both at home and abroad. Sea control—the ability to control who uses an area of ocean—is the basis of most of Canada's maritime activities and requires a surface, sub-surface, and air capablity. In the Gulf, the allies used their aircraft and ships to prevent the Iraqis from bringing in supplies, exporting goods, and attacking the coalition ships. A sub-surface capability was not needed because, as previously mentioned, no one in the region had any submarines.

Off the Canadian coasts, sea control remains a prime naval function. Using ships, submarines, aircraft and electronic sensors, the navy is able to keep abreast of what is going on in Canadian-claimed waters. By having multi-capable ships and aircraft, it is able to help enforce Canadian laws and protect Canadian interests. Without that naval ability to control its ocean areas, Canadian sovereignty would be infringed.

Ships that are able to exercise sea control, to sail in self-supporting task groups, and to defend themselves in a modern war, are also of further benefit: they can be used as floating command centres for land operations in hostile territory. The navy provided just such a service to the army in

Somalia, offering PRESERVER's facilities for command, control and communications, and providing armed Sea King helicopters for reconnaissance and support to the ground troops.

At the base of all of this, however, lies one key factor: the navy must not lose its combat skills, because when needed, they are needed quickly and there will be no time to reacquire those that have been lost. Allowing, for example, its blue water anti-submarine warfare abilities to whither in order to concentrate on a coastal protection role, would leave the navy with limited options in an international crisis. As General John de Chastelain told a Parliamentary Committee,

> ... even if you have a small force that is combat capable, and that maintains all the capabilities of structure, organization, equipment, doctrine and policy, you have the capability to expand on it. If you do away with that capability, you do not have the capability to put it back quickly.
>
> If we can be certain of our future and certain of the threat that this country may face or this country's allies may face, in which they would wish us to play a role, then we can be less concerned about combat capability. If we cannot be that certain, then I suggest we must be very careful in doing away with it.[1]

It is important to have self-supporting task groups

Navies rarely send one ship to participate in an exercise or operation. Rather, a country will send a Task Group or Task Force made up of varying numbers of ships. By taking this approach during the Arabian Gulf War, Canada was able to make a distinctive national contribution to the allied effort.

A key component of the Canadian Task Group was the supply ship PROTECTEUR. She provided the fuel, food, spare parts and other supplies necessary to keep ATHABASKAN and TERRA NOVA, as well as five Sea King helicopters, operational during the extended deployment.

> *Our Canadian-invented one-stop-shop replenishment ship again was more valuable than gold. By modifying PROTECTEUR to have an operational and alternate command capability, as*

---

1. Special Joint Committee on Canada's Defence Policy, *Minutes* Issue No. 1 (March 16, 1994), p. 25.

well as self-defence capabilities, she provided triple worth. She was used as a replenishment ship in the Central Gulf—the only one for the first couple of months—and as a "destroyer" for challenging shipping during the interdiction phase. Finally, and even more valuable, she was the maintenance support vessel for air operations.

Without a Canadian supply ship as part of the mission, the destroyers would have had to rely on the allies for fuel and other consumables, and the Sea Kings would not have attained the high flying rate that they did. By using the maintenance facilities on board PROTECTEUR, the technicians kept the helicopters flying. Lieutentant-Colonel Larry McWha says it "showed what you could achieve at sea if you had the right mix of qualifications and the right kind of tools." By having the shop trades— the machinists and metalsmiths—right on hand, "there was no delay while waiting for the right person and equipment; you could fix things immediately instead of having to nurse them along while waiting." This capability was perhaps best demonstrated by having periodic inspections done at sea—the first time ever. McWha says it "changed our way of looking at inspections; putting aircraft on the line so that there's more time available for flight operations rather than sitting in a hangar waiting for a scheduled maintenance."

The importance of having operational auxiliary-oiler-replenishment (AOR) ships cannot be overestimated. Former Commander of Maritime Command, then-Vice-Admiral John Anderson, underlined the AOR's importance when he noted the limitations which would face the navy if it carried through on plans to pay-off HMCS PROVIDER. He said without a replacement the navy will have to hope that it won't be caught in a time of crisis with its two remaining supply ships in drydock for repairs, scheduled or otherwise. If that were to happen, one option would be to "do nothing." He said, "Where you might have been asked to take on a task, [you would have to say] 'No, I can do it in six months when I have a tanker back but I can't do it now.'" If a crisis erupts, however, and Canada is asked to help out, the first choice would be to work with allies. Another option would be to adapt operations to fit the circumstances, but as Anderson said, "clearly, it limits your ability."[2]

---

2. "Aging supply ships weaken navy's support capability" by Parker Robinson, in Halifax *Chronicle Herald*: July 14, 1992, p. A1. The navy has since decided that PROVIDER, the oldest of the three replenishment ships, will continue in service for a few more years.

Alliance ties and exercises are an essential proving ground for multinational operations.

If ever there was a need to prove that NATO provides an irreplaceable service to international security, look no further than the Arabian Gulf War. For many years NATO has been a proving ground for multinational operations. The allied training and procedures, with their emphasis on interoperability, served as the base upon which the 18 navies in the Gulf—not all of them NATO members—conducted their successful operation.

Canada's allied ties also proved immensely useful during the Task Group's training en route to the Gulf.

> *Our Western allies were of incredible help. The British provided their Fleet Readiness and Air Defence Unit (FRADU) resources for operational work-ups outside Gibraltar—everything from full missile attacks on the ships to identifying surprise press aircraft. The French provided their Exocet missile simulator aircraft for several valuable hours of anti-ship missile training off Toulon. In Djibouti, the French Admiral operating in the Indian Ocean gave a full briefing for the ships' captains concerning special Gulf operating requirements. The Italians provided the NATO degaussing range in Augusta to calibrate the ships' anti-mine capabilities. The Americans provided invaluable assistance prior to departure by summarizing their lessons for us from years of operations in the Gulf, including the tanker war. Finally, all of the navies in the Gulf provided training in situ which will provide a base for future multinational operations.*

One of the reasons that Canadians were given a key role in the naval war against Iraq was that the ships' communications equipment allowed them to communicate with all of the allies. This flexibility was no accident.

> *Over the years we have consciously sought to have our equipment compatible with that of the United States. This proved invaluable given that the communications, cryptographic, and weapons systems need a common basis for both operations and maintenance. When we were getting ready for the Gulf, we added some British equipment, knowing that they would be major players in the crisis. Some countries, with only national-type communications equipment were hamstrung during the*

war given that they could not receive the complete range of information available.

And finally, the most important lesson of all—

Good people are the navy's most valuable asset.

The ships were jury rigged with a mix of old and new equipment and the crews given a short burst of intensive training for their new role. By any measure, the odds were stacked against the Task Group's success. But added to the mixture was another "first," that in another organization, another country, could have sunk the mission before it even got started. By an extraordinary coincidence, all three ships going to the Gulf had new commanding officers.

Captain Doug McClean, commanding officer of PROTECTEUR, had never commanded an auxiliary oiler replenishment vessel before. He took command on July 7, straight from his work at NATO headquarters for the Supreme Allied Commander Atlantic (SACLANT) in Virginia Beach, Norfolk. His Executive Officer, Commander Frank Scherber, was a submariner who suddenly found himself on the surface of the sea aboard the largest vessel in the Canadian navy. Commander John Pickford, who had previously been the Executive Officer of PROTECTEUR, had taken over command of ATHABASKAN just that summer, and hadn't yet taken the ship to sea before being told he was taking her to a war zone. Commander Stu Andrews took command of TERRA NOVA that summer after serving as Executive Officer of ATHABASKAN. Finally, not only did the ships all have new commanding officers, but so did the squadron—Miller was brand new to his job.

That the naval Task Group was able to acquit itself so well, given all the odds against it, was due to the quality of the navy's people and their training. Miller is enthusiastic in his praise.

> *The ships' companies were incredible: well-educated, tremendous initiators and great thinkers. Individually the people were ingenious, collectively they rank with the best in the world.*

PROTECTEUR's Captain Doug McClean is of the same opinion. He says everyday somebody would come up with a good idea, everyone from the ship's officers to young leading seamen. McClean says the young men and women on board the ships were intelligent young people who, because of the training system we have in our navy, were given the opportunity to think; they weren't just robots. They didn't learn by rote. All of our training meant 'let's leave a little room for a person to think.' And if I hadn't had that we'd have never got it right, becuse there's no way I or just my officers could come up with all the solutions, all the things undone that we had to fix.

That attitude and enthusiasm provided McClean with the trust and confidence needed to do the job of using a supply ship in both its intended role and in the role of a destroyer/escort. He says,

When we pulled into the Gulf I felt that my ship was about 85 per cent combat ready, in terms of being able to fight the ship to the best ability of the systems that we had. We busted our butts to get there and were then down to fine tuning. We were still finding out a few little wrinkles about some of the weapons systems, slightly better ways to manoeuvre the ship perhaps, and some of the young guys were still being trained up. By the time the first patrol was over, I'm sure we were 100 per cent, and we maintained that for the rest of the time I was there.

What was true aboard PROTECTEUR, was also true aboard ATHABASKAN and TERRA NOVA. The men and women who sailed in the Task Group learned quickly, adapted easily, and worked unselfishly.

The sailors we had in the Gulf did a remarkable job of keeping old equipment running. The old ship HMCS TERRA NOVA— boiler driven, 45 degrees Celsius in the engine room. They kept that going almost without a hitch. She was out of commission, I think, for a day maybe, on a small engineering item. And that is just remarkable pioneer stamina of Canadians and I wouldn't want to change that. That's the way we are.

Chronology

Iraq invaded Kuwait on *August 2, 1990.* The international diplomatic community reacted quickly to that act of aggression. At the United Nations, Canada co-sponsored Resolution 660 condemning the invasion and demanding that Iraq withdraw from Kuwait.

On *August 6,* the U.N. Security Council unanimously approved Resolution 661—co-sponsored by Canada—imposing economic sanctions on Iraq. Canada was appointed vice-chair of a newly-established committee to advise the Security Council on implementation of the sanctions.

That same day Prime Minister Brian Mulroney met with President George Bush at the White House. Also on August 6, the U.S. and U.K. announced major troop deployments to the Gulf.

Two days later, on *August 8,* Iraq announced that it had annexed Kuwait. Canada reacted with further sanctions under the U.N. Act.

On *August 10,* Prime Minister Brian Mulroney announced that Canada would contribute two destroyers and a supply ship to the multinational military effort in the Persian Gulf.

Iraq demanded that all countries close their diplomatic missions in Kuwait, but on *August 15,* Canada announced that it would keep its Embassy open to protect Canadians.

The ships and Sea King helicopters underwent two weeks of intense modifications to prepare them for their role. On *August 24,* Canadian Task Group (CATG) 302.3, under the command of Commodore Ken Summers, left the port of Halifax to sail to the Middle East. The Task Group was assigned the following mission:

> "To assist in deterring further Iraqi aggression by contributing to international efforts in support of the U.N. Security Council decision. This multinational effort is set

up to impose economic sanctions against Iraq through surveillance, monitoring and, as necessary, interception, of all inward and outward maritime shipping. It involves the inspection and verification of all cargoes related to shipping as laid down in Security Council Resolution 661."

On *August 25,* Canada co-sponsored U.N. Security Council Resolution 665 which called on states deploying maritime forces to use such measures as may be necessary to halt all inward and outward maritime shipping to ensure compliance with Resolution 661. The resolution passed.

Over the next few weeks, nationals of Canada and other countries were evacuated from Iraq. On *September 13,* Canada co-sponsored Resolution 666 which was modelled on Canadian suggestions for determining humanitarian shipments of food to Iraq and Kuwait.

On *September 14,* Prime Minister Mulroney announced that a CF-18 squadron would be sent to the Gulf to provide air cover for the Canadian ships and to augment the multinational air resources already in place. The squadron was deployed to Qatar on *October 6,* and conducted its first Combat Air Patrol (CAP) on *October 7.* Prior to the outbreak of fighting in January, the CF-18s flew an average of 18 missions daily, in a mix of operations and training.

The government placed the Canadian Naval Task Group on active service on *September 15,* just as it entered the Red Sea.

The next day, *September 16,* the Security Council met at the Ministerial level and adopted Resolution 670 which extended the international embargo to air traffic.

The Canadian Task Group arrived in Bahrain on *September 27* and sailed its first patrol in the Gulf on *October 1.* Over the next three months, the ships operated in three different patrol sectors in the Gulf.

The government's first meeting of its Ad Hoc Committee on the Gulf Crisis took place on *October 11.*

On *October 19,* the Canadian Embassy in Kuwait suspended operations and its diplomatic staff withdrew to Baghdad. They left Iraq on *January 12, 1991.*

The House of Commons, on *October 23,* adopted a resolution condemning the invasion.

The deployment of the headquarters personnel and equipment to Bahrain was completed on *October 27*. The Joint Task Force Headquarters, with Commodore Ken Summers at the helm, began operations on *November 6*.

On *November 29*, the Security Council met at the Ministerial level and adopted Resolution 678, co-sponsored by Canada, that gave Iraq "one final pause of good will". After January 15, the U.N. members would use any means available to force Iraq out of Kuwait.

Still hoping to avert war, Prime Minister Mulroney sent a letter to the U.N. Secretary General on *January 9, 1991*, urging him to visit Baghdad. But the meeting between Secretary General Javier Perez de Cuellar and Iraqi President Saddam Hussein on *January 12*, proved fruitless.

On *January 11*, the Chief of Defence Staff announced that another eight CF-18s were being dispatched to Qatar, as well as a Boeing 707 air-to-air refuelling aircraft and a Challenger jet for VIP transport.

The House of Commons adopted a resolution on *January 15*, reaffirming Canadian action in the Gulf.

The air battle began on *January 16* (the early hours of January 17, Baghdad time). Prime Minister Mulroney announced that the CF-18s had been authorized to carry out sweep and escort missions over Kuwait and Iraq. Also on the 16th, Canada announced the deployment of a Surgical Field Hospital to Saudi Arabia to assist British ground forces.

On *January 22* Prime Minister Mulroney addressed the House on the situation in the Gulf.

The land battle began on *February 23*. By *February 26* (February 27, Baghdad time) the coalition forces had re-taken Kuwait City. Military operations were suspended at midnight, *February 27-28* (0800 hours February 28, Baghdad time).

On *March 1*, Canada's Ambassador to Kuwait, Lawrence Dickenson, returned to Kuwait City and re-opened the Embassy.

The conditions for a ceasefire were contained in U.N. Resolution 686 which was passed on *March 2*. Iraq accepted the resolution the next day.

HMCS ATHABASKAN, TERRA NOVA and PROTECTEUR arrived back in Halifax harbour on *April 7, 1991*.

Index

Date Due

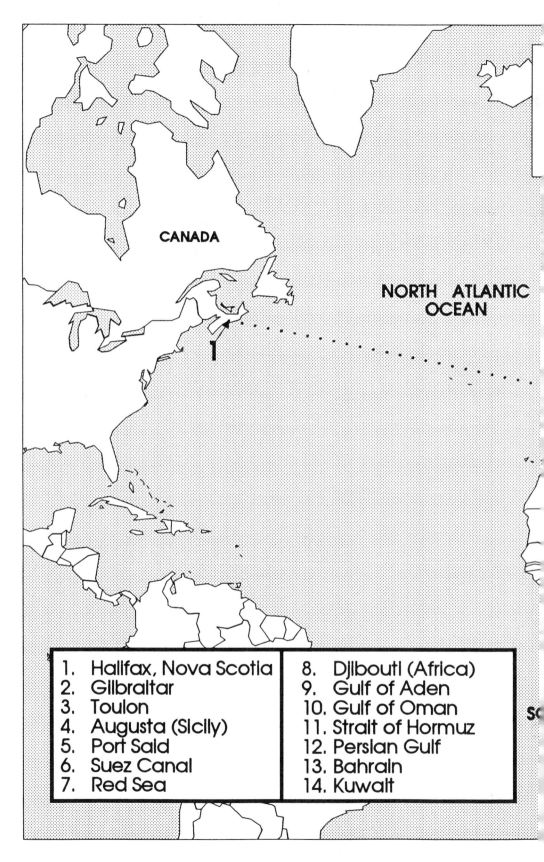

CANADA

NORTH ATLANTIC
OCEAN

1

1. Halifax, Nova Scotia	8. Djibouti (Africa)
2. Gibraltar	9. Gulf of Aden
3. Toulon	10. Gulf of Oman
4. Augusta (Sicily)	11. Strait of Hormuz
5. Port Said	12. Persian Gulf
6. Suez Canal	13. Bahrain
7. Red Sea	14. Kuwait